"What! Still Alive?!"

Modern Jewish History
Henry Feingold, *Series Editor*

Select titles in Modern Jewish History

Between Persecution and Participation:
Biography of a Bookkeeper at J. A. Topf & Söhne
Annegret Schüle and Tobias Sowade; Penny Milbouer, trans.

Assimilated Jews in the Warsaw Ghetto, 1940–1943
Katarzyna Person

The Children of La Hille: Eluding Nazi Capture during World War II
Walter W. Reed

Einstein's Pacifism and World War I
Virginia Iris Holmes

Jewish Libya: Memory and Identity in Text and Image
Jacques Roumani, David Meghnagi, and Judith Roumani, eds.

Leaving Russia: A Jewish Story
Maxim D. Shrayer

One Step toward Jerusalem: Oral Histories of Orthodox Jews in Stalinist Hungary
Sándor Bacskai

"We Are Jews Again": Jewish Activism in the Soviet Union
Yuli Kosharovsky; Ann Komaromi, ed.; Stefani Hoffman, trans.

"What! Still Alive?!"

JEWISH SURVIVORS IN POLAND AND ISRAEL REMEMBER HOMECOMING

Monika Rice

Syracuse University Press

The views or opinions expressed in this book, and the context in which the images are used, do not necessarily reflect the views or policy of, nor imply approval or endorsement by, the United States Holocaust Memorial Museum.

Copyright © 2017 by Syracuse University Press
Syracuse, New York 13244-5290

All Rights Reserved

First Edition 2017

19 20 21 22   5 4 3 2

∞ The paper used in this publication meets the minimum requirements of the American National Standard for Information Sciences—Permanence of Paper for Printed Library Materials, ANSI Z39.48-1992.

For a listing of books published and distributed by Syracuse University Press, visit www.SyracuseUniversityPress.syr.edu.

ISBN: 978-0-8156-3553-6 (hardcover)
978-0-8156-3539-0 (paperback)
978-0-8156-5419-3 (e-book)

Library of Congress Cataloging-in-Publication Data
Names: Rice, Monika, author.
Title: What! Still alive?! : Jewish survivors in Poland and Israel remember homecoming / Monika Rice.
Description: First edition. | Syracuse, New York : Syracuse University Press, 2017. | Series: Modern Jewish history | Includes bibliographical references and index.
Identifiers: LCCN 2017037889 (print) | LCCN 2017038211 (ebook) | ISBN 9780815654193 (e-book) | ISBN 9780815635536 (hardcover : alk. paper) | ISBN 9780815635390 (pbk. : alk. paper)
Subjects: LCSH: Jews—Poland—History—20th century. | Holocaust survivors—Poland—Attitudes. | Holocaust survivors—Israel—Attitudes. | Żydowski Instytut Historyczny im. Emanuela Ringelbluma. | Yad ṿa-shem, rashut ha-zikaron la- Shoʼah ṿela-gevurah. | World War, 1939–1945—Concentration camps—Liberation. | Poland—Ethnic relations.
Classification: LCC DS134.55 (ebook) | LCC DS134.55 .R53 2017 (print) | DDC 940.53/1809438—dc23
LC record available at https://lccn.loc.gov/2017037889

Manufactured in the United States of America

Contents

Acknowledgments · *vii*

Abbreviations · *ix*

Introduction: *In Search of Postwar Memory* · 1

1. The Returning Survivors: *Historical Context* · 17

2. The Central Jewish Historical Commission and Its Project of Documenting Survivors' Stories · 41

3. First Encounters with the Neighbors as Represented in the Jewish Historical Institute Collection · 65

4. Yad Vashem Testimonies in the Context of Israeli History · 86

5. Memories of the First Encounters as Represented in the Yad Vashem Collection · 112

6. Comparative Analysis of the Data: *Memory on a Curve* · 130

Conclusions: *Toward Building a Collective Memory* · 195

Appendix: *On the Value of Quantitative Analysis* · 203

Notes · 207

Bibliography · 227

Index · 249

Acknowledgments

This book and the research that has contributed to it are in part the fruit of my collaboration with and learning from many knowledgeable individuals as well as of generous assistance from several institutions. I would like first to thank Antony Polonsky for his constant academic and personal support. Antony's mentoring is discreet yet essential to growth: by gentle referrals to texts and ideas, he helped me to figure out my own way of proceeding in this research and thus to stand on my own feet as an academic. Nonetheless, at a few moments when the task appeared to be daunting or in times of "crisis," he was always there with fatherly assistance. I am grateful to know this most generous mensch.

Several other scholars at Brandeis University were also important for guiding my academic formation and helping in the progress of this work as well as for their friendship. I thank especially Eugene Sheppard, Ellen Kellman, and Ben Ravid. Sylvia Fuks Fried of Brandeis University Press and the Tauber Institute was crucial in starting me on the road to preparing this project for publication, and I am grateful for her many insights. Karen Auerbach was my study companion and a dear friend who was always willing to share her most helpful observations.

Several other scholars were influential for this book. First and foremost, without Jan T. Gross's shattering impact on Polish historiography of the Holocaust, this project would not have been born. He was also extremely generous in commenting on several chapters of this work and helping to improve it along the way.

Scholars who provided helpful direction and advice include Monika Adamczyk-Garbowska, Omer Bartov, the late David Cesarani, Havi Dreyfuss, Barbara Engelking, Jan Grabowski, Henry Greenspan, Sharon

Kangisser-Cohen, Steven Katz, Zeev Mankowitz, Dalia Ofer, Jakub Petelewicz, Alan Rosen, Alvin Rosenfeld, David Silberklang, Alina Skibińska, Michael Steinlauf, and Andrzej Żbikowski. A long conversation with Joanna Tokarska-Bakir at her hospitable home during her fellowship at Princeton University helped me sharpen my methodological apparatus. Natalia Aleksiun's careful reading of the manuscript and her constructive, substantial review of it pointed me in the direction of correcting certain errors and improving overall perspective, for which I am tremendously grateful.

Aleksandra Borecka of the United States Holocaust Memorial Museum was extremely generous in providing insights as well as in assisting me in obtaining access to archival material. I am thankful also for help from Leah Teichthal and Eliot Nidam Orvieto of Yad Vashem.

During my research and writing, I was supported by several fellowships: a Claims Conference Saul Kagan Fellowship in Advanced Shoah Studies, which also allowed my project to be assessed and improved by feedback from senior Holocaust studies luminaries; a Council for European Studies at Columbia University Fellowship; and the Tauber Institute for the Study of European Jewry at Brandeis University Award.

I wish also to thank Deborah Manion, acquisitions editor at Syracuse University Press, for her kindness, encouragement, and enthusiastic support. Copy editor Annie Barva did a fantastic, careful job of polishing cumbersome expressions and eliminating grammatical pitfalls that nonnative English speakers inevitably fall into, for which I am very grateful.

Finally, I thank my husband, Joseph, and our daughter, Miriam, for their love, patience, insights, and inspiration. Joseph's intellectual challenges to my assumptions as well as his generous aid in smoothing my "second-language" English were invaluable for the creation of this book. Without his constant support, providing me with the "luxury" of being the second academic in our home, this book would not have been written. My love and gratitude go foremost to him and to Miriam.

Abbreviations

AK	Armia Krajowa (Polish Home Army)
AŻIH	Archives of the Żydowski Instytut Historyczny (Jewish Historical Institute)
AYV	Archives of Yad Vashem
CŻKH	Centralna Żydowska Komisja Historyczna (Central Jewish Historical Commission)
CKŻP	Centralny Komitet Żydów w Polsce (Central Committee of Polish Jews)
DP	displaced person
JOINT	American Jewish Joint Distribution Committee
NSZ	Narodowe Siły Zbrojne (Polish National Armed Forces)
PKWN	Polski Komitet Wyzwolenia Narodowego (Polish Committee of National Liberation)
PPR	Polska Partia Robotnicza (Polish Workers Party)
YIVO	Yidiszer Wisenszaftlecher Instytut (Yiddish Scholarly Institute)
YV	Yad Vashem
ŻIH	Żydowski Instytut Historyczny (Jewish Historical Institute)

"What! Still Alive?!"

Introduction

In Search of Postwar Memory

> The past is the remembered present, just as the future is the anticipated present: memory is always derived from the present and from the contents of the present.
> —Amos Funkenstein, "Collective Memory and Historical Consciousness"

On the sunny Saturday morning of July 14, 1945, Chaim Wittelsohn entered the damp room of the local Centralna Żydowska Komisja Historyczna (CŻKH, Central Jewish Historical Commission) in Sosnowiec, a town in the Upper Silesian industrial region of Poland, about forty miles north of Kraków. Six years earlier, at the beginning of the war in 1939, Chaim, a cotton manufacturer by profession, had fled to Lviv in eastern Poland. Thanks to a secret pact between Adolf Hitler and Joseph Stalin, Lviv was then occupied by the Soviets. Two years after that, in 1941, Chaim found himself in Złoczów, near Lviv, on the eve of the German–Soviet war. There, in the castle in the center of town, he experienced one of the most brutal German massacres in Poland, during which 5,000 Jews were forced to dig their own graves, then wait, kneeling, for a benevolent Nazi pistol shot to the back of the neck. This was not a "sanitary murder": in preparation for the final blow, local Ukrainians were organized into a mob to rush at the victims with axes. Chaim fainted while moving toward the ditch, a weakness that saved him. (He also mentioned in the testimony he gave to the CŻKH that 3,000 other Złoczów Jews were able to hide in their hometown and be saved.) Covered by the falling bodies of other victims, he managed later that night to climb up to ground level and escape. He was very fortunate then to find shelter at the home of a Polish peasant woman, who, thinking him a Pole from Ukraine, employed him as a shepherd for two years, until the neighbors became too suspicious of his origins. He had to flee and for months wander throughout the countryside in search of work. Although he was not successful, by a stroke of luck he again came across the old peasant woman who had kept him for two years. Again, she helped him—this time to build a hideout in the forest—and provided him with three square meals a day, useful information, and much needed human kindness.

Like other Jews in occupied Poland, Chaim experienced many close encounters with death. On one occasion, a German division bivouacked right next to his hideout. Chaim again managed to escape, wandering around the countryside and finding temporary employment on farms. Sometime in 1943 (more probably in 1944; the interviewer confirms that Chaim confuses his memories of accurate dates), he reconnected with the good elderly peasant woman for the second time. She was thrilled that he had survived and nurtured him like her own son until the Red Army "liberated" occupied Poland in July 1944. He related to Adela Laufer, his interviewer at the CŻKH, the words that would become the final paragraph of his testimony:

> The Germans had already left the area, so I went with her [to her home]. I was received very warmly; I took a bath [and] changed my clothes and underwear, which she had always washed and brought to me. I ate until I was full, and they didn't want to let me go for a long time. I had to promise that I'd come back to them again, whether or not I found anyone from my own family. In the meantime, I settled in Lublin, where I waited for the liberation of the Dąbrowa mining region. It was only in March that I returned to Sosnowiec, and I consider myself currently to be one of the lucky ones whose immediate family members are still alive—and in Palestine at that.[1]

Only in the last sentence does Chaim report the fact of returning to his hometown; there is nothing more, however, that one can learn about what had happened to him there. The first five months that passed between his homecoming and his testimony must have been filled with encounters with neighbors, friends, acquaintances, and other nameless Poles. He provides no information about any of these encounters, however. We also do not learn whether he found any extended family there in his hometown, although one might suppose that they all were dead because Chaim emphasizes being fortunate enough to have immediate living relatives in Palestine. Concerning those who were still there in his hometown, the Gentile Poles, Chaim's testimony remains silent. The war had ruptured Poland like an unimaginable storm to separate his world and that of his fellow Jews from the world of other Poles; the intervening six years must have made it impossible for the two groups to resume any sort of conversation they had before the war. But Chaim's narrative does not give us any inkling of how the returning Jews of Sosnowiec experienced their arrival home. Did they feel safe? Were they welcomed? Were they threatened? Were they, perhaps, just ignored or treated with a fleeting curiosity similar to that afforded non-Jewish Poles, many of whom were also returning home—from the camps, from the Soviet Union, from the Western front, and from hideouts with the Underground? What were the relationships between Jews and Poles that characterized this moment of attempts to return, to reestablish homes, and to rebuild shattered lives?

Fourteen years after Chaim deposited his war account in Poland, another native of Sosnowiec, Ita Koplowicz, gave a testimony of her survival during the war to Yad Vashem's Department for the Collection of Testimonies on December 27, 1959, in Ramat Gan near Tel Aviv. Like Chaim, she had to leave her hometown during the war, and she had depended on "the mercy of strangers" to survive. Koplowicz's account speaks openly about the antisemitic attitudes of many Poles, some of whom betrayed Jews for a little money or a few articles of clothing. Her style is that of an objective observer. She notes an inhuman indifference that set people against each other during the Warsaw Uprising of August 1944[2]—and not only along ethnic lines. She cites an example of Gentile Poles refusing to give shelter to an elderly Gentile widow who had lost her son in the Uprising. She also does not shy away from pointing out instances of Jewish collaboration with the Nazis or of a decline in moral standards among Jews existing under circumstances that seemed to impose deadly choices on them. She also displays a sensitive ear to the nuances of Polish attitudes; she recounts an instance in which she spoke to an "intelligent Pole" who admitted that "the Germans realized very well that we Poles helped them to assault the Jews."[3]

Ita, who had run a pharmacy with her husband before the war, was fortunate to find a protector in one of her German customers, a certain Herr Weiss. He provided her family with official papers that would guarantee their safety, warned her about an incoming *Aktion* against the Jews, and helped them move to Warsaw, where it was easier to find a hiding place. Ita managed there to hide herself and her daughter in two separate locations; her husband, meanwhile, joined the Armia Krajowa (AK, Underground Polish Home Army), passing as a Gentile. Throughout the war, various Poles frequently threatened the Koplowiczes with denunciation, took financial advantage of them, and subjected their young daughter to cruel treatment while they were in hiding. In this aspect of their rescue, they were totally powerless. Nor were things much better after the war, as Ita's short but informative narrative suggests:

> During the first days of February 1945, we reached Sosnowiec by several means of transportation. We few were the first ones [to come]; apart from us, there were just a few other Jews. I remember when one Pole told me then: "Do you know, lady, how many Jews have returned here?" The Poles did not see the thousands of murdered Jews of Sosnowiec, only the meager bunch of those who managed to survive, but even these ones were bothering them. Antisemitism had always existed in Poland, but now, after additional training from the Hitlerites, it began to grow. Even my tiny daughter, who had started going to school, was suffering because of that. The nun-teachers were giving an example themselves, bullying Jewish kids.
>
> After a while we recovered our pharmaceutical store and ran it until 1950, until the moment of our departure for Israel.

Although Ita provides almost no dates, names, or detailed episodes, her account of her postwar arrival home is anything but silent. Her testimony depicts an image that is clear and persuasive in its simplicity: a Pole's anger regarding the number of returning Jews is a sign, for her, of the greater phenomenon of Poles' hostility to the miserly number of Jews who managed to survive the infernal Nazi hunt. She portrays such anti-Jewish hostility as genetically connected to prewar antisemitism in Poland and relying on its witnessing of the Nazi process of Jewish extermination for its greatest impulse to brutality. In the end, even Catholic nuns attacked schoolgirls for their Jewishness. The picture that emerges offers a gruesome, convincing explanation of why the Koplowiczes had to leave Poland for Israel.

Chaim's and Ita's testimonies concerning their return to Sosnowiec, like many other testimonies from Poland and Israel that refer to towns from all over Poland, speak differently of similar experiences and remain silent on different topics. These moments of silence sound different tunes. Chaim's memories and the memories of multiple other survivors who recorded their war histories with the Jewish Historical Commission in Poland during the immediate postwar period appear to express themselves according to certain patterns. These patterns, indicative of a collective memory, are transformed, however, once the survivors recall their wartime pasts later in a different place: Israel. In general, in Israel the survivors appear more outspoken in expressing their memories about what happened to them when they returned to their homes, and they tend to see Polish hostility as one continuous historical process that prompted them to leave the country and to come to Israel.

In each case—in Poland immediately after the war and in Israel a decade or so later—the record of the memory of the Holocaust survivors was exposed like a photographic negative to a different range of light. In each case, survivors were expected—or, at least, it appears that they thought they were expected—to recall their wartime and postwar histories in a different way. Each country and each era were positioned in different contexts, which appear to have lent color to these memories.

This book has grown out of a desire to understand both kinds of narratives and both sorts of perspectives that the returning Jews expressed in their testimonies. The determination to pursue this project followed the need to enter the world of the survivors and to consider their own interpretations of what was happening to them during the first volatile moments of arriving home after the war. To what extent were they allowed to come home? Had anyone warned them about anti-Jewish assaults at home? Had anyone extended to them any badly needed help, perhaps a warm meal, a set of clothes, or a few kitchen pots? How did these survivors speak about these moments of arrival to "their own people"—the Jewish interviewers in Poland—at a time when the ghastly scale of German mass murder was only beginning to be officially discovered and when the necessity of deciding to stay in Poland or to leave hung heavy in the air? How would they remember these same moments of the return home once they found themselves in completely different circumstances, in the relative safety of their own land, and from the perspective of looking back on a time already past?

This book is an attempt to situate the patterns of memory of Holocaust survivors within the changing geopolitical realities of the two countries where their memories were recorded. In early postwar Poland, the newly Communist Holocaust epicenter, monoethnic tendencies crowded out public expressions of Jewish culture and Jewish memory. In the Israel of the 1950s and 1960s, in contrast, a parallel pressure to portray survivors as heroes and partisans discounted the experiences of "ordinary" survivors who did not engage in armed anti-Nazi resistance. Differing, complex parameters governed the recording of these memories of the survivors' reception at the hands of their former neighbors. My goal has been to uncover these parameters so as to understand better how the survivors themselves might have seen their own encounters with Polish Gentiles after the war.

A number of questions can be considered to analyze and frame these two sets of Holocaust narratives: When were they created? Who was speaking and to whom? In what language? What were the historical, political, cultural, and social contexts within which a testimony was rendered? What questions were asked? What questions did the survivors *think* were being asked? To what extent did the survivors attempt to protect themselves or their rescuers by revealing more or less about postwar Polish–Jewish interactions? To what extent did they thus attempt to supply more justification for leaving Poland or to establish their Zionist credentials? What about the violence against their Gentile rescuers that many returning Jews reported? Was the postwar violence politically motivated, directed only at certain Communist sympathizers who might have happened to be Jewish, or was it specifically aimed at Polish Jews, whatever their political leanings?

A close reading of the testimonies of Chaim Wittelsohn, Ita Koplowicz, and others like them from Poland or Israel becomes an exercise in distinguishing one picture from the interposition of multiple images in order to re-create one collective memory from multiple sets of cultural, political, and even psychological circumstances. Any one testimony may seem not to render a sufficient image, given the many silences and distortions (political, cultural, and emotional) that can influence a narrative. A close reading of two or more selections of multiple testimonies together, however, may permit the researcher to re-create a powerful representation of the experiences common to a Jewish homecoming.

To understand these narratives, I researched two unique collections of testimonies that have not yet been investigated with this particular focus in mind: (1) testimonies gathered in Poland immediately after the war by the CŻKH and currently stored in the archives of the Żydowski Instytut Historyczny (ŻIH, Jewish Historical Institute) in Warsaw (AŻIH Collections 301 and 302, with the letter A standing for "Archives"); and (2) testimonies collected during the 1950s and 1960s by Yad Vashem (YV), the Holocaust Martyrs' and Heroes' Remembrance Authority, in Jerusalem and currently stored in the archives there (AYV Collections O3 and O33).

In Poland, I looked at testimonies collected between the years 1944 and 1950, and in Israel I researched documents deposited from 1955 to 1970. On average, the gap between the times when the two collections were made is about twenty years. The periods I focused on might seem arbitrary, but they make more sense in context. My analysis compares accounts not only from two distinct cultural, geopolitical realities but also from what I argue are two different eras for the survivors. The Polish testimonies span the six years during which the CŻKH's activity was relatively unobstructed and there was as yet some indication that Jewish survivors might be able to recover a semblance of the prewar structure of their communal life. By 1950, when all of the independent Jewish institutions were closed, this hope was crushed, and the Jewish community became even more marginal in Poland. The Israeli testimonies record the voices of victims who were not yet recognized and accepted as fully contributing citizens in their new state. During that era, owing to the trials and conflicts that befell the State of Israel, the voices of the Holocaust survivors would be used to form part of an official narrative to construct the identity of a renascent Israeli nation. It was a process that started with the Eichmann trial in 1961 but was preceded by a polarization of the "Israelis"—who included ghetto fighters and partisans—and the rest of the survivors, manifested throughout two important public debates in Israel: one over reparations from Germany (1952–53) and the other over the trial of Dr. Rudolph Kasztner (1954–55). By 1955, the public realization of the presence of the survivors, who were often perceived in negative terms as victims who had gone to their death like "sheep to the slaughter," was set in a process of change that culminated with the Six-Day War of 1967. By the time the realities of the victory in the war as well as the painful cultural "flashbacks" preceding it sank in for the society, the integration of the Holocaust into Israeli national memory had been achieved. I rounded up to 1970 the end date for the testimonies I selected to use because I aimed to include those voices that followed this extraordinary evolution of collective memory. Therefore, I compare testimonies that function as manifestations of two eras, each with its own characteristics, during which the survivors struggled to give voice to traumatic postwar experiences.

My goal was to uncover any residues of collective memory among the survivors in Poland and Israel, so I researched adult testimonies and diaries because the adult perspective is more likely to lend itself to the formation of a collective memory. Children's impressions of first encounters with Poles may reveal complex, developmental experiences; their tender age, however, most likely complicated their presentation of any self-understanding of a Jewish identity, just as it might have limited the impact of the children's Jewishness on the quality of their contact with native Poles. Adult survivors could appreciate the contrast between "Pole" and "Jew" in a Polish historical context and can be expected to have expressed their impressions in the form of a more mature memory.

Another problem that comes with considering children's testimonies is that the psychological cost of a double identity for a child who was used to hiding is not the same as the cost for an adult. Children in hiding were for their own safety forbidden to identify with their Jewishness. Even after the war, rescuers were not always eager to return children to Jewish relatives or Jewish institutions. Properly speaking, then, Jewish children would rarely have experienced the kind of "first encounters" with Polish Gentiles that are the subject of my analysis. A child could continue living with a sheltering family until a Jewish institution or relative made contact to begin the process of retrieval, a process that the child might have been only minimally aware of. A child would be less likely to recount experiences comparable to those of adults, who returned to a social environment where distinctions between "Polish" and "Jewish" were clearly defined and understood.

Today, interest in the postwar memory of Holocaust survivors in Poland forms part of two broader historiographical tendencies. On the one hand, it falls within the ample range of memory and trauma studies, which—insofar as the Holocaust is concerned—have developed intensely for the past three decades, following a shift toward the perspective of the witness. In Polish historiography, on the other hand, intensive research on wartime and postwar Polish–Jewish relations has been spurred on by the historical and moral public debates that erupted following the Polish publication of Jan T. Gross's book *Neighbors: The Destruction of the Jewish Community in Jedwabne, Poland* in 2001, which were intensified a few years later by the publication of two more works by Gross: *Fear: Anti-Semitism in Poland after Auschwitz* in 2006 and *Golden Harvest: Events at the Periphery of the Holocaust* in 2012, cowritten with Irena Grudzińska-Gross (the Polish versions of these books were published in 2000, 2008, and 2011, respectively).[4] This new Polish critical history has challenged a Polish "historical memory" of innocence and of aid allegedly provided collectively to Jews by uncovering a documented history of Polish violence toward and denunciations of Jews.

In the next section, I briefly outline some fundamental shifts within memory studies that have allowed for readmitting victims' testimony as evidence to form part of the historical discourse.

Memory

The primary framework for memory studies is the concept of collective memory as formulated by the early-twentieth-century French sociologist Maurice Halbwachs. According to Halbwachs, collective memory is, at least in part, a function of the community, which carries particular images, concepts, and notions of the past that bind the collective in a symbolic way. These images, concepts, and notions—or frameworks—are not the sum of the individual memories of members of the collective but a sort of separate, overarching structure of meanings that is used "to reconstruct an image of the past which is in accord, in each epoch, with the predominant thoughts of the society."[5] An individual participates in that framework by acquiring memories, recollecting them, and localizing them in society. The structure of collective memory exists to the degree that it is placed there by individuals; nevertheless, "the mind reconstructs its memories under the pressure of society."[6] Verbal conventions serve as a means to express frameworks of collective memory; it is crucial, therefore, to look at the kinds of narratives that people create as well as at the degree to which these narratives may overlap or subvert the "dominant" discourse.

What is striking in Halbwach's notion of collective memory, however, is the implied erasure of the remembering individual as the bearer of collective memory within the community. Therefore, a researcher studying collective memory must be alert not to assume passivity on the part of the agents of collective memory—the persons who actually remember, recall, and commemorate.

In contrast to Halbwach's dynamic of influence and pressure, recent social history projects are interested primarily not—as Anna Green, a historian of collective memory, points out—in the issue that "individuals draw upon contemporary cultural discourses to make sense of their lives, but [in the issue of] *which* ones, and *why*."[7] In other words, although these more recent projects fully acknowledge the influence of collective memory, they emphasize that the question for the individual subject remains the choice of a particular framework to express that collective memory.

In their important book *War and Remembrance in the Twentieth Century*, Jay Winter and Emmanuel Sivan have also challenged an oppressive understanding of collective memory as expressed in collective acts of remembrance. Responding to a notion that collective memory operates within major forces that have the power to enforce types of remembrance (a view proposed by French historian Pierre Nora, for example[8]), Winter and Sivan indicate the more nuanced social interactions of players who participate and influence each other in creating types of remembering:

> The state is ever-present but it is neither ubiquitous nor omnipotent. Civil society is where many groups try to work out their own strategies of remembrance alongside the state and sometimes against it. . . . Remembrance consists of negotiations between a multiplicity of groups, including the state. Obviously, the partners are not equal. Repression happens, but counter voices may be heard. If some voices are weaker than others, at least in the context of a pluralistic society, this is not only because they lack resources. . . . They may also be weak because of self-censorship due to lack of moral status in the eyes of others, or due to low self image.[9]

Boaz Cohen, an Israeli scholar, has applied Winter and Sivan's findings to his research on Israeli Holocaust historiography. Cohen notes that their theory challenges the mainstream research on collective memory, which emphasizes the manipulation of memory by strong political elites or governments. The application of this theory to the Israeli historiography of the Holocaust is especially appropriate in that multiple groups—survivors, members of *Landsmanschaftn* (mutual aid societies formed by immigrants from the same town or region), former partisans and ghetto fighters, the Israeli academic establishment, and others—proposed different ideas for remembering the Holocaust and exerted different pressures on the Knesset to establish Yad Vashem.[10] I address this issue later in the book, but it is important here to emphasize that scholars have challenged the concept of collective memory as an oppressive force and have proposed an alternative theory that recognizes individual participants as agents of memory.

Scholarship on the Polish memory of the Holocaust, although not a subject of this book, developed in a direction that led to the breakthrough public debates that followed the publication of Gross's book *Neighbors*. In that respect, the now famous publication of Jan Błoński's essay "The Poor

Poles Look at the Ghetto" in 1987,[11] although generally met with a hostile popular reaction, had the positive influence of stirring discussion about wartime Polish–Jewish relations among the intelligentsia.

Even though a few Polish historians did publish methodologically unassailable works on Polish anti-Jewish violence, none of these works ever really broke through to the national popular consciousness; they were either studied or ignored, but in either case only by specialists. In the late 1990s, however, one scholar did study the question of a Polish memory of the Holocaust: Michael Steinlauf researched his subject in situ—studying Polish sources and interviewing Polish participants in the Polish–Jewish dialogue, an approach rare in itself and from a scholarly perspective very challenging. The resulting book, *Bondage to the Dead: Poland and the Memory of the Holocaust*, seemed to employ for the very first time in the Polish case a psychological theory to describe and possibly to explain the Poles' mostly indifferent or even hostile attitudes toward their Jewish neighbors as these Jews were being annihilated. Steinlauf applies to the case of Poland Robert Jay Lifton's concept of a "death guilt" that accompanies the helpless witnessing of a death—a guilt, he says, that was exacerbated in Poland by a common wish that the Jews would simply disappear. Although Poles, according to Steinlauf, "committed no crime, there was nothing to expiate—yet Polish history had loaded the act of witnessing the Holocaust to spring a psychological and moral trap from which there was no apparent exit." Accordingly, "the unacceptable, unmasterable guilt could only be denied and repressed, thereafter to erupt into history in particularly distorted forms."[12] Steinlauf analyzes and "diagnoses" the kinds of Holocaust memory that dominated Polish society, determining that this memory was "wounded" from 1944 to 1948, "repressed" from 1948 to 1968, "expelled" from 1968 to 1970, "reconstructed" from 1970 to 1989, and possibly "recovered" after the fall of communism. His application of psychological notions to assess just how Polish society dealt with the memory of the Holocaust paved the way for Gross's theory of a guilt-ridden, anti-Jewish, Polish aggression and more broadly aided the process of self-reflection on the part of Polish researchers and "ordinary citizens" about Poles' collective memory of the Jews and Polish attitudes toward the Jews.

The larger inspiration for my research was Gross's breakthrough project. Gross's focus—the victims' perspective—has been picked up by Polish historians and other humanities scholars connected with the Centrum Badań nad Zagładą Żydów (Polish Center for Holocaust Research, Warsaw). This center, established in 2003, has been publishing cutting-edge research on newly accessible archival material, unpublished sources, and field studies in the annual *Zagłada Żydów: Studia i Materiały* as well as in various books. Although the range of this new research is broad—literary, philosophical, and historical—the unifying factor is a primary attention to the victims' perspective, an approach that was previously universally lacking in Polish historiography of the Jewish catastrophe even though it was ubiquitous in the treatment of ethnic Polish experiences during the Second World War. In my research, I have followed in particular the approach taken by Barbara Engelking, the first Polish scholar to focus on Jewish victims' experiences. In her recent book *Such a Beautiful Sunny Day . . . : Jews Seeking Refuge in the Polish Countryside, 1942–1945*, Engelking follows Jews who wandered the Polish countryside in search of shelter.[13] Analyzing accounts and memoirs created during and after the war as well as postwar trial reports, she turns traditional Polish historiography upside down, writing an empathetic narrative that considers fragments of records and shards of speech in an attempt to understand the emotions experienced by Jewish men, women, and children desperately trying to avoid recognition and denunciation. In my book, I attempt to follow Engelking in using as much as possible the survivors' own words and resisting to the extent possible the imposition of my own interpretations on their expressions.

Testimony

The current preoccupation with witnessing and testimony in contemporary historiography—particularly in Holocaust historiography—can serve as an illustration of a search for a memory that, according to some, appears to be vanishing. What has been termed "the era of the witness,"[14] beginning with a greater, romanticizing interest in life stories from around the 1970s, became ubiquitous in contemporary culture, eventually influencing how people want their history to be read. In eyewitness accounts, the survivors' firsthand retelling bestows on them an aura of authenticity, which deters the reader from questioning an account, even while validating multiple perspectives that at times may even contradict one another.

Interestingly enough, we can find this same approach being used right after the war. Jewish historians' first attempts to write about the catastrophe in its immediate aftermath not only relied on personal accounts but also advocated their use. Researchers for the immediate postwar historical commissions also tended to write about what was at the time recent history "from the victims' perspective." In the English-speaking world, the psychologist David Boder interviewed displaced persons (DPs) in four countries after the war (most of these DPs were Jewish survivors living in Germany). Boder was particularly interested in the effect of extreme suffering on one's personality as well as in the ethnographic heritage of the vanished Jewish world.[15] Similarly, as I outline later, survivor-historians in Israel advocated writing Holocaust history from a "Jewish victims' perspective" and so became involuntarily embroiled in a methodological conflict with the "indigenous" Israeli historians of a German academic tradition who advocated an "objective," scholarly perspective. Against the background of this conflict, Isaiah Trunk and Yehuda Bauer, two prominent Israeli Holocaust historians, worked from the Jews' perspective. "There is no Holocaust history without witnesses," Bauer asserted. Although testimonies are "intended to mislead," he wrote, their value for research cannot be overstated, for "the Germans tried to murder the murder: they tried to prevent Jews from documenting what happened."[16]

Scholars in the United States have been slow to recognize the value of these accounts, in part because they are following Raul Hilberg's caution about them. It was only quite recently, in fact, that Saul Friedländer formulated a notion of "integrated history" that would incorporate the voices of victims in a recounting of the history of the Holocaust.[17] Similarly, Christopher Browning has turned to investigating personal experiences contained in testimonies of the survivors of the Nazi camp at Starachowice in order to reacquire a perspective that the German legal system willingly discounted and thus allowed the acquittal of a Nazi war criminal.[18]

Cultural and linguistic scholars had already "discovered" testimonies earlier, however, reading them both in terms of what they meant to a specific audience and as a medium of cultural memory. In this field, one case in point is Lawrence Langer's breakthrough investigation of the "deep memory" revealed by oral testimonies, published in 1991;[19] another is Shoshana Felman and Dori Laub's work *Testimony: Crises of Witnessing in Literature, Psychoanalysis, and History*, published in 1992, which confronts the limits of accessing the deep reality of trauma in a witness's account and contains examples of literary and film commentaries on witnessing twentieth-century catastrophes.[20]

Remarks on Methodology

My research studies testimonies to uncover and understand the memories of Jewish Holocaust survivors as perceived and expressed in their own terms. Methodologically, this study is concerned with reconstructing emic categories, as the survivors themselves saw them. In cultural analysis, the use of emic categories signifies the abdication of an epistemological search for explainable behavior; the researcher instead stops just short at the threshold of the world presented by the subjects of his or her research. The researcher's task then becomes to present the subject's world as faithfully as possible, without sacrificing, however, its broader placement within a spectrum of adequately selected phenomena. Following Ward Goodenough, who strove through the use of such emic categories to understand the meaning of particular beliefs and practices,[21] I take each testimony at face value, without attempting to verify its factuality. I then attempt to reconstruct the world that "welcomed" the survivors, who were reaching for their own experiences as expressed in their own words after the war.

Although my research is primarily qualitative, I also perform a limited statistical analysis, typical of quantitative research, of images and tropes that appear more and less frequently in the survivors' testimonies. To analyze the documents, therefore, I employ the fundamentals of grounded theory—a method of qualitative research that uses "a *systematic* set of *procedures* to *develop* an inductively derived grounded theory about a *phenomenon*."[22] Grounded theory, developed by the sociologists Barney Glaser and Anselm Strauss and in use as a method of qualitative research since the mid-1960s,[23] seemed particularly suited for my analysis, in which the data serve as a starting point for formulating a theory about how returning Polish Jews perceived their reception at the hands of ethnic Poles. Instead of trying to find a confirmation or repudiation of a prevailing historical perception that the Polish population uniformly behaved in a hostile manner toward Jewish survivors and that these survivors therefore tended to develop highly negative memories of their first encounters with ethnic Poles, my approach was to see "what was there," what the survivors actually reported, without preconceived notions. Such inductive research—from the ground up, so to speak—allowed me to reconstruct what the returning Jews thought about their neighboring Poles' reception of them and to identify which images appear more or less frequently in accounts recorded at the time. According to a dictum of the founders of grounded theory, "One does not begin with a theory, then prove it. Rather, one begins with an area of study[,] and what is relevant to that area is allowed to emerge."[24]

Regarding the ethnic categories "Poles/Polish" and "Jews/Jewish," one must remain aware that they are, at most, research tools. Ethnic identities are fluid, hybrid, and porous; they may undergo alteration over a lifespan, and so they may be used in contradictory ways according to different contexts. At the time of a "limit-experience," as the Holocaust can be existentially understood, Poles, both Jews and Gentiles, used these clear-cut, even crude, and Nazi-imposed categories. Whatever religious affiliation or personal preference a Polish citizen of Jewish origins might have had, even if she came from an assimilated family that did not identify at all with things Jewish, once cast as a "non-Aryan," she had no choice but to follow those options opened (i.e., not closed) to all "non-Aryans." For lack of a better solution, I therefore rely on this wartime, binary distinction, universally encountered in contemporary Polish–Jewish interactions reported in written documents, although I recognize that it represents an imperfect, semantic demarcation.

1

The Returning Survivors

Historical Context

By the end of the Second World War, Poland and the Poles had been, according to any objective political or social assessment, simply ruined. In a deal sealed at Yalta in February 1945, the supposedly "friendly" transfer of the eastern regions of Poland to Stalin in exchange for a strip of land east of the Oder River was merely a material sign of the political, physical, and emotional truncation that the Polish people had experienced as inhabitants of a central battleground of the war and a harbinger of what they were yet to experience under communism. By war's end, Poland had lost more than 5 million citizens, more than half of whom were of Jewish origin. Ninety percent of the Jewish population had been lost, in comparison to 15 percent of the ethnic Poles. Before the war, Poles had accounted for about 65 percent of a multiethnic Polish state; after the war, the entire population of the People's Republic of Poland could claim to be, for all practical reasons, monoethnic. All of its minorities had been either dispersed or destroyed.

The Christian population of Poland was left exhausted and without resources. The worst of the Nazi terror against the Poles had been directed against the Polish intelligentsia, understood in its widest sense to include not only the intellectuals, writers, artists, clergy, teachers, state officials, and doctors but also lower-level clerks, pharmacists, and small-town officials. It has been estimated that during the war Poland lost about 45 percent of its physicians and dentists, 57 percent of its attorneys, more than 15 percent of its teachers, 40 percent of its professors, half of its engineers, about 30 percent of its technicians, and more than 18 percent of its clergy.¹ Close to 38 percent of university graduates and 30 percent of high school graduates lost their lives;² postwar Polish society stood bereft of a "middle class" that could cherish the values of the Second Polish Republic and lead the country in the direction of restoration. The remaining population was instead divided, as Marcin Zaremba has summarized using the image of two Polands:

> "Poland B": poor and uneducated, with a strong sense of deprivation, full of fears and wounds. More connected with the Church, conservative and traditional, living rather in the countryside and in small towns. It is in her that the Polish Communists placed hopes of modernizing, and primarily within that group that they looked to find functionaries of the system. The revolution from the top, however, had its base—in the marginalized and "disposable" people. It gave them the chance of promotion, and it used their energy, directing it against the survivors of "Poland A," which was in opposition to it.³

Zaremba's recent social analysis of postwar Polish society has filled in a necessary portrait of how the war, the postwar Communist terror, and the systemic changes that accompanied communism affected Poland on a social level. Zaremba analyzes the Polish postwar society in terms of the immense trauma caused by the prolonged terror of war and of the great fear stabbing into the population from many sides: the new political oppression, lawlessness, and a lack of social structures and institutions—in other words, a sort of anarchy, which resulted in an extremely high frequency of brutal crimes, robberies, rapes, "generalized" aggression and violence, and alcoholism. Zaremba attempts, without justifying murder, to understand to some degree the hostilities toward minorities, in particular toward the Jews, in that context of aggression and the transference of that aggression to "strangers."⁴

People were haunted by the ubiquity of death and by extreme poverty, hunger, disease, social disintegration, and atomization. The psychological manifestations of these problems were a fear of death, arrests, and tortures as well as an anxiety for loved ones. The society was initially relieved, of course, to have the war over but was soon disappointed in how a Communist government was imposed on Poles by Moscow and how in a vicious, personal campaign the wartime Polish government based in London and the military Underground that had answered to it were attacked as "Hitler's helpers" and persecuted en masse.

During the first two years after the end of the war—until July 1947—Polish society was also in a state of opposition to and struggle against the oppressive terror. Many continued the physical combat against the Red Army as well as against the Polish army loyal to it, and others expressed their opposition by disobeying the official organs of authority, lending mass support to the Underground, engaging in strikes and manifestations, and voting against the Polska Partia Robotnicza (Polish Workers Party) in a referendum held in June 1946.

We cannot consider hostility and violence against others in postwar Poland without a proper assessment of the brutal context in which the Red Army introduced the new Communist system to the Polish population. Although historians may debate the appropriateness of the term *civil war* for an internal struggle between Underground forces that stood for a prewar government now in exile in London and the official Polish army created in the Soviet Union, together with security and militia forces created to pacify a population that was for the most part vehemently against the Communist system, estimates of the number of victims of these brutal struggles range from 20,000 to 50,000. During the second half of 1944 alone, the Narodnyi Komissariat Vnutrennikh Del (NKVD; Soviet People's Commissariat for Internal Affairs), with the help of the Urząd Bezpieczeństwa (UB; Polish Security Office), arrested and deported to the Soviet interior tens of thousands of members of the Underground connected to the Polish government in London; another 8,500 members were killed in raids and clashes with the Soviet army or with the Ukrainska Povstanska Armiia (UPA; Ukrainian Insurgent Army).[5]

The first postwar years were volatile, especially for the Polish Jews. As the wave of liberation cum Soviet subjugation progressed from east to west, the Jews found themselves suddenly freed and eager to return to their hometowns. The majority of the remnant Polish Jews were not located in historic Polish lands at the time of their liberation; most of them would return from the Soviet Union. Many of them, in fact, would return and then decide to leave again after just a few weeks or months. During 1946, with some hope for a restitution of Jewish life in Poland, many Jews considered staying. The increasing violence, however, culminating in the Kielce Pogrom of July 4, 1946, brutally quashed these hopes and caused the subsequent flight of the majority of Jewish survivors in Poland.

Estimation of Numbers

The census of the Polish population in 1931, the last census taken before the Second World War, counted a little more than 3 million Jews among the close to 32 million Polish citizens—9.8 percent of the entire population. Various adjustments made for the period leading up to the war contribute to an estimation of the Jewish population of Poland of about 3.5 million in September 1939. Following a calculation of Jewish victims during consecutive phases of the Holocaust—the first from the concentration of the Jews in the ghettoes to the final liquidation of the ghettoes; the second from June–July 1941 to the German occupation of the eastern part of Poland, a time that coincided with widespread exterminations; and the third a phase characterized by the so-called remnant and secondary ghettoes as well as the labor camps—the losses among Polish Jewry can be estimated at about 2.7 million, with a death rate of roughly 80.9 percent.[6]

It is nigh impossible, however, to give a precise number of Jewish survivors after the war. In contrast to the practice of singling out Jews for deportation or immediate murder according to a recorded list in many countries, the Nazis did not follow such strict registers in occupied Poland. The postwar situation in Poland, with the loss of close to one-third of its land following the Yalta agreements, made research on those areas that had been appropriated by the Soviet Union impossible. Recently, moreover, there has been a tendency to lower estimations of the numbers of victims of the Second World War, including Polish Jewish victims: the number of Jewish victims, once estimated to be 3.3 million, has more recently been estimated at about 2.9 million.[7]

Attempts to give an approximate estimate of the numbers of the Jewish survivors in Poland in the immediate postwar period are also impeded by the difficulties inherent in the fluidity of the Polish social and political order at the time: although the Polish government relied on Jewish organizations to provide a count of returning Polish citizens of Jewish origins, these counts were made difficult by the constant migration of survivors around Poland as well as by the reluctance of the possibly numerous and unaccounted for survivors to declare their Jewish identities and register with Jewish organizations.[8]

What is known, according to the documents of the Centralny Komitet Żydów w Polsce (CKŻP, Central Committee of Polish Jews), is that by January 1946 more than 106,000 people had registered as Polish Jews. If we add to that number those survivors who did not reveal themselves as Jews, the estimate of survivors could range as high as 120,000. The number of Jews returning from the interior of the Soviet Union remains an even greater puzzle, beginning with the question of how so many had found themselves in the Soviet Union in the first place. It is estimated that from 300,000 to 600,000 Jews were deported in 1941, and they, like the rest of Polish population, would have encountered a tragic plight: multitudes appear to have perished in the gulag or in prisons or from hunger, war, and epidemics.

The first organized repatriation of Polish Jews from the Soviet Union (following an agreement in July 1945) comprised survivors from the Ukrainian, Lithuanian, and Byelorussian Soviet Socialist Republics—altogether almost 55,000 Jews.[9] Apart from this organized repatriation, individual returns of Jewish survivors were already taking place in the fall of 1944 because of the porous nature of the eastern borders.[10] The greatest influx of Polish Jews from the interior of the Soviet Union, however, took place between February and September 1946. According to Yehuda Bauer, of the 200,000 Polish Jews who were in the Soviet Union, about 175,000 returned to Poland, and by June 30, 1946, there were more than 240,000 registered Jews there.[11] Following the experiences of violence against Jews on Polish soil between July 1946 and June 1947, in particular the Kielce Pogrom, approximately 100,000 to 120,000 Jews left Poland, of whom about 80,000 made the move through organized Zionist emigration. Altogether, during 1945–47, more than 150,000 Jews left Poland either legally or illegally, half of whom departed just after the Kielce Pogrom. Nearly 100,000 Jews still lived in Poland as of 1947.[12]

Many incidental findings indicate, however, that the actual Jewish community was significantly larger than statistics might otherwise suggest. In 1948, William Bein, the director of the American Jewish Joint Distribution Committee (JOINT) in Poland, estimated that several thousand Jews still lived under "Aryan" papers.[13] According to Karen Auerbach's research on the postwar lives of families in Warsaw, half did not register with any Jewish institution,[14] and, according to Małgorzata Melchior's analysis, twenty-four out of twenty-six survivor interviewees did not leave any account of their experiences with the CŻKH).[15] The problem of a new "marranism"—hiding one's Jewish identity as the Jews had done during the persecutions in fifteenth-century Spain—was noted and sometimes ridiculed or treated with hostility, even by other Jews. These survivors' choice of identity was dictated by fear and a social need to belong.

Survivors from the Soviet Union

Those Jews who had survived the war in the Soviet Union came home weighed down by a starkly different baggage of experiences, memories, and expectations than that which oppressed those who had lived through the German occupation in Poland. First of all, in spite of the harsh circumstances of deportation to the Soviet interior, many more family members managed to survive together there than did the Jews in occupied Poland, where the survivors were usually the only individuals left out of entire families. When these deportees were allowed to return to Poland, however, they usually came back with literally nothing but the coats on their backs, in contrast to the Polish returnees from the eastern Polish regions, who could bring some of their possessions (including livestock) with them. The Jewish survivors, who were for the most part refugees from central and eastern Poland, did not manage to save any of their material possessions. The Jews who survived the war were thus the ones most affected by the question of the recovery of property.[16]

Another important question was the survivors' ability to return to the workforce to support themselves. About 20 to 30 percent of them were unable to perform any work at all because they were invalids or sick or elderly persons, and children up to the age of sixteen composed about 20 percent of the returnees (approximately 30,000). Men, who survived the Soviet imprisonment in greater numbers than women, amounting to 55 percent of the registered repatriates, had already been forced to increase their work qualifications (from 30 to 70 percent of them had to do so), particularly in manual industrial jobs (for example, as miners or as workers in other heavy industries), in which Jews previously had rarely been employed.[17] Now, in the new Communist reality, the CKŻP, expecting that the old occupational structure of the Polish Jews—different from that of the Gentile Poles—might potentially become a seed of the return of anti-Jewish hostilities, worked to make the Jews more productive by retraining them in occupations deemed more in harmony with the ethos of a future workers' paradise. In fact, this labor issue affected many people, not only Jews, for the war and the new sociopolitical-economic system had changed the social and political expectations of human work. The Jewish repatriates from the Soviet Union, however, included a large number from the intelligentsia—teachers, journalists, literati, artists, actors, social and political activists—who would organize and fill the Jewish leadership positions in Poland. Most of them spoke Yiddish.[18]

This group of survivors seemed to have the least idea of how total and gruesome the Jewish annihilation in occupied Poland had been. Certain reports might have reached them somewhere in the depths of the Soviet Union, although it might have been hard for them not to dismiss the totalizing character of the German onslaught on the Jewish community as mere Communist propaganda. The reports that reached Polish Jews in the Soviet Union were for the most part extremely careful in assessing the scale of German murder of the Jews and even unwilling (perhaps under the influence of the Communist authorities) to note that the Nazis had singled out the Jews for total extermination.[19] Yet even those who believed the more accurate reports could not have fully grasped the near-total extent of the annihilation. The possibility that upon returning to one's hometown or village one might not encounter even a single surviving Jew or a single surviving Jewish building was incomprehensible. To that initial shock was soon added the realization that Jews were not at all welcome among the ethnic Poles. The latter apprehension often came while a returnee was still on the train home: soon after the train crossed the Polish border, anti-Communist partisans would attempt to compel the Polish Gentile repatriates to give up the Jews among them, at which point the returning Jews were typically beaten or killed "for cooperation with the Soviets."[20]

Survivors from the "Aryan" Side

As many as 30,000 to 60,000 Jews may have been saved by going into hiding within the territory of the General Government—that is, the German zone of occupation; the statistics, however, are inconclusive. After the war was over, many of them chose to remain under an "Aryan" name and identity and neither to register with Jewish organizations nor otherwise to reveal their background. This group had already learned to use camouflage to survive, some by hiding completely from sight, others by hiding in plain sight, assuming the appearance and mannerisms expected of a Polish Catholic. Many apparently preferred to maintain such an assumed identity after the war for its comparative safety and anonymity.[21]

During the war, some Jews took their survival completely into their own hands—for instance, by arranging hideouts in the forests—or else organized themselves and joined forest camps or partisan groups. Forest camps began to be arranged around the second half of 1941, while partisan groups began to develop around the spring of 1942 (most often with the assistance of the Soviet army). The Polish Underground army did not usually accept Jewish fighters, and both individual soldiers and even entire units of the AK and the Narodowe Siły Zbrojne (NSZ, National Armed Forces) were involved in killing Jews in hiding.[22] The greatest challenge for the Jewish groups in the forests was to find food. At some point, many had to resort to stealing, for most of the peasants did not want to provide for them. Many of these Jews, however, did manage to join the Polish army by the end of the war and so took part in the liberation. It is estimated that among the armed Jews and the Jews hiding out in the forests, 2,000 and 3,000, respectively, managed to survive the war; the rest were killed.[23] After the war, the partisans formed their own combatant Jewish organizations but were ultimately forced to disband and join the only combatant organization allowed in Communist Poland, the Związek Bojowników o Wolność i Demokrację (Union of Fighters for Freedom and Democracy).[24]

Survivors from the Camps

Probably the third-largest group of survivors came from the German concentration and forced labor camps. Those who survived the extermination centers were an extremely small group, numbering fewer than 200 people (including 100 men from Treblinka). Precise numbers are unavailable, but estimates indicate that about 50,000 to 80,000 Polish prisoners were liberated from concentration camps, among whom were an unknown number of Polish Jews.[25] To make the matter even less certain, it is not known how many of these former prisoners returned to Poland and how many remained in DP camps. The CKŻP reports that about 17,000 registered Jews returned from the camps by the middle of 1945.[26] Estimates that Jewish camp survivors numbered between 20,000 and 40,000 are therefore plausible.[27]

About 15,000 Jews from all over Europe, half of whom were Polish, were liberated from the camps in Lower Silesia. These survivors organized themselves into the Komitet Byłych Więźniów (Committee of Former Prisoners), later transformed into a Komitet Żydowski (Jewish Committee) in Dzierżoniów. In June 1945, the Jews of Lower Silesia organized their first conference, at which the strong intention of remaining in Poland and beginning a new, creative existence was expressed.[28]

The survivors from the camps usually returned on their own because the Polish administration, in spite of its declared intention to arrange for planes and other transportation, was very slow to act and, indeed, quite chaotic. The arrivals of survivors from the camps appear to have been initially met with indifference in Polish society, irrespective of the survivors' ethnic origins. Once the Poles suspected a Jewish background, however, they apparently threatened these camp survivors with the same discriminatory and hostile treatment as the rest of the Jewish survivors.

The camp survivors attempted to join various Polish combatant organizations, with differing results. Occasionally, an application was denied without explanation; some applicants, however, received a reply indicating their unsuitability because of a "non-Aryan origin."[29]

Arrivals

At the beginning of 1946, a delegation of the Komitet Organizacyjny Żydów Polskich (Organizational Committee of Polish Jews), which had been formed in Moscow in July 1944, arrived in Poland to prepare places to receive Jewish repatriates from the Soviet Union. One of the CKŻP's departments took care of the practical side of arranging for accommodation, food, information, and registration.[30] It had already been decided that Lower Silesia, a new territory where even ethnic Poles were predominantly immigrants, would be a relatively safe place to begin Jewish settlement.[31] When Jewish repatriates from the Soviet Union started to arrive, thirty-five special houses (with a total capacity of nearly 7,500), ten specially built barracks, twenty-three hostels, nine homes for seniors, and eleven children's homes awaited them. During the summer of 1946, special "people's kitchens" were distributing close to 250,000 meals per month.[32] Although all of those initiatives were financed by the Polski Komitet Wyzwolenia Narodowego (PKWN, Polish Committee of National Liberation), the survivors' immense needs required still greater resources, which were filled in part by gifts and funds from JOINT and from the Organizacja Rozwoju Wytwórczości (or, in Russian, Obchestvo Remeslenogo Truda [ORT], Association for the Promotion of Skilled Trades).[33]

The survivors' physical and mental condition was disastrous: 60 percent were estimated to be sick or otherwise unable to work, and every third Jew suffered from tuberculosis and required intensive, long-term care. Many had progressive limb paralysis or even symptoms of starvation edema.[34] Lacking in clothes and other basic necessities, they wandered from place to place in search of relatives or a place to sleep. The shelters for returning survivors, which often spontaneously sprang up in buildings lacking beds, windows, water, and bathrooms, were emergency arrangements for homeless Polish Jews that at least allowed them to congregate with people of similar experiences.

The majority of the survivors who remained in Poland after the war chose not to settle in their prewar localities. Some moved away, motivated by a need for safety, and for others the empty houses, streets, and squares of their hometowns, now deprived of Jews, had the appearance of a ghost town. The greatest number of returnees came from central and eastern Poland, which, as I suggested earlier, raised the question of the recovery of their prewar property. Although some property could eventually be recovered, the Jewish population was often simply afraid to raise the issue because their neighbors had manifested enough indifference or hostility toward them already. In attempts to avoid conflict, the authorities promoted Jewish settlement in the western Polish lands, the so-called recovered areas assigned to the Polish borders redrawn at Yalta. Following the greatest influx of Polish Jews from the Soviet Union during the first six months of 1946, when at least 140,000 Jews returned to Poland, the majority (86,000) were directed to live in Lower Silesia because of security concerns.[35] Only a little more than 2,500 survivors of that group decided to return to their hometowns.[36]

First Impressions

Diaries, memoirs, personal documents, interviews, literary texts, and *yizkor bikher* (memorial books) describe the survivors' great longing to return to their homes, to find out who else had survived, and, most often, to revive some semblance of their prewar existence. Reaching their homes, however, witnessing the extent of the destruction, and finding out that no one among their families and friends had survived and that their "place"—in its Jewish meaning—had been eradicated often became an occasion for despair. General impressions of destruction, abandonment, and solitude frequently surfaced in the descriptions of their first visits to their former Jewish settlements, expressed in words connoting demolition and eradication—*destroyed, burned, desecrated, defiled, alienated, cold, homeless,* and *lost.*[37] Ruins, silence, the absence of other Jews, the desecration of synagogues, ritual baths, and cemeteries—all made shocking impressions, revealing to the survivors that the remnants of hope they had cherished of reuniting with their families and friends and of rebuilding some semblance of the prewar Jewish communities were a delusion in the present reality. This disillusionment was deepened by the fear that started to creep in with the first "friendly" warnings that it might be "better" for the Jews to leave their former homes alone.

The survivors recorded any positive or helpful reactions from Polish neighbors in a laconic, factual way. These references were generally to individuals, not to society as a whole or even to sections of it.

Discrimination

The security reports of the new Communist government reflect the atmosphere of fear and discrimination that is also described in Jewish communal reports. Instances of singling out Jewish survivors not only for particular bureaucratic hurdles but also for neglect while in obligatory state care or even for physical attacks began to occur as soon as the survivors entered Polish territory: "A repatriate-Jew," stated one report, "already after crossing the border comes up against a quite unfriendly attitude of nurses, of the Red Cross (recurrent batteries of the Jews by train workers, etc.)."[38]

The CKŻP reports as well as personal memoirs and testimonies note the hostile surprise shown by Poles to the returning Jews, which they expressed in explicit questions or in glances or "looks," as David Sfard writes in his memoir: "Riding a nice stretch of road from undestroyed Praga [a district of Warsaw on the east bank of the Vistula] through the fantastic and strange ruins of Warsaw, I became convinced one more time that those 'looks' were present not only at the airport, and not only in a dream. They accompanied me with a cynical smile and gave me a noble title, with which the Polish nation honored the Jews who miraculously survived the Nazi beasts and their Polish helpers: 'left-overs' [in Polish, *resztki*], pronounced with a specific sneer and with spite."[39]

Regional research confirms that lower-level officials conducted their own discriminatory policies against returning Jews in spite of directives "from the top" (the Political Department of the Ministry of Public Administration) to remedy the unjust trends.[40] The county head of

Biała Podlaska, for example, attempted to prevent Rabbi Berusz Aurbach from fulfilling his functions and refused to register arriving Jews because "they deal with illegal trade, buying various objects from transiting Soviets, which affects very adversely on the economic, social, and cultural relations of all the inhabitants of Biała Podlaska."[41] In Dęblin-Irena (near Kraków), Jews were informed that they could legally settle in only three cities: Lublin, Włodawa, and Żelechów. In Jodłowa, the Stronnictwo Ludowe (Popular Front Party) decided at a meeting in July 1945 to expel the Jews from town and then carried out the decision. In Łódź, separate registration cards were printed for Poles (white) and for Jews, Germans, and Gypsies (yellow). In Sanok, temporary identity cards were stamped with a Ż for "Żyd" (Jew).[42] Many anti-Jewish administrative hurdles were raised especially in the Kielce and Lublin regions.[43]

Specific acts of employment discrimination were directed at Jews in state-run workplaces; official documents and complaints testify to that. In one case, a governor from Lower Silesia (part of the "recovered lands") reported that "all work places are being opened, but only for those who do not have a glaring Semitic appearance."[44] At certain times, Polish workers were against employing Jews in a given factory; at others, in the same way that the Germans rounded people up for forced labor during the war, Jews were picked up on the streets to work in the mines, and their ability to find accommodations depended on their employment in the mining industry.[45]

Murders

Murders represent the peak of a mountain of hostilities that Jewish survivors experienced on their return home. Recent research on postwar anti-Jewish violence in Poland owes its dynamic development to a series of debates that followed the publication of Jan T. Gross's books—in particular *Fear: Anti-Semitism in Poland after Auschwitz*. This research utilizes currently available records of trials based on the so-called August decree (*sierpniówki*, from *sierpień*, August)—that is, the Decree of August 31, 1944—regarding "the punishment of fascist and Nazi criminals guilty of murder and of torturing civilians and [prisoners of war], and of traitors to the Polish Nation."[46]

The issue of the confiscation of Jewish property during the war has been proposed as a primary cause of postwar anti-Jewish hostilities and aggression.[47] The wartime expropriation (or "Aryanization") of Jewish property by the Nazis was witnessed and to some extent inherited by the Poles as those who were "next in line." Property that the Germans had stolen but not sent back to the Reich and that they were not able to take with them when they fled the front was left to the Polish neighbors by default. Apart from the systematic German robbery of the Jews, the Polish neighbors were active in the immediate conversion of Jewish objects (such as clothes, furniture, and other things) as soon as the Jews were herded away for deportation and sometimes even before that. In a postwar situation of exacerbated poverty bordering on the threat of famine,[48] this converted property was now seen as rightfully earned and truly needed by the population. During the war, the conversion had already been considered a fait accompli. Roman Knoll, head of the Foreign Affairs Commission in the Office of the Government Delegate for the Homeland, reported to the Polish government in London in 1943:

> In the Homeland as a whole . . . the position is such that the return of the Jews to their jobs and workshops is completely ruled out of the question, even if the number of Jews were greatly reduced. The non-Jewish population has filled the places of the Jews in the towns and cities—in a large part of Poland this is a fundamental change, final in character. The return of masses of Jews would be experienced by the population not as restitution but as an invasion against which they would defend themselves, even with physical means.[49]

It was Gross who radically proposed that postwar anti-Jewish violence was a result primarily of the Polish population's material gains and their hope of further enrichment. The framework of his thesis is Polish involvement in the Holocaust and in the conversion of Jewish property. Since the publication of Gross's research, the question of Polish participation in the appropriation of Jewish property has no longer been considered taboo. Historians in Poland have been receptive to publicizing reports and documents as well as evidence of the plunder of Jewish homes. Sources that have been brought to light provide circumstantial evidence testifying to the Poles' abandonment and isolation of the Jewish minority doomed to Nazi annihilation. The continuation of this plunder after the war, when Jewish property left with Poles for safekeeping or converted by Polish neighbors could no longer be recovered, contributed to an atmosphere of fear and terror, which the following letter from a survivor captures with bitter sarcasm:

> If a man, who, in the eyes of people, has already been a corpse to such a great extent that one did not have to feel constrained toward it, turns out suddenly to be alive—it is an embarrassing situation. . . . Most of the Jews who are alive, after all, are telling of similar experiences in very different variations that, even though they were there, people never would suspect; they flung themselves onto their things, and, therefore, as many embarrassing situations were created as there are Jewish survivors. Apart from that, many people who must return their property—house, land, or shop—to the returning Jews feel hurt: "Why do ninety-five percent of those who have some Jewish property not have to return it, and I, specifically, have to, because I have the bad luck that a (for example) Rozenbaum survived?" Some do not want to return deposits, and so they do not return them. This is one side of the current antisemitism—perhaps not the most important one, but an unavoidable one.[50]

Another explanation for postwar anti-Jewish aggression is the long-standing prejudice against the Jewish minority, with political and religious origins. On the one hand, a prewar stereotype, that it was the Jews who were responsible for bringing communism to Poland (in Polish, żydokomuna, "Judeo-communism"), became exacerbated by rumors of the allegedly friendly welcome that the Polish Jewish community in the East had extended to the Red Army in September 1939.[51] This public perception, well documented in reports sent to the Polish government in exile, persisted after the war as a general conviction that the new Stalinist government was stuffed with Communists of Jewish origins. Although participation in the postwar Communist apparatus was certainly high among the surviving Jews (estimates vary from 13 to 37 percent of Jewish participation, depending on the section and level of state institutions),[52] the real issue was one of perception. Krystyna Kersten insightfully captures the irony of such a perception: "There is no doubt that the legend of symbiosis between the Jews and the power established by Communists is just a legend. . . . As has already been emphasized by many authors, one Jew was enough to make an institution 'Jewish' in the common opinion. And if this institution had previously been stigmatized with this label (for example communism, or freemasonry), any person could become a Jew. And so, [Bolesław] Bierut [—Polish Communist leader of non-Jewish origin] was perceived either as a figurehead—when the number-one person in authority was seen in [Jakub] Berman [—Polish Communist leader of Jewish origin]—or, ordinarily, as a Jew."[53]

The Polish Gentiles tended to see communism as "Jewish business," even though, as research shows, it was in fact the Polish *classless* people (the so-called people in between, the déclassé, the dispossessed and lumpen proletariat) who were the support base for the new postwar order.[54] Among the Jews, silence and sometimes actual support for the government despite the brutal methods employed by the Communist authorities to pacify Polish society stemmed from the perceived security that the official Communist ideology provided to all citizens irrespective of ethnic background and from the protection that the authorities provided the survivors when violence escalated. Although Communists were in the minority in the CKŻP compared to Zionists and Bundists, they trusted that only the new PKWN government would effectively stand in their defense.[55] Some non-Jewish Poles interpreted this silence and support, however, as a full embrace of the invading army and its political ideology. Kersten also notes that for Poles the frustration of coming out of the war as an object rather than as a subject lay at the root of the search for a scapegoat; the real enemy (the Soviet Union) appeared too big and powerful to attack, so they channeled their aggression toward the weakest target available, which for this generation was embodied by the Jewish minority.[56] The violence against the Jews perpetrated by the anti-Communist Underground was most starkly motivated by a desire for the "ethnic cleansing" of the remnant Jewish Poles. The members of the National Armed Forces

(NSZ) were particularly hostile to the Jews throughout the entire occupation, and at least several dozen murders motivated by antisemitism during the war could be attributed to this section of the Underground.[57]

After the Red Army's winter offensive in January 1945, the conspiracy between the AK and the NSZ began to grow, extending to tens of thousands of people within a few months. Some murders of Jews committed by members of these two forces after the war appear not to have been motivated exclusively by political reasons (i.e., the wish to stop incoming Communists). Antisemitism, robbery, and even unplanned circumstances (such as an error in targeting a victim) might also have been equally responsible. Antisemitism, however, did lie behind the most notorious mass murder—apart from the Kielce Pogrom—which was perpetrated on May 2, 1946, near Krościenko (in the area of the Tatra Mountains) by the anti-Communist partisan division commanded by Józef Kuraś, who was also known as "Ogień" (Fire). Ogień's division attacked a transport truck carrying twenty-six Jews who were attempting to flee Poland illegally. The division shot eleven of them and injured seven.[58]

Recent research on anti-Communist propaganda in the areas of Kielce and Lublin confirms that anti-Jewish emphases were present and often prominent in Underground publications. Ryszard Śmietanka-Kruszelnicki has documented the fact that these materials contained anti-Jewish propaganda that was not much different from Nazi propaganda, with the added motif that żydokomuna, Judeo-communism, was responsible for all of the ills of the new state.[59]

With respect to direct violence, Alina Skibińska counted cases of murder in more than 150 localities all over Poland, emphasizing that official representatives of security organs as well as individual soldiers and officers of the Polish army very frequently took part in these attacks. Even some of the judges during the trials of those who perpetrated attacks against Jews were not immune from occasionally ridiculing Jewish victims and witnesses in court.[60]

To be sure, these murders should be researched in terms of identifying the Underground's motives. The remnants of the Underground army conducted its own war on the supporters of either the Communist dictatorship or its policies. In one of most gruesome examples, toward the end of 1944 in the area of Białystok the Underground murdered three ethnically Polish families (altogether thirteen people) because of their acceptance of the Communist agricultural reform.[61]

Another important component of the postwar violence was the reborn "black legend" of so-called ritual murder, characterized by rumors that Jews were kidnapping and murdering Christian children. In its latest version, the Jews, weakened and mostly annihilated by the war, were allegedly forcing Christian children to provide them with blood for badly needed transfusions. Legends and myths of Jews as vampires had enjoyed a long tradition and a unifying purpose that had manifested itself in Poland at times of social crisis in particular.[62] The postwar situation—with its Soviet terror, with the newness and instability of its political structure, and with a starving and generally ill population—yielded a fertile terrain of fear and terror in which anxiety, aggression, and a search for scapegoats could easily take root. The power of the symbolic function of blood in re-creating life (e.g., sacrifice, blood spilled for one's country, blood as a renewing power of an organism, and so on) was deeply present in the vocabulary and imagery of Poland's survival narrative during the war. In that context, the myth of the blood libel constitutes a kind of profane inversion of the nobility of sacrifice contained in the patriotic narrative. The fact that in each pogrom, whether merely attempted or actually executed, the carrier of anti-Jewish aggression was some form of fear of the death of Polish children is tragically documented even among the militia, who sometimes spread rumors about the alleged kidnapping and murder of Polish children by the Jews.[63] This dangerous legend worked to incite a violent crowd in each postwar pogrom that occurred in Poland: in Rzeszów on June 12, 1945 (no victims there, but some Jews were killed in neighboring localities); in Kraków on August 11, 1945 (one killed, five injured); and in Kielce on July 4, 1946 (forty-two killed, forty to fifty injured).

The intensity of anti-Jewish hostility created an atmosphere in the country that has been described as "pogromlike" (in Polish, *pogromowa*).[64] What is debated is whether the murders and attacks on the Jews displayed features of ethnic cleansing against the Holocaust survivors and whether the underlying hostility against them was universal enough to justify placing it in that category of violence. As Andrzej Żbikowski has asserted,

> The murders of the returning Jews did not evoke efficient condemnation or a decisive counteraction from either the society or the new, Communist authorities. This part of Polish society that did not condemn these murders would justify the murderers with [the supposition] that the Jews, supposedly, had become a pillar of Communist rule and had collaborated massively with the Communist political police. . . . Left de facto to themselves, the Jewish survivors reacted to the wave of murders with a widely felt sense of a lack of security as well as, perhaps, with exaggerated ideas about the scale of these murders and, in the end, with a panic-stricken flight from the country.[65]

Another debated issue is that of the number of Jews killed during the first years after the war. Estimates range from several hundreds to 2,000.[66] David Engel, who until recently provided the only statistical estimate based on archival research of postwar anti-Jewish violence, assumes that the number was smaller, but at least between 500 and 600.[67] Although his analysis is based on careful investigation of Polish documents as well as on personal testimonies and memoirs, it still lacks, according to Żbikowski's criticism, any reference to available JOINT materials in Poland or to reports on the state of security placed in the Ministry of Interior archives.[68] In spite of these limitations, Engel's research has brought to light a series of well-documented conclusions: for instance, the worst month for the safety of Jews was March 1945, when more than ninety Jews lost their lives in Poland. Engel also delineates the most dangerous areas for the Jews: the districts of Kielce, Lublin, and Warsaw. He points to certain surprising statistical relationships: for example, the lack of a correlation in space or time between the murders of Jews and the killings of non-Jewish Communists who were targeted by the Underground as well as the rather high death toll for Jewish women and children (17 percent and 4 percent, respectively), compared to the much lower death toll for non-Jewish women and children (7 and 2 percent, respectively).[69]

Drawing conclusions from these relationships, Engel asserts that Jews were killed for different reasons—and at different times—than why and when Poles were murdered. For the most part, the Jews were killed during the spring and summer of 1945, when the survivors from German camps and from the hideouts were coming home and about a year later when the greatest wave of repatriates from the Soviet Union arrived. Żbikowski adds another factor to these connections by also correlating the number of murders with the greatest number of survivors in a given area: in particular, the Kielce district had a large number of survivors, partly owing to the employment of many Jews by the military plant Hasag, where they had been liberated. Another area where there was a correlation between the number of Jewish survivors and the frequency of murders of Jews was Rzeszów.[70]

It is also important to assess the material and psychological conditions of the Polish population in any discussion of violence against the Jews in this period. In Zaremba's invaluable study, one of the most striking facts is that the areas he describes as the most prone to postwar terror (by the Red Army soldiers, who were robbing, killing, and gang-raping Polish civilians to the same extent they were taking these actions against Germans) and the most exposed to dire poverty, to a lack of food, as well as to the spread of social pathologies (such as alcoholism) overlapped significantly (although not exclusively) with the areas that were most dangerous to the Jews—for example, the Białystok, Rzeszów, Lublin, and Kielce districts.[71]

Historians are also in agreement that at least 200 Jews were murdered during the so-called railway action—a series of attacks, mostly by the NSZ, on trains that were transporting repatriates from the Soviet Union.[72] This number represents only fatalities; the number of nonfatal injuries was not recorded. Because nobody stopped to check whether the Jews who were brutally pulled or thrown from the trains were in any way engaged in promoting the Communist system, one may reasonably conclude that these acts of violence were directed against the Jews as Jews.

The survivors' community, for its part, was not passive in the face of Polish violence. If forewarned by a sympathetic Gentile, the survivors might flee to larger towns and cities; alternatively, they might try to defend themselves or to ask the authorities for protection. In July 1945, General Franciszek Jóźwiak, chief commandant of the Citizens' Militia, issued a special command "for the defense of life and property of the

Jewish population in Poland," which obliged the militia to exercise special vigilance over the places where Jews resided and which provided the Jews with additional protection in case of danger.[73] On the survivors' side, the Komisja Specjalna (Special Commission) of the CKŻP was charged with coordinating self-defense actions from the time of the Kielce Pogrom in July 1946 until March 1947. The Special Commission delegated more than 200 groups, numbering 2,500 armed men in all, to defend nearly 400 Jewish institutions in Poland. These groups would eventually have to intervene more than 2,000 times on behalf of the survivors. Among the areas of special danger were Bytom, Białystok, Szczecin, Bielawa, and Otwock. In Legnica, moreover, they prevented a pogrom incited once again by the rumored disappearance of a Polish child.[74] According to Żbikowski, the ethnic-cleansing goals of the most radically nationalistic prewar parties were now on their way to being fully realized within a few years after the war.[75]

Based on the archival data, historians generally agree that attacks on Jews almost ceased by the fall of 1946—that is, after the Kielce Pogrom. By 1947, a certain peaceful status quo concerning the dwindling postwar Jewish community seemed to have been reached because the Jews' situation improved in terms of both physical well-being and security; the tide of Jewish emigration from Poland correspondingly ebbed. Nevertheless, warnings that a "mood" to carry out a pogrom had been observed are still found in security reports from as late as 1949.[76]

To conclude this outline of the extent of anti-Jewish murders in postwar Poland, one must acknowledge that, as in other cases of mass violence and ethnic hostilities, the exact number of victims and the circumstances of their deaths will likely never be fully known. For the purpose of this book, however, the more important aspect of the situation is a Jewish *perception* of a pervasive threat toward Jews from non-Jews. It is understandable that the actual hostilities affected the survivors more than their neighbors' neutral or even positive reactions to them did. CKŻP reports record the survivors' shock at the violent reactions against the returning Jews, which were even more incomprehensible to the repatriates from the Soviet Union.[77] Rumors of murders in their vicinities, in the villages, and on the trains were so horrifying for the survivors after the experiences of annihilation at the hands of the Germans and of the Stalinist persecutions in the East that even if the perceptions of Polish violence may have been exaggerated (which present research has been unable either to confirm or to deny), such exaggerations would nonetheless be psychologically understandable.

Reasons for Leaving

The flight of the Jews from Poland became a continuous phenomenon once a perception of Polish hostility had become universal among the survivors. The greatest waves of emigration corresponded to the most violent periods: during the first wave, from July 1945 to October 1945, 40,000 to 50,000 Jews left Poland. In the second wave, which culminated after the Kielce Pogrom and took place from May 1946 through September 1946, about 100,000 Jews emigrated. Therefore, although close to 300,000 survivors returned at some point to Poland within the first three years after the war (from July 1944 to July 1947), after that period only about 90,000 remained.[78] The majority of the fleeing survivors received assistance from the Brichah (Hebrew for "flight") organization, which arranged for both legal and illegal transfers of Jews to Palestine. After the significant emigration of the first two postwar years, the exodus continued, albeit slowly, until 1951, when Poland closed its borders to all emigration. At that point, no more than 70,000 to 80,000 Jews remained in Poland.[79]

Explanations for the Jewish postwar exodus from Poland form a kind of mirror image, a reversal of perspective, of explanations for postwar Polish anti-Jewish violence. The reasons why Holocaust survivors elected to leave Poland have been debated in Polish historiography ever since the publication of Gross's book *Sąsiedzi* (*Neighbors*) in Poland in 2000, which provoked a public debate on Polish attitudes toward Jews both during and after the war. Before that point, this issue and that of a generalized Polish silence about the plight of Polish Jews were not tackled beyond a few publications circulating among specialists, so they never made it into the public discourse. These issues were, to be sure, complex and could not be freely discussed, given the character of the Communist regime. It is important to emphasize, however, that during the first postwar years, despite the Communist surveillance state, all citizens continued to strive for freedom and prosperity to the extent possible, and many would have welcomed a chance to exit the pauperized society. The populace may therefore have regarded the exiting Polish Jews with envy.

One possible explanation for the massive Jewish exodus after the war looks at the survivors' Holocaust experience and points out the psychological difficulties of remaining in a country in which the members of one's own family (usually all of them) had been annihilated. Regarding this explanation, Bożena Szaynok and Natalia Aleksiun have proposed the notion of a "cemetery syndrome."[80]

Another explanation offered for the Jewish exodus is the fear or even terror that the Polish population raised in the survivors on their return home. This idea, fully developed in Gross's book *Fear*, is confirmed in the research Irena Hurwic-Nowakowska conducted immediately after the war. In formulating her sociological study of the psychological condition of Polish Jewry, Hurwic-Nowakowska distributed 13,000 questionnaires to Jewish survivors in Poland between 1947 and 1950. She received only slightly more than 800 responses, which could indicate either that many survivors had left Poland or that those remaining were unwilling to discuss the sensitive topic of Polish–Jewish interactions. Although it is thus difficult to consider such a sample to be entirely representative of the Jewish population of Poland at the time, it is significant that the survivors who did respond perceived the greatest problem for their community in Poland to be that of the existence of Polish antisemitism *during* the war. Hurwic-Nowakowska later drew the conclusion that this perception stemmed from the immediate postwar years, when antisemitic hostilities were a matter of daily experience.[81]

Documents and reports deposited either by or with the CŻKH or with the PKWN's Jewish Section testify as well to the survivors' feelings of alienation and hostility, even when they did not explicitly experience overt hostility from the Poles. For example, one report from the Lublin area dated September 1944 states: "If, taking into account the level of safety, the Jews in Lublin feel relatively well, the Jews in the provinces—with small exceptions—live in continuous fear. Since the Germans have left, [there have already been] cases of the murders of Jews, which are being repeated sporadically and which lead the remaining Jews to despair, and a relatively large group of Jews is afraid to come out from their hiding places."[82]

The sheer fact remains that the greatest exodus occurred immediately following the atrocious pogrom against the Jews in Kielce, which caused a panic among the beleaguered survivors and drove some of them in a massive move to the largest cities, where they could live scattered among the population, and drove others across the Polish borders. Those who had retained their Christian names after the war felt "vindicated" in the end, convinced of the comparative safety of their chosen strategy. Following the Kielce Pogrom, the relative stabilization of Jewish life in Poland in 1947, the possibility of legal emigration until 1951, the removal of Zionist activists from the CKŻP, and the shutting down of almost all Jewish organizations,[83] the Jews in Poland entered into the hidden, inconspicuous life of a tiny minority of survivors. These Jews, many of whom would still attempt to leave Poland during one of several anti-Jewish Communist campaigns, found it necessary by then to renounce any dream of a peaceful life in the land of their ancestors.

The reasons that the majority of Polish Jews emigrated from Poland were thus complex and multifaceted—economic, political, religious—and any one of them could be a sufficient explanation for the exit of the remaining Jews from Poland. Nevertheless, two appear to be the most prominent: fear of the Polish population and the "cemetery syndrome."[84]

2

The Central Jewish Historical Commission and Its Project of Documenting Survivors' Stories

As Jewish historians in occupied Poland became aware of the uniqueness of the catastrophe they were facing, they attempted to record it, either in individual efforts or in war-defying collective initiatives. This work did not stop once the war was over. Realizing the scope of the near-total annihilation of the Polish Jews, researchers, teachers, and writers took on the personal obligation to report for posterity on the unprecedented destruction of the Jewish people.

Not surprisingly, the first postwar collective historical initiative was formed in Lublin, one of the epicenters of the Holocaust, on the outskirts of which the Majdanek concentration camp was located. Researchers within the Central Jewish Historical Commission were the first to appreciate the role of the survivors' personal accounts, and they worked tirelessly to collect records referring to what had just happened. The CŻKH eventually gave rise to the formation of the Jewish Historical Institute in Warsaw, and it was thanks to these early pioneers of personal testimonies that today we have, in the ŻIH alone, more than 7,000 narratives that refer to experiences during the Holocaust. The ŻIH houses the Polish collections of testimonies that are the subject of this portion of my study, and so it is appropriate that I outline here the origins of the methodological framework followed by the CŻKH's collectors of survivors' testimonies. Such an overview may yield a hermeneutic tool for re-creating the memories shared by the survivors in the immediate postwar reality.

It is fitting, here, to point out the uniqueness of the CŻKH within the Communist landscape of postwar Poland; its countercultural presence, improbably preserved by a few persistent individuals; and its singular role in creating the still untapped treasure of the first postwar survivors' testimonies. At the same time, its tumultuous history, the "in-gathering" and "dispersion" of its founding figures, and their consequent emigration from Poland testify to the unique and stormy history of the remnant of Polish Jews after the catastrophe as well as to the continuity of a historical research project that traveled with the emigrants across cultures and continents.

From the very beginning of the liberation of the territory that had once belonged to prewar eastern Poland, Jewish historians throughout the European continent set out to document the unparalleled events of the Jewish annihilation. Philip Friedman reports that such attempts took place in fourteen countries: Poland, Austria, Bulgaria, Czechoslovakia, France, Germany, Great Britain, Greece, Hungary, Italy, Romania, Sweden, Switzerland, and the Soviet Union.[1] The reasons advanced for engaging in such documentation are multifaceted. Laura Jockusch enumerates five: (1) to give a testimony (moral obligation); (2) to assist in bringing justice to both perpetrators and victims (legal redress); (3) to prepare documentary material for future research (historiography); (4) to commemorate the dead through history writing; and (5) to continue "a distinct eastern European Jewish tradition of history writing as a response to catastrophe."[2] To some extent, these earliest attempts at postwar historical research on the Holocaust were a continuation of archival and documentary activity that took place during the war. In Poland, they were also indicative of the historiographical currents that were of interest to Polish Jewish historians.

Historical Antecedents of the
Central Jewish Historical Commission

The creation of the Central Jewish Historical Commission was not a deus ex machina event for Jewish scholarly activity in Poland but a continuation of traditions that dated as far back as the early nineteenth century. The most obvious antecedent was that of early Jewish scholarship in Warsaw, which derived from the tradition of the German *Wissenschaft des Judentums* (science of Judaism) and which allowed for the formal development of this historical discipline among Polish Jews while also providing them with training. Moreover, what Friedman has termed the *khurbn forshung*, Yiddish for "destruction research"—the tradition of research on catastrophe—was the most important of the methodological approaches that gave rise to the CŻKH's collection of survivors' testimonies.[3] From that tradition, the circle of the Oneg Shabbat—Hebrew for "joy of the Sabbath," so named because the volunteer researchers in this circle would meet on the Sabbath to exchange the results of their research—arose as an underground group of researchers started by Emanuel Ringelblum in the Warsaw Ghetto, providing a more direct continuity between the war and the postwar historical activity of collecting and analyzing documents.

The Early Jewish Historical Tradition in Polish Lands

As far back as the early nineteenth century, Jewish historical scholarship was represented by the Towarzystwo Krzewienia Nauk Judaistycznych (Association for the Propagation of Judaic Sciences) and later by the Instytut Nauk Judaistycznych (Institute for Judaic Studies), the Główna Biblioteka Judaistyczna (Main Judaic Library) in Warsaw, and the Yidiszer Wisenszaftlecher Instytut (YIVO, Yiddish Scholarly Institute) in Vilna.[4] Although Warsaw could not boast a level of Jewish scholarship on a par with the scholarship in Lwów (present-day Lviv) or Kraków, it did develop its own historical circle, which eventually founded its own academic institutions.

The beginning of institutional Jewish scholarship in Warsaw can be traced to the opening of the Szkoła Rabinów (School of Rabbis), an institute of secondary education, in 1826. After its closing in 1862, a remnant of its library collection was serendipitously rescued from an antiquarian book shop and recovered to the library of the Great Synagogue on Tłomackie Street. This remnant was later transferred, through the Main Judaic Library, to the ŻIH's library.

Rafał Żebrowski reports that the library on Tłomackie Street, officially opened in 1881 (together with its accompanying historical commissions), became "a genuine academic institution and likewise was perceived as having grown from the spirit of the *Wissenschaft [des Judentums]*."[5] Its academic *spiritus movens* was the distinguished historian and preacher Samuel Poznański.[6] The proper Institute for Judaic Studies was established owing to the efforts of his successor, Rabbi Mojżesz Schorr, together with certain Jewish members of Parliament, who secured part of its funding from the Ministry of Religious Affairs and Public Education.[7] The institute opened in 1928 with the following professors: Mojżesz Schorr (rector), Majer Bałaban, Jakób Kahan, Icchak Schiper, and Abraham Weiss. This opening was a symptom of the growing cultural and academic activity of Polish Jewry between the two world wars.

The curricula of the Institute for Judaic Studies, in spite of many practical difficulties—for example, the institute was without its own *locus* for many years; only in 1936 did it move to the rooms of the Main Judaic Library—were highly demanding, requiring students to pursue simultaneous studies in humanities at Warsaw University. Although its main emphasis was pedagogical, its research bore fruit in numerous publications, including the ten volumes of its own journal, *Pisma* (Writings), issued before the war.[8] As Marian Fuks points out, the institute was "the first Jewish educational institution in Europe with an academic and pedagogical curriculum that included secular Judaic studies as well as theological studies."[9]

During the fruitful interwar period, the restitution of the Polish state, the consequent rebuilding and opening of educational institutions and archives, as well as the development of a free, uncensored Polish historiography had an impact on the work of Jewish historians in Poland. Although relatively little interest was displayed by *Polish* historians in focusing on the history of Polish Jews, with only a few exceptions, historians of *Jewish* origins were nevertheless encouraged to pursue their research.[10] Three of these scholars are today considered among the greatest historians of Polish Jewry: Schorr, Bałaban, and Schiper.[11]

In broad terms, Bałaban, who represented the "older" generation of historians, occupied himself with monographic studies of Jewish institutions and personalities, and Schiper, also belonging to the "older" generation, focused on patterns of social development as well as on certain largely ignored economic aspects of Jewish history. The "middle" generation of historians, in the words of Artur Eisenbach, "introduced into the historical science the national and social approaches of secular Jewish culture."[12] Among their interests, economic history and social history were predominant. This generation included Friedman, Ringelblum, and Raphael Mahler. The "young" generation, concentrated mainly in Warsaw, tended to belong to the Warsaw Historical Section of YIVO. Among them, Eisenbach, Isaiah Trunk, Rafał Gerber, and Josef Kermisz published works before the war and were later involved in the CŻKH.[13]

Khurbn Forshung

The postwar Jewish historians relied on the *khurbn forshung*, a unique historiographical genre that, Jockusch reports, was "centered on interdisciplinary, social-science oriented, and proto-professional research methods and geared to achieving moral and material redress."[14] This genre was developed by the autodidact historian Simon Dubnow in response to the Kishinev Pogrom of 1903; about a decade before that, he had already proposed its goals and principles in an essay he wrote after the expulsion of the Jews from Moscow in 1891.[15] In the essay, Dubnow defined the Jews as a national group held together by a "historical consciousness," the support of which requires the study of the Jewish past. In contrast to the premises of *Wissenschaft des Judentums*, the German-speaking tradition of an academic, elite-focused study of Jewish history, Dubnow called for "passion" and "heart" in researching the mystery of the Jewish past and for recruiting people connected with Jewish record keeping as well as amateur historians to help collect communal records (*pinkasim* in Hebrew), personal documents, and the recollections of "ordinary" Jews.[16] In the same essay, according to Jockusch, Dubnow also differed from his contemporary Jewish historians in Russia, who were focusing on legal matters and following strictly legal documents in their archival studies.[17] His project thus was meant to strengthen the Jews' national identity by enlisting "the whole nation," not just the academically employed elites, into the writing of its history. To some extent, Dubnow followed the beginning of ethnographic research, in which interviewers or collectors of documents (*zamlers* in Yiddish) provided the picture of everyday situations on the ground—what we today might call, with some approximation, an *Alltagsgeschichte*, "everyday history," that employs a human-centered, ethnographic approach. It was, however, a nationally oriented ethnography. Following the Kishinev Pogrom, with its 47 dead and nearly 500 wounded, Jewish communities began to organize their self-defense, and a group of Odessa intellectuals sent the poet Hayim Nahman Bialik to collect eyewitness testimonies. From this group, Dubnow provided Bialik with a series of detailed questions with which to interview witnesses concerning the occurrence of violence in the pogrom; its causes; its development; the role of Christians before, during, and after the pogrom; and other related topics. These questions, for example, also inquired about the roles of the local Christian and Jewish authorities, their responses to the pogrom, and the aftermath. Bialik was likewise to visit hospitals and to gather exact information about the numbers of dead and wounded and any available information about perpetrators and bystanders. He was to provide photographs of the victims when possible, to estimate material damages (so that the estimates could then be presented to relief agencies), and to evoke public protests against the abuses committed by the czarist regime.[18]

The methods commissioned by the Odessa intellectuals stood in sharp contrast to the scientific methods of the *Wissenschaft*, which were based on written sources and employed by university historians who preferred to focus on a more remote Jewish past. The Dubnowian approach, which was later followed in chronicling other pogroms, relied on a grassroots collection of contemporary accounts, both personal and official, in order to preserve the immediate picture of each catastrophe just as it had occurred. Primarily, then, the accounts relied on victims' testimonies. This approach was in part necessary, for the perpetrators would not likely give testimonies to Jewish interviewers, and in part intentional, designed to gather a first-person perspective of an event that would be available only by interviewing the victims. As David Engel has noted, the task of recording everything connected to the pogrom was a component of a "popular self-help," "the broad Jewish public struggle for physical safety and material wellbeing [sic]."[19] The evidence collected through testimonies, documents, and photographs could be and was used in the international arena as a political tool to attract attention to injustices and abuses perpetrated on the Jewish minority in eastern Europe.

The new historiography of collecting ethnographic evidence and personal testimonies became even more pronounced and deliberate during the First World War, when Jewish communities of the Russian Pale of Settlement became a target of violence by marauding troops. The ethnographer and writer S. An-Ski (Solomon Zainwil Rapoport) and two other writers, Isaac Leib Peretz and Jacob Dineson, were major figures in this movement, which called on fellow Jews to write down what they witnessed in order to procure testimonies for future political arguments for Jewish rights: "Be your own historians!" they admonished. "Don't depend on others! Record, make notes, and collect!"[20] Several Jewish institutions answered that call and even established a "war archive" for collecting eyewitness accounts. Throughout the war and afterward, the new style of writing history became more popular and well known, and it served the Jewish community as an archival base within which to document a need for social reforms in their "host" countries, mainly Russia. During the pogroms in the Ukraine (1917–21), another group of intellectuals, headed by Elias Tcherikower (albeit again supported by Dubnow), formed the Redaktions-kolegye oyf Zamlen un Oysforshn di Materialn Vegn di Pogromen in Ukrayne (Editorial Committee for the Collection and Research of Material Concerning Pogroms in the Ukraine) and managed to collect several thousand eyewitness accounts as well as other documentary materials on the pogroms. These materials were then transferred to Berlin for safekeeping.[21]

Some of the methods Tcherikower employed were later used by YIVO, created in 1925 in Berlin and Vilna, from initiatives by Dubnow, Tcherikower, and others. There again, as in the earlier stage of Dubnowian research and in contrast to the tradition of *Wissenschaft*, the emphasis was placed on "the sociocultural, economic, and political developments of Jewish society in the past and the present at the center of their analysis. Accordingly, they developed an interdisciplinary concept of Jewish scholarship that combined the fields of history, sociology, philology, demography, ethnography, economics and pedagogy, using methods from the social sciences."[22]

This developed interdisciplinary approach, utilizing personal documents and eyewitness accounts, was continued during the Second World War by Ringelblum's unique project—Oneg Shabbat. The notions of history writing to build a common national identity and practical self-defense in times of danger thus continued into the period of the Holocaust.

Oneg Shabbat

The Oneg Shabbat project inherited and perpetuated the methodological tradition of *khurbn forshung*. Several of the survivor researchers who founded the historical commissions after the Second World War came from this tradition and from the Oneg Shabbat circle. Ringelblum, the founder of the Oneg Shabbat project, was a Polish Jewish historian of Marxist Zionist convictions who headed YIVO's Warsaw branch before the war, taught history in a high school, conducted research on Polish Jews, and published numerous articles and books. Together with Dubnow, Ringelblum believed that Jewish identity was a matter of a people, not of a religion; as a consequence of this identity, the history of the Jewish people could not be exclusive to the elites and rabbis but would have to include "common" people collectively gathering and writing their own histories of their communities.[23] Historical research as a popular and communal enterprise, with ethnographic appreciation for everyday expressions of the culture of "real people," was the mode of collaborative effort that Ringelblum developed in Oneg Shabbat.

Apart from following Dubnow's methodology, Ringelblum also inherited his two-sided mission of writing history: (1) the immediate, relief- and justice-oriented goal (the "defensive" tradition, connected with political activity) and (2) the "redemptive" purpose of endowing the Jewish people with a unifying understanding of their own past.[24]

Ringelblum collected historical artifacts from the beginning of the German occupation of Poland. His scientific activity went hand in hand with his social activities; by 1933, he was involved with JOINT, and in

1938 he became its permanent employee.[25] Through JOINT, he organized help for Jewish refugees sent from Germany, who were trapped in Zbąszyń on the western Polish border.

After the outbreak of the war, Ringelblum became the head of the social sector of Alleynhilf (Jewish Self-Help), a major social aid organization in the Warsaw Ghetto.[26] From his post, Ringelblum supervised the activities of "house committees" in the ghetto—self-organized groups of tenants attempting to provide basic resources in the face of increasingly harsh ghetto conditions—and organized a system of public kitchens.

By November 1939, Ringelblum extended his research activity to other people—those who typically were also involved in Jewish Self-Help—by creating the Oneg Shabbat. The circle included permanent staff as well as one-time contributors, who were usually refugee leaders of communal organizations and could describe the events that had taken place in their hometowns before they managed to flee to Warsaw.[27]

About fifty of the group's permanent members were not academics. Ringelblum, fearing literary embellishment by professional writers and journalists, preferred amateurs from among the intelligentsia and craftsmen, who were for the most part active in left-wing political parties.[28] He strove for methodological objectivity, emphasizing the use of many perspectives to describe one event as well as a focus on future audiences so that the researcher's judgment would not be visited upon the events described.[29]

The Oneg Shabbat staff collected all sorts of material relating to the German occupation as it affected the Jewish community: reports and official accounts; personal testimonies, letters, and interviews; as well as leaflets and tickets testifying, for example, to cultural and political activities within the ghetto. Everything mattered: not even candy wrappers were deemed unimportant for preservation. There were postcards from Jews deported to "unknown destinations," poetry by Władysław Szlengel and Yitzhak Katznelson, a script of a popular ghetto play, and many photographs.[30] The group conducted surveys and wrote monographs on specific topics. Prizes were awarded for written depositions.[31] At the beginning of 1942, the circle focused on the wide-ranging project of reporting on the first two and a half years of Jewish life during the war. One branch of this project was research on ghetto women conducted by Cecylia Słapakowa; another was research on the life of the ghetto street; still another focused on the ghetto children.[32]

When the Great Deportation to Treblinka began on July 22, 1942, Ringelblum ordered that the archive be buried.[33] He himself was caught in the round-up of Jews and sent to the Trawniki labor camp. After a complex rescue operation in June 1942, Ringelblum went to "Krysia" (affectionate code name for his secret hideout), where more than thirty Jews were hidden by the Wolski family. His research activity continued even there. A second cache of the Oneg Shabbat archive was buried in February 1943. When "Krysia" was denounced and discovered in March 1944, all of the Jews hidden there, together with their male Polish rescuers, were imprisoned and shot.

To a large extent, the first researchers and activists of the European Jewish historical commissions after the war continued the tradition of the Oneg Shabbat, the secret project initiated by Ringelblum in the Warsaw Ghetto. As Jockusch has documented, some CŻKH members expressed the explicit conviction that they continued Ringelblum's efforts through their postwar activities.[34]

The Beginning of the Central Jewish Historical Commission

On August 29, 1944, five weeks after the Red Army's liberation of Lublin on July 22, five Polish Jews—Marek Bitter, Menachem Marek Asz, Jehuda Elberg, Mieczysław Szpecht, and Ada Lichtman—founded a *historishe komisye* (Yiddish, "historical commission") there to collect Jewish testimonies in order to describe Jewish suffering perpetrated by Germans in occupied Poland. Even before the first meeting, however, these survivors used, as a guide for their interviews, a questionnaire that focused on Nazi persecutions, Jewish responses, and Polish–Jewish relations. Once they had accumulated the first hundred testimonies, their goal was to publish them to inform Jews all over the world of the plight of Polish Jews as well as to aid the Polish government in its investigation of German war crimes.[35]

This historical commission attracted new collaborators, among them Philip Friedman, who, according to Rabbi Dawid Kahane, had also already been conducting research on the Jewish community of Lviv in the summer of 1944.[36] When Friedman reached Lublin, he was asked to reorganize the Lublin commission into a nationwide institution: the Central Jewish Historical Commission was established on December 28, 1944.[37] The CŻKH, now headed by Friedman, was subordinated to the Central Committee of Polish Jews (CKŻP), the body representing the entire Jewish community to the Polish authorities.[38] Among the founding members and collaborators who soon joined the CŻKH were the folklorists Melech Bakalczuk and Nachman Blumental; the writer Rachel Auerbach and the lawyer Hersh Wasser (both previous collaborators in Oneg Shabbat); the historians Kermisz (Bałaban and Ringelblum's pupil and author of studies on Polish and Jewish history), Eisenbach, Trunk, and Noe Grüss; and the Hebrew poet Abba Kovner.[39] The CŻKH's goals were primarily to document the extermination of the Jewish people and to publicize the extent of the Nazi crimes.

Heralds of Testimony: Friedman and Auerbach

Philip Friedman

Friedman, founder and first director of the CŻKH, came from Lviv and studied in Vienna, where one of his teachers was Salo Baron, with whom he developed a deep friendship. He wrote his dissertation on the archival study of the Jewish struggle for equality in Galicia and then, like Ringelblum, taught at a Hebrew high school in Łódź, at Łódź University, and at YIVO in Vilna.[40] Also like the founder of Oneg Shabbat, he published extensively before the war; one of his more than 130 prewar works was an important history of the Jews in Łódź. His interest lay primarily in economic and social problems as well as in confrontations between the followers of Haskala and Hasidism. In that emphasis, he followed Schiper, focusing on detailed local studies combined with overarching analysis.[41]

Having lost his wife and daughter in Lviv during the war, Friedman emerged from hiding on the "Aryan" side and immediately, as mentioned, began performing research on the German occupation in his hometown. In November 1944, he moved to Lublin, and in January 1945, just as the Polish Provisional Government was moving to Warsaw, he and the CŻKH relocated to Łódź.

Friedman developed his methodology of sources in part owing to what was available and in part out of his striving for historical objectivity. Although the first (soon to become preeminent) study of the Holocaust by Raul Hilberg was to rely primarily on official German sources,[42] Friedman immediately asserted in a paper he presented in 1948 that "German sources are biased. They must be balanced and complemented by Jewish records and statements—interviews with Jewish survivors, reports by Jewish groups and individuals, and biographical materials." Factual accuracy was not the only concern: "The inner Jewish history, the sufferings and the spiritual life, are rarely or falsely reflected in the German sources, and must be studied in Jewish sources." He recognized the enormous outpouring of memoirs and chronicles following the Holocaust, which had evoked "thousands of Nathan Neta Hannovers," referring to a Jewish chronicler of the Khmelnytsky Uprising in the seventeenth-century Polish Lithuanian Commonwealth and its disastrous effect on the Jewish community in Poland. He also cautioned against "the works written by inadequately trained amateurs, zealous and ambitious, but using unchecked materials and unreliable sources, credulous, taking all for granted, sometimes striving for sensationalism to bring their work into the market." He advised that such attempts, although psychologically understandable, must be taken with great caution and should warrant careful training of interviewers collecting testimonies. The training should utilize sociological methods (interviews and questionnaires) rather than historical methods so as to gain "more and better material" and to gain it speedily because "the living source of information is diminishing from year to year, and the memories of the living fade and grow distorted with the passage of time."[43]

Except for Friedman's caution with respect to writing and collecting personal accounts, there can be little doubt that a focus on a Jewish perspective and on Jewish sources was part of his struggle to rescue Jewish history from the victors' attempts at its erasure. In part, personal testimonies could fill a gap where sources were not yet available. In writing his monograph of the destruction of the Jews in Lviv, Friedman pointed out the "absolute lack of original data and authentic official documents," which forced him to reconstruct the stages of the destruction "based on the experiences of the author himself, partially on the memoirs, oral history, and testimonies given by other witnesses of the events."[44]

Rachel Auerbach

Another person crucial to the project of collecting the testimonies was Rachel Auerbach, a Yiddish writer and activist from Galicia with a folklorist's gift for observation of everyday customs and language. In Lviv, she studied psychology and wrote for Yiddish cultural journals. Beginning in 1933, she pursued a literary career in Warsaw, publishing in both Polish and Yiddish literary journals. During the war, Ringelbaum appreciated her organizational and literary talents and asked her not only to assist in Jewish Self-Help but also to observe and write on various topics, including the soup kitchens, literary life in the ghetto, and others. Completely from scratch, Auerbach created a soup kitchen for writers and journalists, sourcing the necessary equipment and furniture by her own efforts.[45] The kitchen's goal was to support the lives of starving writers so that the words of a dying people would not die with them. One of her assignments was to write down the account of an escapee from Treblinka in the fall of 1942.

After the war, as one of only three survivors of the Oneg Shabbat circle (together with Hersh Wasser and his wife, Luba), Auerbach was essential to the project of recovering two out of the three milk cans containing the Oneg Shabbat archives buried by its staff (the first can was unearthed in September 1946, the second in December 1950, but the third was never located). She did not stop writing. Working for the Główna Komisja Badania Zbrodni Niemieckich w Polsce (Main Commission for the Investigation of German Crimes), she visited Treblinka in November 1945 and two years later published a chilling account in Yiddish of the machinery of the death camp, an account inspired by the testimony that she recorded in 1942.[46] For the Żydowska Komisja Narodowa (Jewish National Committee), she wrote on the Great Deportation in Warsaw and on the massacre of the Jewish intelligentsia. Working at CŻKH's Łódź branch, she collaborated on preparing a guide for the taking of testimony and marshaled the publication of some witness accounts in Yiddish and Polish.

What can be gathered from the impressions Auerbach left on those who met her is that she preferred to remain close to her people and that she had the ability to do so even at those moments when political friction could divide the Jewish community. Before the war, she had been interviewed frequently by Shmuel Lehman, a well-known Jewish folklorist and ethnographer, about the music and customs of the Podolian Jews. In her war writings, Samuel Kassow reports, "Auerbach conveyed what she saw and observed in evocative, powerful language that made her writings an indispensable source for any cultural or social history of the Warsaw Ghetto."[47] Her style of bringing unique Jewish personalities to life remained close to the tradition of the Yizkor, the remembrance of the dead, which she recalled being recited in the synagogue built by her grandfather in Łanowce.[48]

In 1950, Auerbach moved to Israel, most likely as a result of the Communist takeover of the ŻIH and the perceptibly diminished prospects that it brought for being able to work toward the proper documentation and commemoration of the Holocaust. There she founded the Department for the Collection of Testimonies in Yad Vashem, where she was fully devoted to listening and writing down the survivors' stories. In the academic circle there, which criticized a reliance on personal accounts and preferred a traditional historiography of researching official documents, Auerbach (together with Kermisz and Blumental, who also found themselves in Yad Yashem) represented the tradition of history practiced by Ringelblum and continued by Friedman, a tradition in which competent but "ordinary" Jewish people who treasured Jewish sources, as opposed to sources provided by the victors, made a collective effort.

The Work of the Central Jewish Historical Commission, 1944–1950

In March 1945, the CŻKH moved to Łódź, which became the center of Jewish life after the war. The commission was aided at first by correspondents from all over Poland working for its local branches, which numbered twenty-five at its peak, before eventually being drastically reduced owing to budgetary limitations.⁴⁹ The leaders guided the documentary efforts in the local branches and attempted to create a set of standard methodological procedures that could be efficiently followed. Friedman, the man behind this methodological plan, left Poland in the summer of 1946; Blumental then became the commission's director.⁵⁰

As mentioned earlier, the CŻKH's goal was primarily to document what was deemed unprecedented in the recent catastrophe for European Jewry. The historians were aware that the world around them might write a victors' narrative, where Jews would be mentioned only marginally. Schiper had already expressed such thoughts when he was in the Majdanek concentration camp, before he was murdered: "They may wipe out our memory altogether as if we had never existed[,] as if there had never been a Polish Jewry, a Ghetto in Warsaw, a Maidanek."⁵¹

The CŻKH's documenting activity was also perceived as a form of commemoration. Where no traces of Jewish graves were left, historical artifacts and personal accounts preserved what could be saved of a world that had vanished. In that aspect, the commission continued the mission of the Oneg Shabbat archive.

The commission also counted among its goals to further the struggle against the ideological roots of the destruction of Jews, in particular antisemitism, as well as to bring its perpetrators to justice.⁵² To this purpose, the commission collaborated with the Main Commission for the Investigation of German Crimes, which supplied documents to the Polish delegation at Nuremberg.⁵³ The cooperation between the two commissions was very close; Friedman, for example, was at the same time head of the CŻKH and a member of the Łódź branch of the Main Commission.⁵⁴ Auerbach, as noted earlier, likewise worked for the Main Commission.

The CŻKH also collaborated with the Ministry of Justice, the Public Prosecutor's Office, Poland's Military Mission in London, and certain Jewish groups abroad. Its members testified in the trials of Nazi war criminals in Poland and prepared personal testimonies on Treblinka, Belzec, and Sobibor to be presented at Nuremberg, just as Auerbach would later prepare for the Eichmann trial. As Natalia Aleksiun notes, the fact that the Main Commission used the term *Polish nation* rather than *Polish society* when naming victims of the Nazis in Poland may have alienated the Jews and marginalized their particular experience of persecution and destruction.[55]

Eyewitness accounts were seen as crucial tools in achieving both scholarly (documentary) and legal goals. The agenda of the founding meeting of the CŻKH in the autumn of 1944 confirms that the gathering of testimonies would be its principal mission.[56] Developing a methodology for interviewing survivors was of primary importance, and so in 1945 the first instructions and questionnaires for *zamlers*, the interviewers and collectors, were published.

A team of researchers under Friedman prepared the standard questionnaire, while Kermisz wrote the methodological introduction. In it, he noted with satisfaction that the CŻKH's work as well as its staff had been growing intensely, to the point that it required a standardized procedure to assure that the interviewers' time would be best used. For that purpose, the CŻKH created "the post of 'instructor,' whose duty it [was] to travel among the centers, giving advice and keeping the work on track."[57]

Kermisz's methodological introduction illustrates the CŻKH members' motives and goals to collect personal narratives of the Holocaust experiences:

> The Central Jewish Historical Commission in Poland has set before itself the goal of collecting documents and materials detailing the history of the Jewish martyrology during the German occupation. It has done so under the conviction that, unless proof of German wrongs and crimes are gathered, it would be impossible to present in its entirety the immeasurable breadth of suffering, misery, and gigantic mass murder, which demands that just punishment be meted out without exception to all German criminals and their helpers. Through the efforts of the Central Historical Commission, a large number of documents have thus been gathered. It is characteristic that the proof of German crimes arises most definitively from their own records and documents, which reveal the grim truth of the camps and crematoria. The numerous photographs of *Aktionen* and executions that were kept by the Gestapo and KriPo [Kriminalpolizei or Criminal Police Department] have the same significance. Unfortunately, the original documents held by the Historical Commission, of which the majority pertains to the Łódź Ghetto,

are in many instances only fragmentary. Moreover, there are no original documents pertaining to the fates of a number of towns and villages. Therefore, the Commission continues to spare no effort to obtain such documents. For this reason, it is incumbent upon the few remaining Polish Jews still alive to aid the Historical Commission in this task, applying all of their strength towards helping to collect proof against the German criminals. By fulfilling this noble charge, they will become, in some measure, executors of the last will of the martyrs, who, with their dying breaths, fervently desired that the crimes committed upon them would not go unpunished. We must not forget, however, that the Germans tried at all costs to erase any trace of their crimes. They burned bodies and destroyed documents and files towards this end. But such crimes cannot remain hidden! Luckily, the number of living eyewitnesses suffices to present the history of the Jews' martyrology and the German crimes in adequate measure.

The lack of original documents—taken away or destroyed by the enemy—should not prevent us from uncovering the entire truth.[58]

Kermisz's methodological remarks contain passionate exhortations that were meant to prevent the German plan of total Jewish annihilation from being finalized by allowing silence about and the lack of punishment for the atrocities. He appealed directly to Jews' solidarity with the "martyrs" to save the records of "the immeasurable breadth of suffering, misery, and gigantic mass murder." Although the Jewish population was for the most part destroyed, the evidence contained in witnesses' words should not be eradicated.

Through this heart-wrenching appeal, Kermisz continued the last desperate plans of the dying Oneg Shabbat members to "record history." In some of the last messages recorded by the group and recovered by the survivors after the war, the realization that they would not see liberation is set against a hope to be able at least to provide a historical witness. Nineteen-year-old David Graber, for instance, ended his account of how he buried the collection of the archive with a chilling expression of realism:

What we were unable to cry and shriek out to the world we buried in the ground. . . . I would love to see the moment in which the great treasure will be dug up and scream the truth to the world. So the world may know all. So the ones who did not live through it may be glad, and may feel like veterans with medals on our chest. We would be the fathers, the teachers and educators of the future. . . . But no, we shall certainly not live to see it, and therefore I write my last will. May the treasure fall into good hands, may it last into better times, may it alarm and alert the world to what happened . . . in the twentieth century. . . . We may now die in peace. We fulfilled our mission. May history attest for us.[59]

Apart from the call to serve history, practical advice for interviewers incorporated the basic principles of field research according to an emic approach: the survivors should be questioned in an individualized manner, allowing for their personal intelligence and competence to create a testimony; a connection should be established to facilitate openness; the survivors should be able to speak freely on what they feel most competent about, so as "to help the witness[es] *shed as much light as they can on issues they are most familiar with*"; and the data collector should never embellish or change anything in the testimony, which should provide the survivor's personal perspective of the events. For the CŻKH's *zamlers*, therefore, "the most precious element in a witness's testimony is what they personally saw or lived through. It is the task of the data collector to pour the direct impressions and experiences of the witness onto paper, keeping as much as possible in their style and words—and to pass it on thus to the researchers."[60]

The questionnaire itself reflected the CŻKH members' interest in giving a full description of the impact of the German extermination plan on the Jewish community. After providing personal details, each interviewed survivor was asked briefly about the demographic profile of his Jewish community immediately preceding the war and about the influence of the first German anti-Jewish laws, whether they resulted in flight, limitation on movement, or the arrival of refugees. The questionnaire paid special attention to eliciting from the survivors all possible mentions of any limitations or persecutions of the Jewish minority and to explain how these limitations and persecutions may have affected Jewish individuals in practice (sections I–IV). It also inquired about the Germans' and "local" population's and authorities' attitudes toward the Jews (section III). Section V was devoted to the establishment of the ghettos, with special attention paid to the Judenräte, or Jewish Councils, which the Nazis required Jewish communities to establish in the ghettos as a means to enforce occupation law. Its subsections explored the economic aspects of Jewish survival, religious and cultural lives in the ghettoes, the people's "everyday" customs and social relations, and facts about the liquidation of the ghettoes. Section VI was devoted to camp life, with emphasis on living conditions, details of tortures, and cases of collaborators or helpers. Section VII asked about social moods among the Jewish population, rumors, and news that people shared as persecuted companions. Sections VIII and IX dealt extensively with the Jewish resistance and the partisans. Section X asked about hideouts and bunkers, and section XI about the life on the "Aryan" side. The rest of the interview provided an opportunity for the survivor's personal remarks as well as for the possible mention of any particular German cruelty. It also inquired about significant Jewish personalities and the plight of Jewish books. Only in one small section among the sixteen did the questionnaire ask about a survivor's postwar situation: in section XII, "Personal Experiences and Specific Facts the Witness Observed," three short questions addressed the circumstances surrounding the survivor's liberation:

1. How did the witness survive ("Aryan" papers, bunkers, partisan groups)?
2. When and under what circumstances was the witness freed?
3. Did the Jewish survivors lose anything after liberation (material losses, human losses)?[61]

The relatively small proportion of "postwar" questions with respect to the interview as a whole may suggest that the postwar situation was not yet a topic of interest for the CŻKH or perhaps that it might have been a dangerous topic to explore. The majority of the questions led to the description of unprecedented deeds of persecution and annihilation as well as to the Jewish community's and Jewish individuals' responses (both positive and negative—the latter through the acts of collaborators) to this onslaught. It is not, therefore, surprising that the survivors focused on the facts of the unraveling genocide and on their own successful attempts at survival.

According to Jockusch, the CŻKH employed on average about 100 workers in all of its branches, most of whom were women. They were paid monthly salaries of 5,000 to 10,000 złoty and provided with health care and, for those living in Łódź, free lunches.[62] *Zamler*s, however, were paid only rarely, only if their contributions were of superior value, and only if they could be counted on regularly. Apart from being acknowledged as donors to the collection, they would also typically receive the CŻKH publications. The CŻKH had no qualms about gently correcting overzealous or biased *zamler*s in their work. It is impossible to assess their educational and social backgrounds or their ages, but the instructions do make it clear that their task was considered a great moral responsibility. They were admonished to give a faithful account of a testimony and had to sign their protocol as they would any legal document:

> *Under no circumstances may the data collector change anything in the witness's testimony.* . . . The testimony itself cannot be altered, since it has the same value as a witness's account before a court. Therefore, once the testimony is taken down, the data collector should read it out to the witness and the witness should sign it personally, so that they take full moral responsibility for their testimony.[63]

The idea to use *zamler*s and interviews, as outlined earlier, came from the Dubnowian concept of history as a collective effort; indeed, the survivors were coming to the CŻKH branches on their own, even while they were also encouraged, via the Jewish press and posters, to join the documentary project.[64] The task was also seen as a moral duty: "The blood of our martyrs, our relatives, is still fresh. It screams to us and calls upon us not to forget!"[65]

Most *zamler*s volunteered their services in response to appeals by the CŻKH. Their work could help them to create a meaningful situation for themselves after the war, as evidenced in some of their statements to the commission: "When Mrs. Hirsz visited us in the hospital she invited me to work for the Jewish historical commission [sic]. This invitation is the most beautiful present I have received these days. This work will give my life a purpose. I take up a broad project, because in Lower Silesia there used to be a network of camps."[66] By the middle of 1946, the CŻKH *zamlers* had already gathered about 1,800 interviews; a year later the CŻKH had accumulated more than 3,000 testimonies, which became the basis of the more than 7,000 testimonies that make up ŻIH Collection 301. Apparently, various branches placed different emphases on the collected material: the Kraków branch, for example, collected more than 1,300 testimonies during the first three years because of its proximity to the liberated camps. The Katowice branch, however, focused on archival material and documents.[67] Friedman drew attention to an inner struggle within the CŻKH: the leadership in Łódź favored scholarly activity, whereas the members in Kraków as well as other left-leaning groups within the CKŻP "advocated a policy of publishing for popular consumption, to serve propaganda purposes and fight against fascism."[68]

The CŻKH was active in preparing exhibitions in the former camps of Auschwitz and Majdanek. Their efforts also brought about a number of pioneering analyses with respect to various aspects of the Jewish extermination. Maurycy Horn relates that during the first three years of the CŻKH's activity, several dozen separate publications appeared, which he describes as "impressive": the most notable among them are Friedman's book on Auschwitz (the first book on the camp based on official documents and survivor testimonies) and Michał Borwicz's book on the Janowska camp in Lviv.[69]

The CŻKH also published a selection of diaries and memoirs as well as studies of destroyed communities based on personal testimonies. In all of these endeavors, the authors relied on eyewitness accounts, in part because of the unavailability of outside sources, thus creating what Friedman would later term "Judeo-centric" history.

In May 1947, the CKŻP board of directors decided to move the CŻKH and its branches to Warsaw and to transform it into the Jewish Historical Institute (ŻIH). CŻKH members had postulated the need to create a scientific Jewish institute from the beginning. At the end of 1946, then, Eisenbach proposed in the press that the ŻIH be created.[70] The transformation of the CŻKH into the ŻIH was accelerated by the rebuilding of the prewar seat of the Institute for Judaic Studies at 5 Tłomackie Street. The new ŻIH began its activity on October 1, 1947; its first director was Blumental, who up to that point had been the CŻKH's director, and its vice director was Kermisz. Its board included Eisenbach, Trunk, and, as general secretary, Gerber.[71]

The ŻIH was to face several difficulties in a Poland that was officially liberated. The move to Warsaw and certain structural problems caused its research activity to be severely restricted, resulting in a lack of publishing during its first two years.[72] In 1949, two years after the ŻIH's formal inception, some of its board members moved to work in the state administration, and others (Blumental and Kermisz, for example, with Auerbach to follow in 1950) immigrated to Israel. That same year almost all of the independent Jewish institutions in Poland were closed, including the CKŻP. As a result, the ŻIH formally realized its independence as an organization, although from 1952 it would be subordinate to the Polish Academy of Sciences. Before closing, however, the CKŻP had managed to appoint a new director for the ŻIH: Bernard Mark, Communist activist, journalist, scholar, and the author of a short work on the Warsaw Ghetto Uprising published in Moscow in 1944.[73] Although Mark's articles published in the *Biuletyn Żydowskiego Instytutu Historycznego* (the official scholarly publication of the ŻIH) use Marxist vocabulary and sometimes depend wholly on Marxist ideology to explain historical processes, his research nevertheless seems rather unbiased and valuable despite its contemporaneous phraseology.

Summarizing the first five years of the activity of the CŻKH/ŻIH, Friedman had nothing but praise for "that small group of Jewish historians, joined by a group of young students and amateurs . . . [who] attempted to carry as far as possible the brilliant traditions of Polish Jewish historiography." He also hinted at the destructive Communist ideology and at how state control was placing a limit on what could at the time be achieved in the field of historical research:

> There is little hope for a rebirth of Jewish historiography in Poland. There are no Jewish masses left in Poland; experienced and distinguished

historical scholars are lacking; and interest in Jewish historical study has given way to other tasks and aims, which now dominate the Jewish scene in Poland. Many members of the [ŻIH] have left Poland. Yet, this small group of Jewish historians, under the most unfavorable conditions, has managed to create imposing archives and a museum, collect great treasures of Jewish scholarship and art, develop a large publishing house, and contribute serious scholarly work. This must be recorded as an unusually impressive achievement.[74]

Since its very beginning, the Jewish Historical Commission served purposes that would normally be fulfilled by various institutions. After the liquidation of independent Jewish institutions in Poland in 1949, the ŻIH became even more intensely the center of Jewish life in Poland, combining its scholarly, educational, social, and—particularly during the first years after the war—communal roles.

All CŻKH branches participated actively in collecting survivors' testimonies. By the middle of 1946, seventeen volumes of testimonies had been published in Polish and Yiddish; these testimonies came primarily from Polish Jews and described the destruction of Polish Jewish towns. Up to this point as well, the CŻKH had published (or patronized the publishing of) several pioneering historical works on the Warsaw Ghetto Uprising, the Łódź ghetto, the camps, and other aspects of German occupation.

By 1945, Friedman had already published documents on the Auschwitz camps. Research on the primary sources provided a basis for thorough studies of the situation of the Jews during the Nazi onslaught.

The ŻIH has published the periodical *Bleter far Geszichte* (Pages of History) in Yiddish since 1948 and the quarterly *Biuletyn Żydowskiego Instytutu Historycznego*, in Polish with English and Yiddish summaries, since 1950. Certain invaluable primary sources, such as Ringelblum's letters and notes, were first published in these periodicals. During the first two decades of the CŻKH/ŻIH's existence, the commitment to researching the period of destruction resulted in "several hundred essays, articles, works from primary sources, reviews and other minor titles published in the academic publications of ŻIH and many other periodicals and publications, as well as scores of books."[75] The worldwide scholarly community's interest in ŻIH publications has been demonstrated by many translations, including excerpts from Ringelblum's *Notitsn fun varsher geto* (*Notes from the Warsaw Ghetto*),[76] the collection of documents referring to the extermination of the Jews, and others.[77]

It appears, however, that the CŻKH/ŻIH's most important contributions to the "field of Holocaust studies" remain the very creation of the field based on its emphasis on personal perspectives expressed in the unadulterated voices of the Holocaust survivors themselves as well as its unique collection of documents left by these survivors. The pioneering work by the survivor-researchers on the "ruined garden" of Jewish life in Poland as well as their commitment to interviewing the last surviving witnesses of the Jewish annihilation against all attempts by the Communist regime in Poland to silence them and against the hostile environment of the Polish population were a gift whose significance cannot be overvalued. As Jockusch has noted, these researchers "introduced methodological innovations that would enter the academic study of the Holocaust only decades later, in the 1980s and 1990s. Most notably, they pioneered the development of a victim-focused Holocaust historiography that used both perpetrator as well as victim sources."[78]

3

First Encounters with the Neighbors as Represented in the Jewish Historical Institute Collection

The early survivors' testimonies collected by the Jewish Historical Commission (later the Jewish Historical Institute) focused on that brief moment of transition between the return of the Jews and their decision to remain in Poland or to leave it. These collected accounts, therefore, may provide a glimpse into the state of a decimated Polish Jewry living through an unstable moment of transition: the war over, the new order not yet crystallized, and the few Jewish survivors, like their Christian compatriots, having little idea how the temporary change in power might ultimately affect them. Was Joseph Stalin correct in his assertion that communism would eventually settle into place, fitting Poland "like a saddle on a cow"? Would the West acquiesce to Soviet aggression, allowing the Soviet Union de facto control of Poland, as during the first, "free" elections that immediately preceded the Kielce Pogrom of July 4, 1946?

Testimonies given in the immediate aftermath of the war can be characterized as being situated in a context of uncertainty. Jewish survivors might have tried to revisit their homes, but in the long term their future plans might have depended on what they found there—any surviving relatives, any possible structure with which to rebuild a once-ruined life in the context of the new political reality that was coming to be. My research begins from a recognition that those thus polled would have recorded their experiences in a state of relative insecurity compared to the rather settled situation of those survivors who would contribute their accounts after the passage of time and often after their own transfer to safer lands had insulated them to some degree from the immediacy of the situations they were describing.

Analysis

The ŻIH testimonies and memoirs contain relatively little information on the postwar period in general or on Polish–Jewish relations in particular. This lacuna appears to be the result in part of timing: a majority of AŻIH Collection 301, spanning from 1944 to as late as the 1990s, consists of documents dating from the end of the war and immediately thereafter, but those early testimonies that are the subject of my research (1944–50) are focused for the most part on the issues of annihilation and survival during the war. Collection 302 (the Memoirs Collection, numbering 339 memoirs and diaries) contains even fewer references to the postwar period owing to the subject it focuses on: its narratives, written during the war, often end at the peak stage of annihilation (the summer of 1942), so that even if a survivor were to have deposited another testimony later, the previous document would have been considered already finished. In a telling example, one such memoir, divided into three parts, ends with a description of liberation, followed by a cryptic note: "I will describe what followed, in Part Four" (testimony of Janina Masłowska, AŻIH 302/182). One realizes that even in 1955, when this memoir was deposited, one might have searched in vain for the promised "Part Four." Even if Janina Masłowska wrote and delivered to ŻIH an account of her postwar life in Poland, it could not be fully relied on as an honest narrative concerning Polish–Jewish relations because of the state-imposed Communist policy of silence on this topic. In the milieus of politics, culture, and publishing, Jewish contributions were practically invisible in the Poland of that time.

What, then, can be found in this unique collection concerning the first impressions that Polish Jews had of their neighbors after the war? Following the questionnaire prepared by the CŻKH, the testimonies were structured according to the following pattern:

1. Life before the war (including information about Jews in their hometowns).
2. The beginning of the war and the onset of (German or Soviet) occupation, forcing the Jews into ghettos.
3. The process of extermination, *Aktionen* (usually precipitating a decision to hide).
4. Enduring: hiding until liberation or surviving the concentration or extermination camps in occupied Poland or Germany.
5. Liberation (most commonly described in a single sentence).

When we study the narratives, it becomes evident that questions were asked so as to elicit a story of the annihilation of the Jewish people and of each survivor's unique circumstances of survival. In other words, it was important to record *who* and *what* were killed (the Jewish communities described in the first part of an interview) as well as *how* the interviewee survived (the story that followed). The issue of the survivor's return to his or her home did not necessarily form a part of this picture, and we may legitimately ask why. One possible answer—apart from the rather obvious fact that the trauma, the unprecedented break with the past of the Polish Jews, was what dominated the minds of the CŻKH researchers—may be that asking about postwar experiences might have elicited negative impressions concerning interactions with ethnic Poles, which could endanger the Jewish community's convenient invisibility in the landscape of postwar Polish society and disturb the Communist government's tacit approval bestowed on that community through the support of its institutions. I do not mean to suggest that there was a routine, explicit, interior censorship at work in the CŻKH: in fact, the collection contains multiple accounts of attacks by Polish individuals or bands on unsuspecting Jewish survivors during and after the war; the CŻKH was clearly aware of its interventionist opportunities and collaborated with the Polish authorities to obtain protection for Jewish survivors. Nevertheless, although some accounts do mention Polish–Jewish interactions after the war as a separate subject, the question of the survivors' postwar life was in general not of interest to the CŻKH.

Individuals' statements concerning their current situations tend to be scarce and laconic. Unlike children's testimonies, which often contain a few sentences or paragraphs on postwar life because the young survivors would frequently create narratives to describe a transition to "Eretz" (the Land of Israel), for which an orphanage or kibbutz would have provided preparation, the adults' testimonies that extend to a moment of liberation usually mention it in one factual sentence as a kind of terminus. One occasionally also finds a mention of those who managed to survive, for example, with the help of Christians, but unaccompanied by a description of the survivor's postwar plight.

In this chapter, I propose what I think is a useful categorization of the Jewish survivors' encounters with Polish Gentiles as described in some of the survivor testimonies collected in Poland during the years 1944–50. I have formulated it based on what I found in the narratives, guided by the premises of grounded theory. The categories are not to be read as exclusive, however: what the data suggest to me, rather, is a series of concentric circles within which the images that each account projects may be situated, where there is some degree of overlap according to the intensity of each.

Negative Memories

1. Rumors or News of the Murder of Nearby Jews

Decisions to leave Poland seem typically to have followed once an accumulation of antisemitic episodes in a survivor's postwar life had reached a tipping point. At the center of the concentric structure of memories, then, one can find the experience of fear—fear motivated by the incredulous realization that Jews could be still killed in Poland after the war, this time by Poles. That fear is evidenced in various ways, most directly in rumors or in the actual reports of the murder of nearby Jews. Table A.1 in the appendix illustrates that roughly 40 percent of the documents that refer to the postwar period mention such a rumor or report, and most of these documents are in Polish.

Specific examples indicate the way in which such memories are presented in these accounts. Szmul Lerer (AŻIH 301/104) states tersely at the end of his account that of the more than 300 prisoners who managed to escape from Sobibor, only 30 survived because "the AK-*ovce* [members of the Underground forces] helped, by any means possible, to exterminate that small bunch of Jews that survived the Hitlerian murderers." Mojżesz Goldblatt (AŻIH 301/2093), for his part, reports that after he returned to his hometown of Grajewo, he had to flee again because

> bands are ravaging there. They also know about me that I am a Jew because I stood in front of the military commission and told them my real name; there is nothing to hide anymore—the Germans are gone—but you have to hide again because again the fascist pigs [Polish antisemites] are attacking, murdering, and—where should you go? To Silesia, there are more of your own. I will embrace my own. I presently have my own children, a little son and a little daughter, I work as a barber, and time goes by quickly.

There is more in this unedited, broken-speech testimony than first appears on the surface: an acknowledged need to hide after denying any official need to hide ("the Germans are gone"); a desire to find some remnants of the Jewish community and to live within familial bonds; and the matter-of-fact account of attacks by Poles on the remaining Jews, following an expression of disbelief that such a course of action would ever occur after the war. Such is also the language of the testimony by Lejbko Goldberg (AŻIH 301/1869), who describes attacks on Jews on a train:

> On September 18, 1946, four Jews were riding on a train from Międzyrzec to Biała Podlaska. About 10:00 a.m., right after the station of Sokuła, the train was stopped by a band of people (about one hundred persons) armed with machine guns and automatic weapons. With a cry—*Turn in the Jews and Soviets!*—they started to push everyone from the train and check their identification papers. One of the Jews, Srulek Zylberstein (who had been a partisan near Minsk), being afraid that they would kill him, started to run away. The bandits shot him while he was escaping. They also killed a woman, Genia Adlerstein from Biała Podlaska (a former Auschwitz inmate), having first checked her papers. A certain Polish scout girl, riding in the same carriage, told the bandits that there were four Jews on the train.

Attacks on Jews traveling by train were in fact so common that they became known in the literature as the "railway action." The designation may be confusing to the extent that the term *action* may imply a coordinated effort. No historian yet has indicated any united force behind these attacks, which rather bear the features of spontaneous collective violence made possible by a social consensus concerning the victimization of "the other."

2. Direct Threats or Attacks against One's Person

Actual violence or threats against one's person are mentioned in about one-fifth of the researched testimonies, given in almost equal parts in Polish and Yiddish, with a slight predominance of Yiddish.

If we combine the first and second category, the memory of physical danger to returning Jews, whether to oneself or to others, is mentioned in more than half the sample. A majority (two-thirds) of this half were written in Polish, about one-third in Yiddish, and only one in German.

By comparison, the general language distribution of my sample was 73 percent in Polish, 25 percent in Yiddish, and one percent in German. The linguistic distribution of reports of violence is therefore close to that of the sample as a whole, with a slight tendency among the survivors to resort to a "secret language" when reporting on violent encounters with Poles. Safety of speaking among "one's own" contributed to a greater openness in revealing difficult and unflattering opinions about the majority population.

Nearly all of these accounts, it must be noted, are written in a dry, officious language, devoid of any hint of personal reflection. Elias Magid (AŻIH 301/2019), for example, describes in a rather unemotional style an encounter with three men on a night train: "From my accent they realized that I was a Jew. When the train was at full speed, they told me that I would not get to Międzyrzecz because I am a Jew. Before I had a chance to say anything, they hit me with a piece of iron and threw me, unconscious, from the moving train. I fell under the wheels of the train. By some miracle, I survived, although I lost both my legs. I lay for nine months in a hospital, and now I am a cripple."

It is possible that such matter-of-fact language may testify, first of all, to the shock of what was happening to these Polish Jews after their previous annihilation. The word *again* or expressions such as "the murders continued, this time by the fascist Poles," seem indicative of a kind of abdication of the language, which, unable to convey a reality of unremitting doom, resorts instead to the simple and commonplace approach of a police report, neutral and matter of fact in its style yet harrowing in its detail.

With a more literate witness, the tone of a report might occasionally be caustic or bitterly ironic. Such is the deposition by Dr. Henryk Stecki (AŻIH 301/445), who, in submitting his reply to a questionnaire from the CŻKH, gives the CŻKH permission to publish it only anonymously because, as he explains, "I still remain in the Polish environment, and its relation to the Jewish question is generally known. I had an opportunity to experience it in my own skin."

At the end of his account describing his survival under an assumed "Aryan" identity, Dr. Stecki adds a short moral and political reflection:

> Because a new generation of Poles of democratic convictions has not yet grown up, I dare say that for the present Polish society the Jewish "problem" as such will still exist as long as there are only a few Jews remaining in Poland. I would wish that an appropriate conclusion be deduced from this statement for the future. Finishing my story, I will also add that, having returned to Kraków, I learned that two to three weeks after I left the village where I was recently staying [hiding as a Pole], a rumor started to circulate that I am a Jew. After the liberation of this area, I was already threatened with death, and the people who protected me—as pure as the driven snow—were threatened with lynching and arson. Therefore, the German sowing has not gone to waste.

The few accounts I encountered that do provide a more personal, emotional reflection are by women. These accounts elaborate on feelings such as the fear that the returning survivors experienced upon realizing that the murder of Jews continued even after the war. In one account, Rachel Kosower (AŻIH 301/4418) reports revisiting her former hiding places immediately after the liberation, assisted by the Red Army soldiers, to gain some information about her family; her sister, in the meantime, wished to remain home, claiming that she had nothing to be ashamed or afraid of, thus suggesting that Kosower's journey had more to do with fleeing home than with acquiring knowledge. Kosower tried to discourage her sister from staying at home, and her testimony poignantly reveals her state of mind:

> My thought was as follows: the people [Poles] are exasperated, we are defenseless, the war is not yet over. Surprises are possible. Ciechanowiec is a small town. In a transitional period, it is much safer to be in a big town. . . . So we remained, but because those few Jewish families moved to Białystok fearing bandit attacks, we started to think seriously about moving. . . . As quickly as possible, I tried to leave this little destroyed shtetl, which filled me with fear, especially after the terrifying news of murders in Wysokie Mazowieckie, Czyżew, where many Jews died. On July 23, 1945, the last group of Jews left Ciechanowiec. . . . We lived in constant fear. My sister and I slept in the attic, barricading doors with iron slabs. . . . The atmosphere was full of anxiety and fear.

Then one day a group of Underground (AK) members, somewhat known to her family, arrived in the town. Kosower narrates the encounter in these words:

> They drank at our place a whole container of beverage. When, late at night, my brother Meir came back—I simply lost control of myself. I had an impression that the whole world was in on a conspiracy against me. It is possible that all of the experiences sharpened my sensitivity that way. After the arrival of my brother, I lost my patience completely. There was an exchange of sharp words. . . . My brother even wanted to run away with me somewhere, but he could not stand up to [our sister] Chawcia. At last, in greatest agitation, I left the house. I left my last fifty złoty at home. Whether it was stubbornness or fate, I don't know. I only knew that I would go mad that night. My unforgettable ones [i.e., loved ones] remained. They locked the doors. I entered a neighboring house, which had been uninhabited for some time. As long as I live, I did not have such a night. . . . In the morning, Ajzyk Grzybek knocked at my windows:

—Are you there?
—I am.
—Rachel! Get up!

A horrible thought shook me: "My dear ones are no more." I got up from the floor, ran out, saw a terrible picture. As I was later told, the bandits entered through a broken window. My brother begged the murderers for mercy; he wanted to leave everything. There had to have been a terrible fight because he was not shot, but his head was cut off. My sister ran away from the room to our neighbor, Helena Paduchowa, but she [Helena] drove her [my sister] out from her apartment, and the murderers killed her with a shotgun. I was driven by an unnatural power. I pushed the barricaded door myself and fell fainting into the river of brotherly blood. The Polish neighbors did not want to give the water to wake me up.

After these horrendous experiences, Kosower was taken to Białystok (probably by some neighbors, who apparently at the time did not reveal the fate of her sister), and there the Jewish Committee put her in a hospital: "The doctors did everything to save me. An entire team was keeping constant watch over me. I left sick, poor, lonely, with an inhuman legacy of pain and fear. I have never returned home again."

This unusually long and emotionally revealing testimony is rather an anomaly among the early postwar accounts. Kosower's account, imbued with the harrowing terror of a frozen past, demands to be read, re-read, and analyzed, and it escapes all generalizations that I might try to impose on the majority of these accounts. In a highly unique style and with emotional depth, it may give a voice to an unknown number of Polish Jews who either could not or would not record similar postwar experiences. The climate of fear verified in the other testimonies, however, argues against diminishing the importance of Kosower's account on the grounds that it is anomalous or somehow unique. In that climate, it instead appears instructive.

3. Various Negative Societal Reactions

Just as common as the memory of the physical danger accompanying first interactions with ethnic Poles is the memory of various other negative societal reactions, present in about 41 percent of the sample. I have included in this category those general impressions of hostility from the Polish population that had not yet risen to the level of violent threats or attacks. These pejorative reactions are expressed in the following forms: expressions of fear experienced by rescuers—reflecting hostility toward those who extended assistance and thus, by implication, toward those who received it (including threats, attacks, and even sometimes the killing of those who helped the Jews); the passive attitudes of members of the militia in the face of physical attacks on the Jews; discriminatory actions by state officials and administrators (including train conductors); the defilement of Jewish graves; and expressions such as the infamous question "What! Still alive?!"

The death penalty for those who aided the Jews had been instituted exclusively in Nazi-occupied eastern Europe. In an interesting, if cruel, irony of fate, the postwar situation of those heroic Poles who risked their own and their families' lives to save Jews became a ghastly shadow of the situation experienced by the survivors themselves. The rescuers felt "shame" for helping Jews during the war (even for rescuing children), were afraid to admit the help they had rendered, and sometimes went into hiding to avoid reprisals at the hands of their neighbors. These rescuers suffered robberies, beatings, and even death from armed bands, hooligans, and members (alleged or real) of one or another underground branch of the anti-Communist army. On occasion, they had to flee and even to be rescued by the Jews whom they had formerly saved. Young Pinches Gruszniewski (AŻIH 301/1990), for example, narrates that after the war while he was still staying with the peasant who had rescued him, a woman arrived from another village: "I heard her saying," Gruszniewski testifies, "that she had been hiding Jews, and now she is afraid of revenge from the forest bands; they have already attacked her several times, they were shooting at her, they robbed her of her horses, [and] they demanded gold." Another young man, Władysław Siekierka (AŻIH 301/3681), likewise notes not only his great anticipation of liberation but also the disappointment he experienced after it actually occurred: "But it was not as we had imagined; the peasant was ashamed in front of his neighbors that he had hidden the Jews, and, again, we were returning by night [i.e., trying to hide] after two years, to our hometown."

On occasion, when rescuers suffered beatings, the most frequently mentioned perpetrators were those identified as "forest bands"—that is, members of the NSZ or the AK. These anti-Communist groups, whether imposters or true former AK or NSZ troops, ravaged the eastern villages of the newly drawn Poland in an attempt to reverse the Red Army's brutal invasion and occupation. Although their primary targets were Soviet and Polish Communists, Jews were also sometimes branded as Communists for reasons of personal or political convenience known only to the bands' leaders.

Szmul Garber (AŻIH 301/3535) reports that after the war, unable to find any living relatives in his hometown, he decided to return to his rescuer, Bolesław Pogorzelski, and to work on his farm. The relative peace in which they first lived did not last long, however; the rescuer was soon harassed and attacked by the "forest bands," who learned that he was hiding a Jew. They invaded his home and brutally asked his wife whether they were not "ashamed, as Catholics, to hide the Jews." They beat the man, robbed his house, and demanded that he "return" the Jew at some point to another town, after which the man's stolen things might be returned. Pogorzelski and his wife begged Garber to leave for Białystok, where he eventually ended up and where he would host his rescuer's family in frequent moments of danger. Garber later invited this family to find a more permanent place in Białystok, but they were unable to move due to family considerations.

We should not automatically assume that the actions of these "forest bands" are to be identified with the response from the society at large. Nevertheless, the support the society seemed to give such groups may testify to a broader consensus regarding the postwar treatment of the Jews. In Rachel Kosower's account, quoted earlier, her own neighbors aided an AK raid on her house and refused to help the wounded victims. Perhaps out of a continuation of a wartime antisemitism and possibly out of fear of retaliation from the Underground, Polish neighbors may once again have adopted a passive or even a supporting stance toward the murder not only of the Jews but also of their rescuers.

Regarding one particularly brutal case concerning "revenge" taken against a rescuer, Abram Lipcer (AŻIH 301/1260) testifies that after a failed attempt to kill a survivor, members of the newly formed

Communist Citizens' Militia (which had a reputation for frequent drunkenness) approached the survivor's rescuer in order to ask him a rhetorical question, "Why have you rescued a Jew?" They then beat the rescuer, too, breaking a rib. The rescuer then complained to a Soviet captain, after which the vengeful militia commandant engaged in a campaign to trump up charges that the rescuer had collaborated with the Germans.

In some cases, rescuers were even killed. Lejb Hofman (AŻIH 301/1092) notes with sorrow that Wacław Szpura, who had sheltered him and his companions during the occupation and "who was like a father to us, whom we called among ourselves *our rabbi*," was murdered by other Poles after the war because "he was helping the Jews."

One may also illustrate a general societal hostility toward the Jews with numerous instances of official discrimination by clerks, state officials, the militia, the military, and the courts. Such instances were part and parcel of collective anti-Jewish violence in Communist Poland and have been well documented in the literature on the Kraków, Kielce, and Rzeszów Pogroms; they confirm other sources and so tend to reinforce a particularly convincing image.

Abram Lipcer's account, quoted earlier, describes a militia commandant, apparently acting on his own, who used his newly gained power to exact revenge against a rescuer and to persecute a survivor. Testimony by Mordko Berger, Dawid Gruenbaum, and Sara Mahler (AŻIH 301/1357) describes an attack against Jews on trains carrying repatriates from Lviv. It appears from their account that the bands that boarded the train near Tarnów did not spare even a pregnant woman and that the other passengers on the train, including some members of the militia, remained passive all the while. One family and some other militia men, however, apparently did defend the attacked Jews. (However, the way in which this fact is noted in passing raises the complex issue of how aid and protection appear as both a bright spot and a dark memory of violence in these accounts.) In a somewhat different case of violence on a train, Eli Ulicki (AŻIH 301/1828), a survivor from Mauthausen, was recognized by the conductor "as a Jew," after which the train was stopped. The conductor tried to force Eli off the train, which would doubtlessly have happened had not a woman and a Red Army soldier risen to his defense.

Icek Lerner (AŻIH 301/2802), who survived a murderous attack by one of his "rescuers," recounts his futile quest to bring justice to bear on the man who had murdered Lerner's wartime fiancée and her child. Neither multiple reports to the militia nor arrest orders nor consistent appeals to courts of higher importance could bring this man to a proper trial. At each step, Lerner's attempts to initiate the trial were dismissed. He finally left Poland for Sweden and then returned with a renewed hope for justice. We do not learn from the testimony whether his hope was eventually fulfilled.

Regarding what are now considered iconic questions expressing a similar idea in various forms—"What! Still alive?!" "Why are so many Jews returning?!" "Didn't Hitler finish you off?!"—the Polish testimonies refer to a surprisingly small number of such reactions once the war ended. I have found such expressions to be more numerous in accounts of wartime events but was able to find only one example from the postwar period. (This does not mean that there are no other examples in the entire AŻIH Collections 301 and 302, merely that in the pool of testimonies that showed promise of containing descriptions of postwar situations— my "active" sample—only one testimony containing such an expression was found.) That example is from an account (AŻIH 301/687) in which a certain Samuel Rajzman describes encountering a forest ranger who was known to have killed Jews hiding in the forest. After the war, the ranger appeared to be more humble, although he uttered an ambiguous-sounding welcome: "Well, boys, you remained alive" (in Polish, "Cóż, chłopcy, zostaliście przy życiu").

Another surprising finding is that the question of appropriated Jewish property, often indicated as one of the reasons why the Polish population was hostile to the returning survivors, is almost never mentioned in Jewish testimonies after the war. Only one testimony—that of Róża Reiner (AŻIH 301/4633)—contains a complaint that peasants from her village refused to return the things she had left with them. It is possible that owing to the timing of the depositions no such accounts could be given as yet. The survivors might still have been contemplating recovering or might actually have been at some stage in the process of recovering their property, so they might have been unlikely as yet to have reported on the outcome. It is also plausible that in the grand scheme of things the question of property was entirely marginal to the issue of finding one's relatives.

4. Postwar Hiding

Another memory that contributes—at least by implication—to a general picture of social hostility awaiting the returning survivors is the recollection of postwar hiding. About 18 percent of the testimonies in the data set mention attempts to pass as ethnic Poles after the war. Five describe physically hiding, which usually took the form of remaining for a while at a rescuer's home or in a wartime hiding place. Rachel Kosower's evocative account, quoted earlier, brings to life an image of the survivors hiding ("Again!") in the attics and barricading doors "with iron slabs." Dawid Nassan (AŻIH 301/3262) remained with his rescuer for two weeks after liberation. After that time, the rescuer took him secretly to a Jewish doctor to be "reclaimed" by a Jewish community. In Władysław Siekierka's account, he and his family found themselves "returning by night after two years, to our hometown."

Although some survivors felt it was safer to continue hiding in their wartime hiding places, more of them decided to retain their "Aryan" identity and to pass as ethnic Poles even after the war,[1] thus lending credence to the existence of the "new Marranos" phenomenon described by Henryk Shoshkes.[2] This need to hide is related in a dry, curt, matter-of-fact manner. In one instance of a Jewish Nazi collaborator (AŻIH 301/3329)), it was hard to determine whether the survivor was hiding under "Aryan" identity to protect himself from antisemitism or from a trial for collaboration.

Finally, negative societal reactions could also be described in the sort of cryptic language that we find in Nuchim Perelman's account (AŻIH 301/2327) of his return to his hometown: "I found there, unfortunately, the ruins of the house and the unfriendly attitude of the local population, [which] forced me to leave my home area." Not knowing exactly what this "unfriendly attitude" might have consisted of, we can merely speculate that his "welcome home" may have included anything from hostile looks and the silent treatment to negative remarks, threats, and even attacks.

Before turning to describe the positive memories of Polish–Jewish interactions, I would suggest that the categories "negative societal reactions" and "postwar hiding" may also be joined with "threats and physical attacks" because together they sketch a picture of hostility on the part of the surrounding population. Altogether, these negative-category memories are mentioned in 80 percent of testimonies, making this general category of memory applicable to a great majority of all "active" ŻIH accounts (note, however, that several negative memories could be recorded in the same document). Seventy-five percent of these negative memories were recorded in Polish, 24 percent in Yiddish, and one percent in German. Furthermore, it is, in fact, somewhat surprising that these negative testimonies appear to reflect almost exactly the language proportion of the "active" data set as a whole. Such a consistency would seem to indicate that internal censorship through resorting to a "secret language" was not an issue when a survivor chose to report a negative impression.

Positive Memories

About 23 percent of the selected ŻIH accounts yield positive memories. The negative accounts, of course, reflect a more drastic outcome; mere statistics do not tell the whole story. In the positive accounts, moreover, even the good memories are still mixed with some negative ones. Most commonly, the positive memories are memories of wartime rescuers continuing to render aid and assistance or of someone defending a survivor from antisemitic harassment.

The help offered could be of a short-term nature. Leon Epstein (AŻIH 301/2042), for example, wrote upon leaving the camp in Wesoła:

> I realized that the Germans were gone, I wrapped myself in a blanket and went out to the nearby hut. There I learned that the Germans are no more and any moment now the Red Army will enter. The owner of the hut, named Olej, washed me, as I had a wound on my hand, [and] gave me clothing and the first piece of bread and a bit of coffee. He told

me to leave because he was afraid, in case the Germans would return, that they would kill him and me. I left and went through Jaworzno and Chrzanów to Kraków.

Eli Ulicki, quoted earlier, was indeed saved by a single woman's opposition to his harassment by a train conductor. To be sure, a Red Army soldier enforced the woman's demand, but without her intervention things might well have gone according to the conductor's plan. Following Ulicki's narrative, an interviewer, whose role in general would have been to summarize the survivor's account, reflects on Ulicki's experiences (AŻIH 301/1828):

> On the margins of that event, it must be remarked that in Mauthausen, after the liberation, people had already tried to persuade Ulicki not to go to Poland because they keep on murdering Jews there. Yet his heart was driven to his hometown, which he desired to see after the catastrophe and maybe even to find some relatives or loved ones. Besides, he didn't believe these rumors, and he thought that after what the Jews experienced, they would be carried on [the people's] shoulders. The episode with the train conductor was a strong blow to him.

Ulicki, the account continues, returned to Białystok, wept when he saw the ruins of his home, and was taken care of by a Polish acquaintance, who kept him in his home for three weeks, providing basic assistance and care. Ulicki mentions a few other Poles who aided him in finding the necessary resources to begin his life anew. His account presents us with a complex mixture of attitudes on the part of the population, both friendly and hostile, that were likely the survivors' daily bread. Most typically, the contrast was between group hostility and individual help. Of the instances of help, however, we receive only glimpses.

There were nevertheless some rather astounding examples of care and help extended to the returning Jews. Mieczysław Żurawski (AŻIH 301/376), one of three inmates to escape the Chełmno death camp, was received with caring hospitality by a nearby Polish villager. Żurawski told the interviewer:

I went to the nearest house. Here I found out that the Germans had received orders to leave the area. I was received very warmly. I soaked my leg and bandaged it. A woman took care of me. She was the first person I told about the recent events. The next day someone I knew from Chełmno showed up; he recognized me. He remembered the Jew going to work in handcuffs. He told me everything had already been liquidated. An hour later the Russians arrived. I felt completely free at last. I returned to Chełmno, where my hosts received me very well. They called me a Jewish hero who did not give in to the Nazis. They told me that there was one Jew left whom the Germans did not manage to take care of yet. That was Szymon Srebrnik.³

Chaim Wittelsohn (AŻIH 301/531), whose testimony was quoted in the introduction, describes help from a peasant woman and other people in Sinowoda village immediately after the war:

The Germans had already left the area, so I went with her [to her home]. I was received very warmly; I took a bath [and] changed my clothes and underwear, which she had always washed and brought to me. I ate until I was full, and they didn't want to let me go for a long time. I had to promise that I'd come back to them again, whether or not I found anyone from my own family. In the meantime, I settled in Lublin, where I waited for the liberation of the Dąbrowa mining region. It was only in March that I returned to Sosnowiec, and I consider myself currently to be one of the lucky ones whose immediate family members are still alive—and in Palestine at that.

Such human gestures as those depicted in the preceding quote were not the most typical help given to the survivors indicated in the sample. More often, help might consist of a friendly warning that "bands" in the neighborhood were going to attack the local survivors or an act of direct sheltering from an anti-Jewish attack. Thus, in a novelized memoir, Hela Ken (AŻIH 302/210) recounts that a friendly Pole on a train warned her not to go alone to Garwolin because "reactionary bands," ravaging there, might kill her.

Survivors' accounts recalling positive encounters make up about one-fourth of all of the "active" testimonies in AŻIH Collections 301 and 302. Although some accounts mention a short-term intervention by a member of the Polish population, a few describe longer-term aid to survivors in need, which was probably known in the neighborhood and which would seem to contextualize ethnic Poles' responses to the desperate needs of their Jewish compatriots.

"Silent" Memories

Four percent of "active" documents in AŻIH Collections 301 and 302 refer to some aspect of postwar life but without indicating what the interactions with Poles were like. I have designated such accounts "silent," although it is admittedly an awkward term: such testimonies and memoirs seem "silent" only by the implication that if Jewish interaction with ethnic Poles had a strong enough impression, positive or negative, we might assume they would merit a mention or even only a veiled hint (as sometimes occurred with negative impressions).

It is likely, however, that in these accounts other aspects of the survivors' postwar existence took precedence over their relationships with the Gentiles. I have chosen to construe here nothing more than that these survivors' silence on the matter of the quality of their relations with Poles simply indicates that it was not enough of an issue to them to merit any mention in their accounts. Anatol Weksztajn (AŻIH 302/204), for example, wrote a long memoir of 200 pages, 150 of which discuss his prewar education, his love adventures, antisemitism in Poland, and other questions. His family was of an assimilationist background, and he weaves many heartfelt stories of Polish aid as well as betrayal into his war narrative. In the final paragraph, concerning his return to his hometown, he includes the following report:

> My first action in Łowicz after expelling Hitler [sic] was the rebuilding of the Jewish cemetery, completely destroyed by these "bloodsucking beasts." Grave slabs taken away or broken . . . I managed to put back

several hundred and to cement thirty-six of them straight, like they used to stand.

My grandparents' monuments were untouched. Even the iron crates were left alone, although iron parts had been taken from the whole of the cemetery. Apparently, the destruction of the cemetery was a specialty of the local *folksdeutsche*. Because my brother was a son-in-law of their once-favorite pastor Oppman, they left the monuments in peace.

Of the synagogue, which I had rebuilt before the war, not a trace was left, and it was a large, four-story building, [capable of] containing several thousands of people. It was purchased for parts from the Germans by my one-time clerk from the time of war 1914–1918. For her, there is one description: a scoundrel.

To some degree, Weksztajn's narrative is a continuation of his life story in prewar Poland, where some Poles were scoundrels, there were burglaries at the Jewish cemetery, and his family's assimilationist past protected it to a certain extent, even as its members lay in their graves. Yet in spite of the antisemitic behaviors, which the author seems to have become used to, there is no visible trace of any particular societal attitude, whether adverse or propitious, toward himself. In some curious way, his memoir seems even to present a life somewhat undisturbed by the war and the Holocaust, and although he does mention the deaths of his family and friends, his prewar existence, including his attempts at salvaging the Jewish cemetery, continues undisturbed by any mention of the social climate of the postwar years.

Cemetery Syndrome

Expressions that can be interpreted as testifying to the "cemetery syndrome" are extremely rare. They do not reflect directly on Polish–Jewish interactions. However, their rarity seems to provide a contrast to some historians' thesis that the "cemetery syndrome" was the dominant postwar emotion among Polish Jews and their greatest reason to leave Poland. As unique examples, some such expressions can be fully quoted here. Tojwie Blatt (AŻIH 302/190) finishes his memoir entitled "God Has

Turned Away from Us" (in Polish, "Bóg się od nas odwrócił"), in which he describes the rebellion in the Sobibor death camp, with the following passage: "I was to be happy, to kiss soldiers that I met, to jump for joy. I am free, after all; I can go wherever I want, shout loudly—*I am a Jew*—and no one will dare to touch me—so why am I not happy? I am not crazy from joy. . . . I am alone. . . . [O]nly now this fact reaches the depth of my consciousness. Where is my home???"

An even more explicit expression of "cemetery syndrome" is found in the testimony of Rywa and Cypa Szpannberg (AŻIH 301/451), who at the end of their account reveal what they have learned about the "mystery" of the disappearance of the Jews from their small town:

> We came out to freedom, went to our little town; houses burned down, few people, individuals, only ten persons. Our house stands, not too much destroyed, but people who were living there, worked, were suffering all those years, they wanted to have something for the future; they are dead now; the cursed Germans ripped life out of them and hid the traces of a horrific crime. But after three years the key to this riddle where the Germans put those people was found: in the trash heap, about two kilometers away from town, in a huge ditch twenty-five meters wide, fifty meters long, and thirty meters deep, there is a brick wall; that is where the older people are lying, children, young, girls in full bloom, they all lie there murdered. This was their last passage in their life. There is no trace of a shot, because the German put the living ones and sprinkled them with earth, and people suffocated because of the lack of air. It is possible even to recognize some people. We saw it with our own eyes, a very painful and tragic sight. It forced us to run away from this land where we lost our parents, relatives, etcetera, to be among our brothers and sisters, who will take interest in our experiences and our lot.

Another quotation comes from Moszek Pantofel (AŻIH 301/2195): "Our life is and will be hard on the thresholds of our hometowns. No one will welcome us; no one will lend us a hand. Ruins everywhere; our homes are destroyed. We are strangers in our hometowns. Our wounds are incurable. Our tragedy continues."

The overwhelming and hopeless thought that the liberation did not bring true consolation and unification with one's family was the ultimate anticlimax to the anticipation and hopes that had kept survivors alive during hiding. In Pantofel's case, it is the sad realization of being a unique witness of unique times that brought some meaning to his lonely postwar existence: "Yet, in spite of all that, time will heal our pain; [it] will cure our wounds. We will live, we will work—that is what our destiny desires. We have remained yet a handful of witnesses of all that has happened here."

4
Yad Vashem Testimonies in the Context of Israeli History

Those Holocaust survivors who left Poland in order to settle in Eretz Israel, the Land of Israel, soon found themselves in the unprecedented circumstances of becoming citizens of a novel Jewish state. In contrast to a diasporic existence, in which statehood and nationality were disconnected for the Jewish minority, Israel provided the Jews, the survivors in particular, with an experience of national self-agency. It also provided them with Zionism—a national ideology and a cultural project that could attract and embrace the incoming refugees, just as it would shape and color their memories of the past.

In following the testimonies of survivors from Poland to Israel to reconstruct the survivors' interpretations of what transpired during their first postwar interactions with Gentiles, let us take a closer look at what kind of culture, ideology, and attitudes toward survivors the refugees encountered in Israel. Was anybody interested in where they came from or in what they had left behind? Was the Israeli population curious, indifferent, embracing, or, perhaps, strangely hostile to the refugees' experiences of annihilation at the hands of the Nazis? Who listened to their stories, and how were they being interviewed for historical research? Finally, during the period 1955–70 (the period researched for this part of this study), how did Israelis' attitudes toward the survivors develop? What historical events and social context may have influenced their progress, and, conversely, how might such an evolution have affected the survivors' memories of their first contacts with Gentiles after the war?

In the Israeli context, Zionism seems to be the most important and dominant ideological and cultural background, paradigm, and subtext at the same time that it underwent its own significant modifications. Zionism is a notion that covers multiple and sometimes even contradictory ideologies of the "return to Zion" and that prides itself on a vast and growing bibliography, but I focus here primarily on Zionism as a state-building ideology that attracted many of the newcomers to the Israeli state. Once the state had been created, Zionism served as a tool of national cohesion, a unifying principle that affected Israeli culture in many aspects, including the state's defense plans, its education, and its research paradigms. In particular, Zionism affected how the Shoah (Holocaust) was being interpreted and used in the broader context of building Israeli statehood. It also significantly influenced how native Israelis perceived and welcomed the refugees from Poland.

In this chapter, I consider such influences to delineate the context in which the survivors in Israel started to or continued to tell their stories.

The Yishuv and the Survivors

What attitudes toward the incoming Holocaust survivors were found in the Yishuv, the Jewish population in prestate Palestine? Although the advantages of a massive Jewish immigration that could help the Yishuv leaders create a political fait accompli and eventually be incorporated into the armed forces used in the War of Independence were ultimately perceived, the initial reaction to the survivors arriving in the Land of Israel was affected by the Zionists' "negation of Exile": "the total rejection of what was viewed in Zionist thinking as deformed and anomalous Jewish existence in the diaspora."[1]

In fact, the image of the survivor-immigrants posed a challenge to the founding principle of the rebirth of the Jewish state.[2] Often undernourished and even emaciated, nursing both physical and psychological wounds, and most often the lone survivors of families or even communities, the survivors seemed to be the embodiment of everything that was wrong with the Jewish Exile: the many scars the survivors carried were an ultimate proof of the futility of the diasporic wishful thinking about the possibility of a reasonable existence for Jews among the Gentiles. At the same time, the ultimate coupling of the Jewish tragedy with the rebirth of the Jewish state helped to create a "new" national identity.[3]

The survivors were regarded as weak and hopeless, even when they managed to some extent to rebuild their lives and to accommodate themselves to difficult circumstances in the Land of Israel. The most infamous words about and against the survivors were significantly uttered by David Ben-Gurion, Israel's founder and first prime minister: "A mob and human dust, without language, without education, without roots and without being absorbed in tradition and the nation's vision."[4]

The emissaries and soldiers from the Yishuv who visited the DP camps in Europe used other derogatory and patronizing expressions. Shame and contempt in reference to the survivors were likewise freely exchanged in the Israeli press and official communications, if not directly in the survivors' presence: "Are these the kind of immigrants you're sending us? . . . We want *haluzim* [pioneers], people like us, the kind of people we are used to."[5]

In contrast to the critical and patronizing attitudes toward "ordinary" survivors, which were expressed from the foundation of the state through the 1950s, native Israelis felt that the ethos of the ghetto fighters and partisans supported the Zionist foundations of the state and were attracted to it. The admiration toward the small minority of survivors who actively took up the struggle dated from the Warsaw Ghetto Uprising of 1943 and increased as the emissaries from the Yishuv encountered Brichah activists, fighters, and partisans. Further on, the arrival of Ruzka Korczak, a leader of the Vilna partisans, in Israel and her lecture tour there significantly changed the notion of who some of the survivors of the Shoah were as well as which ones it would be more desirable to remember and single out as examples.[6] When the poet Abba Kovner, leader of the Vilna Ghetto resistance movement, arrived in 1945, followed by the charismatic couple Zivia Lubetkin (in 1946) and Yitzhak "Antek" Zuckerman (in 1947), leaders of the Warsaw Ghetto Uprising, "the gulf between the heroic image of the ghetto fighters and the partisans and the image of the 'ordinary' survivors in general" only widened.[7]

The leaders of the Warsaw Ghetto Uprising and the leaders of underground activities in other ghettoes enjoyed the status of national heroes.

They resided together in a kibbutz of their own creation, Beit Lohamei Ha-Getaot (Ghetto Fighters' House), and they attempted to define and lead Holocaust memorialization according to their fighting ethos.[8] That ethos included specific criticism of the Judenräte, or Jewish Councils, during the war, and general criticism of the rest of the population, which had "refused" to participate in the armed struggle. While the fighters and partisans were still in Europe, they had not spared bitter words blaming the Yishuv for its perceived isolation from the Jews living under the Nazis, but, significantly, once they entered Eretz Israel, their criticism of it was muted. It is possible that the immediate military needs of the state that was being born as they watched as well as the need to assimilate themselves into the new society prevented them from dwelling on what they had seen as the Yishuv's abandonment of the Diaspora.

The notion of the ghetto fighters' heroism eventually became absorbed into and utilized by the ideology of *mamlakhtiut* (Hebrew for "kingdomship," meaning "statehood" or "statism"), propagated by Ben-Gurion. Indeed, state-sponsored commemoration of the Holocaust centered around that notion. On the way, Gulie Ne'eman Arad argues, "a depersonalized and abstracted 'six million' code [was] appropriated as a sacred taboo, a taboo to be traded exclusively by and for the state. Tinkering with the victims' memory and fine-tuning their reality[,] [the state] used [them] as leverage for persuading the nations of the world of their unrecoverable moral and material debt to the Jewish people."[9]

Although the "six million" served as a rationalization for the creation of the state, only those survivors who actively took part in armed struggle were deemed worthy of being remembered and commemorated. That Zionist subtext stood behind the support of Ben-Gurion and the ruling Mapai Party in establishing a central memorial and research center to the exclusion of memorials abroad, which could be conceived as creating competitive claims to represent Jewish victims.[10]

The Israeli state's ideological goals coalesced, therefore, with that tiny fraction of the survivors—ghetto fighters and partisans—who became the faces of the Holocaust memorialization. This dynamic was manifested in the process of choosing the official name of the Israeli commemoration of the Holocaust, a process that did not begin in the Yishuv until 1948. Although three proposals for a commemorative date were initially offered from three different bodies,[11] in the end the date chosen was the twenty-seventh day of Nissan in the Hebrew calendar. This date was close to April 19, the anniversary of the beginning of the Warsaw Ghetto Uprising but was also removed from any possibility of falling during Passover week.

The discussions and consecutive proposals for the commemoration day seem to confirm the dichotomy in the collective Israeli consciousness of the Holocaust and the survivors, who were divided between a heroic, fighting elite and a majority who were perceived as shameful victims and who, in the words of Abba Kovner, "went like lambs to the slaughter."[12] Yael Zerubavel notes that this "dual classification that marked armed resistance to the Nazis as 'heroic' and lumped all other aspects of the Jewish experience under the label 'Holocaust'" made the Holocaust the "'nonheroic' category."[13] The original commemoration day, passed in the Knesset on March 21, 1951, was called the "Remembrance Day for the Holocaust and the Revolt in the Ghettos," although this name was later amended to the "Holocaust Martyrs and Heroes Remembrance Day," thus omitting the word *revolt*.[14] The law to establish Yad Vashem (YV), the Holocaust Martyrs' and Heroes' Remembrance Authority, submitted on August 19, 1953, was called the "Holocaust and Heroism Memorial Law—Yad Vashem," and the day of commemoration, not established until 1959, was called the "Memorial Day of the Holocaust and Heroism."[15] During those years, the survivors themselves commemorated the Holocaust in their own ceremonies, but it was not until 1961 that observance of the Holocaust became a national observance, with public manifestations such as ceremonies, time off from work, and the sounding of sirens.[16]

At the same time, it is important to note that there were some in the Yishuv even during the war and throughout the 1940s who objected to the distinction between passivity and heroism. The most vocal were Mark Dworzecki and Nathan Eck (both survivor-researchers) as well as Zerah Warhaftig, a member of Hapoel Hamizrahi (Mizrachi Workers, a religious pioneering and labor movement in the Land of Israel), who represented the opinions of religious Zionists.[17]

Some groups of survivors likewise resisted the emphasis on the celebration of armed resistance: "Every survivor knows," wrote Yosef Gar, editor of the *Landsberger Lager Cajtung*, "that he survived by pure chance and that this had nothing to do with either wisdom or heroism. Although the Jews who took to arms should be commended, these were few and far between and their role should not be overstated."[18] "Ordinary" survivors described their suffering in a martyrological manner, which also found expression in the work of the Jewish historical commissions that grew in postwar Europe. Some of that martyrological approach found common ground among the survivor-historians who created the YV's Research Department.

Israel's struggle with how to approach the Holocaust survivors as well as the question of how and what to remember from the recent catastrophe were manifest throughout the years of founding and expanding the project of Israeli Holocaust research.

Silence in Historiography

Probably the most striking feature of the first years of Israeli historiography is its reticence with respect to the recent annihilation. Orna Kenan reports that this "silence of postwar historiography" in Israel existed in strong contrast to the activities of professional and amateur historians alike in the historical commissions set up immediately upon liberation in Communist Poland and in the DP camps in the West.[19] Kenan argues that this sudden cessation of a formerly prolific documentary historical activity can be traced back to the endemic, ideological disputes between native Israeli historians and survivor-historians. Whereas the survivors wanted to remember their defunct families and communities, whether they had actively joined the armed resistance or not, the Israeli Zionist ethos was built on the notion of a strong self-reliance and a military spirit that were not natural to the experience of Jews in the Diaspora. Those survivors who eagerly collected documents and delivered testimonies in the DP camps or for the various European historical commissions do not appear to have radically contrasted armed resistance and "Amidah" resistance through "standing up," the very perseverance in continuing to live against the will of an annihilator.[20] The Jews from eastern Europe persisted in their attachment to the notion of Kiddush ha-Shem (Sanctification of God's Name), a martyrdom that ennobled each Jew's death, even death that occurred in the most humiliating or depraved circumstances.[21] Indeed, as the memoirs and testimonies written mostly in the DP camps suggest, the survivors did not necessarily see a contrast between *churbn* (Hebrew for "destruction") and heroism, but in Israel this contradistinction was to become dominant in the commemoration of the Holocaust during the first two decades of Israel's existence. The survivors instead strove to document their perseverance in the face of unprecedented suffering and the tenacity of their will to live and to carry on.[22]

Because the Israeli public memory of the recent destruction tended to elevate only those who had been heroes of the uprisings or the partisans or those who had managed to mount a physical rebellion, the survivors retreated, by default, into a silence pregnant with memories of experiences at odds with the common, dominant evaluation of the past.

Another compelling explanation for the reluctance on the part of both the survivor-historians and the Israeli historians to delve into historical research concerns a difference in determining the "lessons for the future," in the words of the famous historian Ben-Zion Dinur, minister of education and culture and first president of YV.[23] Whereas the Zionist interpretation of the Holocaust as the inevitable result of life in the Diaspora became an official point of view supported by Dinur and his circle of scholars at the Hebrew University and accepted by the ruling Mapai Party, the survivors tended to draw more universalist "lessons" from the recent catastrophe, lessons having to do more with the human condition, nature, and political (totalitarian) and economic systems rather than focusing uniquely on the situation of the Exile.[24]

Finally, one reason that deterred survivors from engaging in a study of the Holocaust was common not only to Israel but also to other locations in which Holocaust survivors settled: the local inhabitants' general indifference or even hostility to those who had come from "there." In Israel, that hostility seemed like a variation of the antisemitic reactions that awaited survivors in parts of Europe, especially Poland: it was a condescending gaze upon "weak" human beings who "went like lambs to the slaughter." The ethos of the sabra—a muscular, self-reliant, and (agriculturally and militarily) capable settler—was clearly at odds with what was perceived as the passivity of the Diaspora Jews in the face of persecution and murder. That societal disdain corresponded in academic circles to the conflict between Israeli historians of the German intellectual tradition (even if they came geographically from eastern Europe, as did Dinur himself) and those historians from eastern Europe who had experienced the catastrophe. Current scholars see in the conflict that ultimately broke out between the two groups of historians a remnant of a Western, German Jewish ("West-Juden") contempt toward Jewish brethren from historic Poland and Russia ("Ost-Juden") that dated at least to the time of the emancipation of German Jewry in the nineteenth century.[25]

For all of these reasons, the eastern European historians who conducted their documentary activity in Poland or in the DP camps and later found themselves at YV were directly influenced by the state-supported Zionist politics of memory so that their academic output on the Holocaust was rather meager.

Historians in the Yishuv, however, displayed a lack of interest in the recent catastrophe for different reasons. Dalia Ofer has suggested that "intellectuals and historians also insisted that the Holocaust should not be overemphasized. They did not doubt its significance nor [sic] minimize the tragic outcome for the continued existence of the Jewish people. However, most assumed that it was too early to research the period of the Holocaust from an academic viewpoint—the correct perspective was missing and the emotional involvement too strong."[26]

Another explanation has to do with ideological leanings. A Zionism that discouraged studying antisemitism, either in itself or as a leading cause of the catastrophe and as a phenomenon presumably inherent in the Diaspora and irrelevant outside of it, subjugated and interjected the Holocaust as a topic into the Zionist outline. The German educational background of many of these scholars might have been still another unifying reason for their avoidance of the Holocaust as a unique subject: they might have "found it difficult to turn their backs completely on the German part of their intellectual heritage."[27]

Apart from these reasons, Israeli scholars generally abstained from engaging in Holocaust research because they might have seen it as being dominated by East European Jews, whose methodology followed what Kenan calls "the Dubnowian–Anskian tradition of the mass accumulation of primary sources, with the assumption that the gathered documents, once arranged according to a chronology of events, would 'speak for themselves.'"[28] This tradition, as analyzed earlier, is what Philip Friedman called *khurbn forshung*, or research on catastrophe.

Yad Vashem and the Survivor-Historians

Yad Vashem[29] was first created as an initiative by Mordechai Shenhabi, a young Zionist from Volochisk, a town in the czarist empire near the border with Habsburg Galicia, and a member of Ha-Shomer Ha-Tzair (Young Guard). His passion for Eretz Israel was so consuming that he was the first of the movement to arrive there in 1919. During a board meeting of the Keren Kayemeth LeIsrael (Jewish National Fund) that took place after the first reports of the extermination had reached the Yishuv in 1942, Shenhabi proposed the establishment of a memorial to murdered European Jewry.[30] Its commemorative purpose was predominant; the initiative did not yet include strictly academic goals. Nevertheless, Shenhabi was also responsible for arranging in July 1947 the first international conference of Jewish historical commissions in Jerusalem under the auspices of the Jewish Studies Institute of Hebrew University. At this conference, the International Conference on Holocaust and Martyrdom in Our Time, YV defined its twin goals: (1) to create a world center for the gathering of all historical material about the recent Jewish catastrophe and the instances of heroism connected with it and (2) to build a monument to the 6 million Jewish victims, to the heroes who resisted, and to those who risked their lives in attempts to save the Jews.[31]

After a few years of nonactivity (owing in part to the War of Independence, November 1947–July 1949), YV was officially reestablished on August 19, 1953, as a result of the new Holocaust and Heroism Memorial Law—Yad Vashem. The law obligated the new national institution to fulfill the two functions defined during the conference of 1947: to commemorate the martyrs and heroes of the Holocaust and at the same time "to gather, investigate, and publish all evidence about the Holocaust and heroism."[32]

The first president of YV, Ben-Zion Dinur, saw the Holocaust as both the expression of a long-term antisemitic hatred and a redeeming moment that contributed to bringing forth the new Jewish state. He saw YV's role as commemorating the noble memory of the fighters who, through the link to the War of Independence, symbolized the self-asserting power of the reborn state.[33] He was also convinced of Israel's unique role in commemorating the recent catastrophe and perceived other attempts to create memorial centers (for example, the Center for Contemporary Jewish Documentation in Paris, founded by Yitzhak Shneurson) as competitive efforts not deserving of full legitimacy.[34] YV's mission, for him, lay primarily in the area of Holocaust research, which he believed ought to begin with a systematic study of antisemitism.

Dinur's presidency of YV was not without tension with other groups of various interests. His Zionist vision for the new institution was manifest not only in his conviction that Israel is the "mother country" that ought to commemorate and conduct research on the Holocaust, which led to the end of the Diaspora, but also in his uniquely secular approach within Zionism that influenced him to see religious commemoration as a "threat." To a proposal by the Orthodox Zionist Party in 1958 to combine the annual religious celebration on Mount Zion (the traditional burial place of King David and a symbol of redemption), which had begun in 1948, with YV's commemorative activities, Dinur retorted: "The commemoration on Mount Zion borders on idol worship. Everything that is done there is a disgrace which is backed by the Ministry of Religion."[35] Likewise, the YV Executive Board attempted systematically to limit the independence of other commemorative or documentary institutions (in particular the Ghetto Fighters' House) throughout the 1950s, apparently out of a fear of losing authority and exclusivity in interpreting the role of the recent catastrophe in the creation of Israel.[36]

The strongest opposition, however, leading to the conflict that eventually caused Dinur's dramatic resignation from the directorate of YV, came from the survivor-historians (YV was contractually obligated to employ Holocaust survivors), whose background and research strayed often from those of the Israeli-born Zionist historians and from the latter's vision for the institution. Among the important research staff of YV were some of the survivor-historians who continued to stream in from Poland as they became disillusioned about the possibility of free academic activity in the ŻIH in Warsaw.[37] Nachman Blumental and Josef Kermisz, for example, first moved to the Ghetto Fighters' House on leaving Poland in 1949. Their colleague Rachel Auerbach arrived in Israel in 1950, settling in Tel Aviv. After the establishment of YV, Auerbach was appointed director of the Department for the Collection of Testimonies in March 1954. Kermisz and Blumental left the Ghetto Fighters' House and joined Auerbach and Nathan Eck, who during the war had been active in the Polish Underground and principal of the Underground "Tarbut" Hebrew school in the Warsaw Ghetto.[38]

Auerbach had a particular notion of the role of survivors' testimonies; her appointment to YV, therefore, was fortuitous. By 1950, she had already predicted the danger of distortion stemming from relying on the victors' (i.e., German) sources, a distortion that lay in telling "the story of the murderers, but not the murdered."[39] Auerbach held that studying Jewish sources, in contrast, "gives us a picture of reality, which it is possible to use to fill in the already built framework based on official sources."[40]

In her attachment to oral history—or "living testimony," as it was called then—Auerbach was following the methodology of the Oneg Shabbat project, which, according to Ofer, "reflected the desire to provide the fullest possible Jewish account of the events."[41] About comparing testimonies to official documents, Auerbach wrote:

> A Jewish scholar may not be dismissive of the memoir material that constitutes the bulk of documents of Jewish origin. Indeed, it is the surveys of Jewish imagery that gives [sic] us a picture of the situation with which it is possible to fill in the outline based on official documents. As for witting and unwitting errors and distortions, no historical material is ever without them. This is in fact the role of the historian, to compare different versions and different materials and to extract from all those truths and fragments—from all the embellishment and suppression—the nucleus of historical truth.[42]

In Auerbach's view, YV was to provide that Jewish voice of the truth about the Holocaust.

Auerbach believed that the survivors' testimony had a cathartic function, which, although bringing back the pain, could also heal, in contrast to "the stifling of sorrow[,] [which can] cause much damage."[43] For almost a year, Auerbach was the only employee of YV collecting testimonies, and she believed that in order to elicit the survivors' stories in a compassionate way, only other survivors should be involved in recording their testimonies. In fact, it was at significant personal cost that the interviewers helped the survivors to open up to them. Based on her own experience, Auerbach described the labor of "love and suffering" that such work supposed: "For them I suffered all the time and received with love the suffering and the pain bound up in them; for them, I neglected my literary work because I saw in this a mission and an obligation and a justification of the fact that I remained alive."[44]

Finally, Auerbach saw the collection of testimonies as a preparatory stage for the entrance of the Jews in history as its witnesses. This role in collecting testimonies was to "give voice to our sorrow and our fury also at the hour when we will no longer be in the world."[45] This position and her commitment prepared the ground for the inclusion of survivor testimonies in the trial of Adolf Eichmann in 1961. While managing the YV Department for the Collection of Testimonies, Auerbach claimed that her previous work in CŻKH in Poland was not flawless because of the insertion of personal additions, abbreviations, interpretations, and formulations that unwittingly distorted and interrupted the free flow of survivors' speech. For this reason, she suggested to the administration the use of tape recorders, but this suggestion was not met with a positive response.[46]

By 1965, the Department for the Collection of Testimonies under Auerbach's direction had collected about 3,000 testimonies in fifteen languages.[47] As a rift eventually developed between Auerbach and other survivor-historians, however, her work in YV became increasingly a source of personal pain for her.

Among the survivor-historians who left a mark on YV and on Holocaust research in general, Philip Friedman was preeminent. After founding the CŻKH in Lublin, Friedman had worked in Łódź and later in the

American Zone in Germany. He came to Israel for a short period but in 1948 moved to the United States, where Salo Baron, his former colleague and friend, helped him to acquire a research fellowship at Columbia University. Friedman remained in touch with the scholars in Israel and published there, so his collaboration with YV cannot be overlooked or overestimated. Similar to the crucial influence that he had on the scholarly direction of the CŻKH in Poland, Friedman also significantly had an impact on YV's methodology of collecting testimonies and in general on delineating the parameters of the new field.[48]

On the one hand, Friedman recommended great caution when using personal testimonies; he was well aware of the danger of the martyrological approach that tended to permeate them, and he sharply criticized some of the survivors' accounts and research:

> The spirit of martyrology emanating from our literature on the Holocaust prevents a clear-cut view from a historical perspective. True, the sympathizing heart beats in harmony with those of the scholars and authors who could not suppress their emotions roused by the impact of the tragedy. We are dealing here with an outbreak of emotionalism that has had no precedent in our literature. As a result of this phenomenon the material at the disposal of the scholars consisted mainly of one kind, namely of descriptions of the suffering inflicted and the atrocities committed by the Nazis. Thus we were reverting again to the historiographical system of the *Leidensgeschichte* (martyrology), which had become obsolete a long time ago.[49]

On the other hand, Friedman also warned against the "romantic" approach that was apparently present in the publications of the Ghetto Fighters' House, which emphasized resistance. He felt that neither of these approaches stood up to scholarly scrutiny and tended to appropriate a "Nazi-centric" perspective, according to which the Jewish people simply reacted to the actions of the outside world. Friedman proposed instead a "Judeo-centric" perspective in which "the central role is to be played by the Jewish people, not only as tragic victims but as bearers of a communal existence with all the manifold and numerous aspects involved."[50] Owing to the dispersion of the Jewish people as well as to the international nature of antisemitism, such a perspective should also bear universal elements that should be studied not merely as "[the Jewish] nation's internal life" but as a contribution to the understanding of the history of humankind.

The main methodological differences between East European and Israeli historians in approaching the Holocaust lay in their relationship to the original sources and in their understanding of the meaning of the subject itself. Whereas the survivor-historians, aware of the uniqueness of the annihilation that the Jewish people had experienced, saw the collection and documentation of all available material relevant to the recent catastrophe as the primary goal of their work, with analysis to follow once a critical mass of material had been collected, the historians from Israel advocated a critical analysis of facts, although one based on "Zionist goals and aspirations."[51]

Four survivor-historians in particular launched a battle with the YV administration centralized around the figure of Dinur. By taking this fight public in major daily newspapers, they reached beyond academic circles to the wider Israeli population. This battle, which also concerned German material reparations to Israel, started a process of change in the Israeli public's perception of the survivors. The four survivor-historians in question were Auerbach, Blumental (director of the YV Library), Kermisz (director of the YV Archive), and Eck (YV publicity officer).[52]

These researchers felt undermined in their work and unappreciated for having gone through the Holocaust. They believed that their personal experiences were the best qualification for researching the recent catastrophe, as evidenced by their work in the historical commissions in Europe. Their vision for YV was that it should lean more toward commemoration, and they particularly objected to the direction in which Dinur was taking it. His steering of YV toward cooperation with Israeli and Zionist historians was expressed, for example, in the appointment of his disciple, Israel Halpern of the Hebrew University, as the scientific adviser to YV. Dinur also created, in conjunction with the Hebrew University, an academic institute designed to attract young Israeli scholars of the modern period (this institute was eventually named the Hebrew University and YV Institute for the Study of the European Jewish Catastrophe).[53]

The seeds of the conflict between the survivor-historians and Israeli researchers were apparently visible early on. Dinur and his students from the Hebrew University interpreted the Holocaust as only one among many past examples of antisemitism. Dinur's plan for research on the catastrophe, for instance, included "the war against antisemitism," "persecution of the Jews," "the Jewish question," and "hatred of Israel" and could therefore extend to research on the whole period of the Diaspora.[54] The personal circumstances of the survivor-historians, who typically had lost their families during the Holocaust and stood in contrast to the relatively stable Israeli historians, were an added thorn aggravating the survivor-historians.

In 1957, when Yosef Melkman, a survivor from the Netherlands, became YV's director-general, the situation reached a crisis. Melkman, although a survivor, did not find a common language with the survivor-historians from Poland. The four survivor-historians—Auerbach, Blumental, Kermisz, and Eck—published their complaints in the daily papers *Davar* and *Ma'ariv*, claiming that they had been invited to work at YV but were not given a proper opportunity to develop their plans. Following the publications, Eck, Blumental, and Kermisz were temporarily dismissed from YV; Auerbach had already been suspended.[55] When the YV Executive Board gathered to discuss the matter, its members, although surprised and angered by what they considered to be "defamation," felt that because of these dismissed historians' public prestige, it would be best to accept their presence in YV. At the same time, the board expressed multiple grievances against them: inefficiency, unfulfilled promises of writing books, personal sensitivities, and—in Melkman's words about Auerbach's running of the Department for the Collection of Testimonies—"faulty organization" as well as "the phenomenon that frightened me in particular . . . the low output from our department in Tel Aviv."[56] Like this comment, the strongest criticism was directed against Auerbach. Her methods of collecting testimonies were described as erroneous because "she influences the witnesses' accounts: she incites them to talk by bringing up memories and she spends too much time with each witness; in a year and a half she managed to interview only some fifty survivors."[57]

Auerbach defended herself in an open letter to *Davar*, entitled "What the Struggle within Yad Vashem Is All About." In this letter, she presented a vision of a YV that would represent the needs of survivors, "with the people and for the people, not an aloof scientific institute . . . and certainly, not a bureaucratic fortress void of content."[58] The essence of her and other survivor-historians' opposition to Dinur lay in their approach to the survivors' testimonies: "On this, first and foremost on this—hangs the struggle in YV," she emphasized. "On the appropriate treatment of the authors of testimony who are no longer [living] and on the words of the witnesses who are still alive. On the knowledge and the understanding [of them] and on the decision of what to do with them."[59]

Auerbach then accused the Executive Board of deliberately placing hurdles in the way of the survivor-historians: "Researchers like us, who are not part of the 'in-circle,' receive no kind of support, monetary or otherwise. . . . In fact, every effort has been made to dismiss us, one by one, so as to ensure the veterans' total control over the course and management of Yad Vashem."[60]

A dramatic solution to the conflict between the survivor-historians and the Israelis in YV came from the State Comptroller's investigation in 1958, which in its first report pointed to administrative transgressions. That initial report spurred the YV World Council to look into the matter and to make its own recommendations. A special committee of the council soon urged the board to increase YV's commemorative and public activities, as declared in the Holocaust and Heroism Memorial Law. It also recommended that five additional survivors join the board as observers.[61]

Following growing public pressure, the Executive Board announced a compromise. The four employees would be reinstated under certain conditions; all except Auerbach accepted the conditions. She was to be left in charge of only the Polish testimonies, while another supervisor was to manage the testimonies from all other countries.[62] Later in the same year, however, following another evaluation of her work by the directorate, Auerbach was fully reinstated to the management of the Department for the Collection of Testimonies.[63]

During this conflict, both Dinur and Melkman attempted to present the survivor-historians in general and Auerbach in particular as incompetent and emotionally involved; these ad hominem tactics, however, did not go over well: "They [Dinur and Melkman] were amazed that public opinion clearly supported the survivors and by the intensity of this support in the press."[64]

Through the compromise that was reached and following Dinur's resignation as YV's president, the survivors could be seen as gaining public recognition of their unique claim to remember and commemorate the Holocaust.

The Silence of the Survivors

During this time, although the attitudes toward the survivors were slowly changing, the survivors still felt themselves pushed to the margins and often ignored while the country was slowly building its structures and institutions. From a sociological perspective, during the 1950s the Israeli population perpetuated the vision of the survivors expressed in official commemorative practice: it treated the "ordinary" survivors with relative contempt and attached the memory of the Holocaust to the tiny minority of ghetto rebels and partisans, whose heroism provided a link between their past and Israel's present. The survivors, like Holocaust survivors everywhere, felt that they could not share what they had experienced. As one of them put it, "To tell we must until our wit's end, but no one wanted to listen. Only stories on doll-houses were listened to; to all the rest of the horrors, who can listen? They lowered their eyes, as if they were told something too private, too personal, not to be mentioned in public. We learned quickly: Be an Israeli outside and a survivor at home, and even not at home—why burden those dear to you—but only in your heart."[65]

In fact, although the survivors of the Holocaust at some point constituted nearly half of the population of Israel, their lives seemed hidden and unknown to the other half. Their often desperate needs, including immediate and comprehensive medical care, were not obvious to the people around them. To address these needs, the resources of the Yishuv and later the new state were not sufficient. For example, according to a report by Harry Vitalis of JOINT in 1949, the Joint Distribution Committee, of the 120,000 Holocaust survivors who

> had already been examined in the DP camps in Europe, approximately 12,000 needed immediate medical care, including 1,500 with tuberculosis, 400 who were mentally ill, 2,500 who were blind, 3,000 elderly who were in need of long-term care, and 3,000 unemployable elderly in need of welfare. There were 3,000 people who were disabled and required medical support as well as full or partial long-term care, 600 had other chronic illnesses, and 500 children had mental illnesses, disabilities, or other functional deficiencies.[66]

The survivors, as a group of immigrants with a distinctive past, were being marginalized and not properly taken care of by any government agency.[67] Although individual administrative organs attempted to come up with plans for integration, the overwhelming results of the vast immigration of survivors to the Land of Israel were the isolation and clamming up of their community. Multiple state organs and social organizations, including the Israeli Defense Forces and the kibbutz movement, tried to "utilize" the additional manpower represented by the survivors, which was badly needed, but each failed, to some degree, for not understanding the survivors' special needs. Although the Defense Forces, for example, provided a release from combat for sole surviving *sons* of families, it did not generally acknowledge the unique situation of men who were *the sole survivors of entire families*. And in the kibbutzim, which were ordinarily very successful in providing newcomers with socially connected and family-like living, very few survivors were ultimately accepted, and those who stayed (if not immediately recruited to military service) were not always provided with sufficient resources to become contributing members of the settlements.

Language appears to have been the greatest problem for the incoming survivors. The Yishuv did not appreciate the survivors who spoke in a mixture of Yiddish and one or another eastern European language—for instance, Polish—but nor were they eager to provide them with proper opportunities to learn Hebrew quickly and to mingle with the "indigenous" Jews. The kibbutz movement, for example, strove, albeit unsuccessfully, to ensure at least *one day per week* of Hebrew lessons in most of the kibbutzim. The military was even less patient with the survivors; it did formulate a plan to educate them, but the plan was too little, too late.[68]

The silencing and marginalization of the survivors began to be abated over the course of Israel's turbulent history—first during the negotiations over the reparations from Germany and then during the trial of Dr. Rudolph Kasztner.

Changes in Attitudes toward the Survivors

Blood Money and Selling One's Soul to the Devil

It was David Ben-Gurion who initiated the signing of the Reparations Treaty with Germany, according to which the German state would pay monetary compensation to the survivors for their suffering and lost property. Before even starting the negotiations, however, in December 1951 a debate erupted over "blood money," which would polarize the political arena in Israel.[69] Ben-Gurion and the ruling Mapai Party proposed these negotiations with Germany primarily on account of the Israeli state's critical economic needs. Nevertheless, some members of the opposition found that objecting to the negotiations by appealing to the memory of the Holocaust provided them an advantageous political position. Menachem Begin's right-wing Herut Party, for example, hoped to gain some lost public support when Begin compared the government's acceptance of the agreement with Germany to a new "holocaust" and Mapai to the Nazis.[70] The left-wing Mapam Party also refused to negotiate with West Germany, in this case because of its adherence to the Soviet line of "absolving" only East Germany from its responsibility for Nazi-era crimes. The language of Holocaust memory was used explicitly for political gain rather than to work toward compensating the survivors for their sufferings. In the end, the great majority of the survivors accepted their share of the compensation, signing on to the agreement in September 1952.[71]

During the Kasztner trial, the Israeli public was faced with the issue of resistance and "collaboration" in the institution of the Judenräte. The trial started when in 1952 Malkiel Gruenwald was charged with libel when he accused Dr. Rudolph Kasztner, a Zionist leader from Hungary, of collaboration with the Nazis' extermination of the Jews. Although Kasztner admitted that he had negotiated a "trucks-for-Jews" deal with Adolf Eichmann, he claimed to have done it to save thousands of his coreligionists. Gruenwald was acquitted, and Judge Benyamin Halevy reversed the focus of the trial, accusing Kasztner, who was by this time an activist in Mapai, of "selling his soul to the devil."[72] Again, in the ensuing public debate the memory of the Holocaust was misused for political advantage: Mapai leaders were accused of knowing about the exterminations during the war but suppressing that knowledge and thus of bearing direct responsibility for the killing of Hungarian Jews. As in Kasztner's case, the accusations implied, had these leaders informed the public about the extermination in Europe, the Yishuv might have become more involved in rescue efforts.[73] In this political squabble, however, even some survivors, especially those who testified on behalf of Kasztner, were labeled "collaborators."[74] In fact, for some, the collaboration of the Judenräte with the Nazis came to embody the dynamics of the Diaspora's self-government, which, as Shmuel Tamir, Gruenwald's defense attorney, asserted, "in periods of trouble tended to resort to bribery and solicitation."[75]

The verdict of the trial, which condemned Kasztner's cooperation with the Nazis, as well as the public debate surrounding the verdict reinforced the division of the survivors into heroic rebels and passive sheep, a division that reflected characterizations of the self-serving actions of the Judenräte. It should not come as any surprise that at this point the Holocaust survivors' silence became even more pronounced and deliberate. The survivors sought the company of other survivors, preferably those from their own former geographic areas (*Landsmanschaftn*), and chose private (i.e., nonpublic) communal commemorations of the Holocaust. In time, these communal commemorations encouraged transcribing a communal memory into what became the *yizkor bikher*, the memorial books of the destroyed communities.[76] The survivors' remembrance of the Shoah was nonpublic and local in contrast to the public commemorations of the Jewish fighters and partisans, which involved the presence of political figures and the press. The latter memorial celebrations tended to be "Israeli" and "Zionist."[77]

The Eichmann Trial

The third historical moment that transformed the Israeli public's perception of the survivors was the Eichmann trial, which *relied on* victims' testimonies in its proceedings. The trial itself, which took place from April to August 1961, exposed the Israeli public to individual voices of suffering and to moral choices that could no longer be categorized as "weak" in opposition to the fighters' heroic ethos. In the words of Haim Gouri, a poet and journalist covering the proceedings, "It was the trial, with all its dark implications, that unveiled the duality of our existence—the Jews as a murdered people and the story of Israel as a nation sitting in judgment."[78]

In contrast to some historians' opinions about the meaning of the trial for the development of research on the Holocaust, it was not necessarily the issue of *silence* concerning the catastrophe that broke through during the Eichmann trial.[79] It was rather the individuation of victims' experiences that now reached the public, ultimately introducing a new way of understanding and approaching the annihilation of the Jews, a way that Annette Wieviorka has famously termed "the era of the witness."[80]

Hanna Yablonka, in her groundbreaking study *The State of Israel vs. Adolf Eichmann*, convincingly establishes that the Eichmann trial was not a turning point but rather the culmination of a long process, "its high point." In summary, she writes:

> Sixteen years after the end of the Holocaust, the story of the great destruction was related in depth for the first time, and information was turned into knowledge. The survivors were no longer nameless immigrants with a telltale mark on their arms, but people with a personal identity, a unique history, and a tale to tell, to which the nation suddenly had a fierce desire to listen and to embrace. The survivors became the representatives of the lost world of European Jewry, which

was transformed at once from "Diaspora" to "heritage." Israel no longer stood apart from this heritage, but was a part of it, was its continuation. At the same time, attitudes of alienation and shame toward the Holocaust faded away, and the self-critical voices of native-born Israelis grew louder, with regard both to the fact that rescue efforts had been so feeble and to the efforts made by their society to integrate the survivors.[81]

This personalizing aspect of the legal battle between Israel and Eichmann, not the verdict itself, brought to the Israeli public a touch of the real suffering of the people "from there," whom the public had up to that point treated generally, as though they formed an anonymous, passive mass. The trial's emotional toll on the victims was also noted: several victims collapsed while relating their horrifying experiences, and the most dramatic moment came during the short testimony of Yehiel De-Nur,[82] which ended in his fainting while in the witness podium.

As director of the Department for the Collection of Testimonies, Auerbach was in direct contact with Bureau 06 of the Israeli police, which was responsible for the investigation and preparation of the evidence for the Eichmann trial. She confessed later that the authorities were initially interested only in documents that could establish direct proof of guilt. She, however, wanted to bring witnesses "who were in the middle of the horrors and scope of the extermination and who survived nonetheless to tell the story."[83] Her successful cooperation with Gideon Hausner, the attorney general and the chief prosecutor of the case, resulted in her preparing the first witness list, presenting summaries and suggestions for the investigators, as well as preparing background information on many subjects.

The trial seemed to have a "cathartic" effect on the Israeli consciousness of the Holocaust. The novelist Moshe Shamir, for example, confessed that "the force of the testimonies of death at the trial, against the background of our *dolce vita*[,] have [*sic*] caused me, more than anything else, to face the catastrophe for the first time as a personal problem of my own."[84]

The crack that was now forming in the general impression that native Israelis had of the Jews in the Diaspora during the Holocaust, the doubt about the validity of the "heroes versus passive victims" distinction, affected the survivors themselves.[85] Placing their unique, personal experiences at the center of the trial allowed the groups of survivors to begin to reach out to a wider, public audience with publications and commemorative activity in an attempt to challenge the myth of generalized passivity in the Diaspora.[86]

Psychologically, the survivors' "coming out" had a dual effect. On the one hand, the breaching of the distance (or, even, the dissonance) between the survivors' private lives and their public personae, achieved in the outpouring of the testimonies "from there," resulted in an unusually high rate of suicides among the Jewish survivors from Europe—two and a half times as high as that among the Israelis from Africa during 1962 and 1966.[87] On the other hand, the emotional crises that psychiatrists observed among Holocaust survivors were explained as a surfacing of repressed memories, a necessary step to mental recovery. Indeed, medical data seemed to confirm this assessment; as Yablonka reports, "although the trial did have a severe impact on many of the survivors, it was for a short period of time, and the effect was manifested mostly in a reawakening of dormant memories and nightmares."[88]

One of the after-effects of the Eichmann trial was the revisiting of the issue of the role and collaboration of the Judenräte, which came to prominence in the public consciousness through the publication of three famous books that would become controversial in Israel: Bruno Bettelheim's *The Informed Heart* (1960), Raul Hilberg's *The Destruction of the European Jews* (1961), and Hannah Arendt's *Eichmann in Jerusalem* (1963).[89] The underlying attitude toward the Judenräte in these works was highly critical; it accused them of collaboration in the destruction of the Diaspora. Interestingly and somewhat ironically, had these books been written a decade earlier, they might, as Kenan has suggested, have found a positive response in Israel.[90] Now, however, the public came to sympathize more with the victims and to understand their plight in different terms: the question of the extent of knowledge of the Nazis' final goals came to be debated, and the survivors' diaries and memoirs gained greater popularity.[91] Several works appeared that openly challenged both the condemnation of the councils as well as the general assumption of the population's passivity in the face of Nazi aggression. One of these works was a pamphlet titled *As*

Sheep to the Slaughter? (1962), written by the schoolteacher Keshev Shabtai. This work sought to contextualize the occurrence of rebellion under the Nazi yoke in light of the degree of terror and the air of invincibility projected by the German military. Shabtai concluded that no rebellion takes place against a despot who uses terror and that rebellion will not appear until at least some military losses begin to be experienced by that despot.[92]

Another question put in a new light concerned the individuals who served on the councils. As a result of the Eichmann trial, there appeared a tendency to research these individuals' biographies, to see them not only as people who acted as extensions of Nazi control but also as personalities who weighed the obligations of their positions against the meaning of their actions for the Jewish community as a whole, and to discern in them patterns of behavior that were more differentiated.[93]

In historiography, voices critical of the "negation of Exile" were raised, and a more nuanced approach to the Diaspora was suggested. The question of the study of antisemitism, for example, which up to then had been seen as inherently associated with the Exile, was revisited on its own terms; this revisitation did not occur, however, until after 1967.[94] Even though some Israeli scholars still abstained from approaching the Holocaust directly, they henceforth focused on the study of antisemitism, albeit prior to the rise of Nazism.[95]

Saul Friedländer has written that a "protective shield" and a kind of "numbness" are necessary, to a degree, in any scholarly confrontation of the Holocaust. They are "defenses" that one erects to protect oneself from a subject that may bring one to despair.[96] In the Israeli context, such a "protective shield" and "numbness" overlapped with the Zionist tendency to brush off the whole uniqueness of the recent Jewish catastrophe and to approach it merely in terms of the continuation of what has been termed "the longest hatred"—that is, antisemitism.

The Six-Day War

It was finally in the wake of the Six-Day War of 1967, twenty-two years after the liberation of the camps, that the Holocaust became a vivid topic in Israel, if not a vital one as well. The fear of defeat and the threat of "a second

Holocaust" brought to young Israelis an awareness of the link between the survivors' past and their own volatile situation. As Ofer reports,

> During the waiting period [i.e., the two weeks before the outbreak of hostilities] Arab rhetoric consisted of extreme propagandist terminology, including threats of "destroying" Israel, "wiping" it from the face of the earth, and "pushing" it into the sea; Israel had already "existed for too long," etc. These slogans were regularly voiced in mass rallies in Arab capitals, followed by long and inflammatory speeches. Regardless of [the] true intentions of Nasser and other Arab rulers, this constant incitement was taken at face value by many Israelis.[97]

All levels of Israeli society—as revealed in letters to the press, for example—appeared to have grasped the falsity of the proverbial assumption that "barking dogs don't bite." This time around, the Jews would know better what assurances to believe. Journalists, partisans' organizations, and survivors' organizations contacted governments and war veterans' associations in Europe and the United States to ask them to act on behalf of Israel.[98]

Soldiers engaged in the conflict referred to the eerie way they were suddenly being confronted with the memory of the Holocaust survivors, which must have subconsciously permeated their collective memory—a memory formed, as it was, through commemorative ceremonies, visits to YV, and personal encounters with survivors. "We tend to forget those days before the war," one soldier described this experience, "and perhaps rightly so—yet those were the days in which we came closest to that Jewish fate from which we have run like haunted beings all these years. Suddenly, everyone was talking about Munich, about the Holocaust, about the Jewish people left to its own fate."[99]

Expressions of such a "collective flashback" is found in two frequently made Holocaust comparisons in the press: of Egypt's ruler, President Gamal Abdul Nasser, to Hitler and of Czechoslovakia before the Munich agreement of September 1938 to Israel. This time Israeli society succeeded in making a creative and constructive conclusion from the latter analogy: "While the first comparison was adopted by many," as Ofer suggests, "and was elaborated through textual comparisons of the rhetoric of Hitler and Nasser, with regard to the latter, the differences between Israel and Czechoslovakia were stressed. Unlike the Czechs, the Israelis, who had learned the lesson of the Holocaust, were ready to fight for their independence; Jews had already experienced abandonment during the Holocaust and had learned that they could rely only on themselves."[100]

A collective experience of victimization, combined with the euphoria of victory when Israel eventually prevailed in the war, finally seemed to mold the identity of the "Israelis" together with that of the "survivors": "We believed we would be exterminated if we lost the war," another soldier confessed. "We got this idea—or inherited it—from the concentration camps. It's a concrete possibility for anyone who had grown up in Israel, even if he personally didn't experience Hitler's persecution. Genocide—it's a real possibility. . . . That's the lesson of the gas chambers."[101]

The short but powerful threat of annihilation that Israel encountered in 1967 forever shifted the perception of otherness in relation to the people from "there" and allowed the Israelis to forge a more united narrative of the nation, which now did not have to reject the 2,000 years of the Diaspora. The onset of this new identity and the consequent new relationship to the Holocaust survivors, admittedly not without some problematic and contesting voices, crowned the painful yet successful evolution of the tensions present in the difficult merging of the tradition of the Yishuv and the shattered experience of the Diaspora.

5

Memories of the First Encounters as Represented in the Yad Vashem Collection

> We both remained thus like small pieces of a broken ship, neither here nor there.
> —Rivka Nagler-Kramer (AYV O3/3128)

The Yad Vashem archives include the amplest collection of Holocaust testimonies in the world. The earliest accounts, dating from the 1950s and 1960s, were the first deposited by the new survivor-residents of Israel. Although YV collections have been extensively investigated within the general area of Holocaust studies, attention to them as a source for the postwar period has so far focused largely on research into the fate of Jewish children.

A certain continuity between the Polish and Israeli collections stems from the fact that several ŻIH historians eventually immigrated to Israel, where they played a crucial role in developing the YV Department for the Collection of Testimonies, as highlighted in the previous chapter. Rachel Auerbach, one of the three survivors of the Oneg Shabbat group, played a particularly energetic role, passionately devoting her life to recording survivors' voices. The premise from which the YV research staff worked—consisting in a primary focus on the collection of survivors' testimonies—was founded in the realization that the recent catastrophe was absolutely unique and thus ought to be recorded in a new and complex way. These historians also felt that the world's judgment (as represented, for example, by the Nuremberg trials) might diminish the understanding of the extent of Jewish suffering during the Second World War and that such a misrepresentation would need to be addressed by the survivors.[1]

From a theoretical standpoint, the YV accounts, written ten to twenty-five years after the events of the Holocaust by people who had already "arrived" at their ultimate destination, could be expected to display a relative sense of stability. Despite the wars that attended its political inception and survival, the Land of Israel might have been understood as a place of destiny, the fulfillment of an ancient Jewish hope for the recovery of the state, even when the objective conditions might have counseled further emigration. Living in the Jewish homeland should have contributed, on the surface, to a sense of security founded on the ability of self-defense, a strong contrast to the helplessness experienced by victims of both the Second World War and postwar violence. Indeed, many accounts give expression to the simple relief of finally living in one's own "home."

Nevertheless, this political fulfillment of the ancient dream did not bring even a relative sense of security from which the survivors could look back at their past. The revived Jewish state's constant need to assert not only its borders but even its right to exist cost the Israeli population not a small share of anxiety and trepidation. During the difficult first ten years, when the population of the new state almost tripled as a result of the arrival of refugees from Europe and the Arab lands, the economic infrastructure of the new entity had to be built within and against the chaos inflicted upon it by the surrounding Muslim states. Many refugees from Europe decided to move even farther away. Right from the outset, some, especially immigrants from eastern Europe and China, often considered Israel no more than a stopover.[2]

In spite of the difficulties, many stood their ground there, though, choosing to build their homeland with their own hands. It is their voices that I analyze in this chapter.

In General

Whereas the ŻIH accounts express surprise, a sense of the unexpected, and even shock, the memories recorded at YV seem to be more solidified, certain, definite, and categorical. Somewhat analogous to what Dalia

Ofer says of the early records compiled by historical commissions in the DP camps,³ that they had a sense of predetermination that all experiences were leading to a catastrophe, one may arguably detect in the YV accounts an attempt to create a continuous narrative of prewar, wartime, and postwar experiences. Some continuity does exist in the earlier Polish records, but for the most part these records seem rather to display expressions of shock at the totality of the destruction of Jewish life as well as at the continuation of hostilities from the Polish population. Table A.1 in the appendix presents the results of a comparison of the ŻIH and YV testimonies.

Perhaps the most curious finding reflected in table A.1 is that more than one-third (39 percent) of the testimonies selected from YV contain no memories of any Polish–Jewish interaction at all after the war, even though postwar references appear four times more often in the Israeli testimonies than in the Polish testimonies (61 percent to 17 percent, respectively). The relatively scarce mentioning of postwar experiences in the early postwar Polish testimonies, however, is in part explained by the peculiar fact that the interviewers did not always ask about life after the liberation, whereas the "return home" was a routine question during the YV interviews.

Negative Memories

1. Rumors or News of the Murder of Nearby Jews

The most frequently recorded memory of the period immediately after the war (in 30 percent of the YV sample) is that of hearing rumors or news of the deaths of Jews at the hands of the Polish population. The "population" (Polish: *ludność*)—that is, ordinary civilians—appears, indeed, as the most commonly identified culprit. Almost as many accounts point to the AK, but the independent, openly antisemitic, anti-Communist underground NSZ is mentioned only twice.⁴ Looking at the subjective memories, however, without arguing facts, if we put the AK and the NSZ together and add certain ascriptions of murders to "partisans" and to "bands" (the Polish term *bandy* here implies quasi-military formations more than gangs of hooligans), then we can say that the majority of the alleged murders were ascribed to the Underground opposition that was leading partisan activities against the Communist takeover of power, and, as those testimonies confirm, against the Jews.

Various Underground agencies, "bands," and "partisans" are quite frequently mentioned in the same account, signaling that the provenance of a given violent group was not exactly determined. A multitude of perpetrators may also denote a perception of a generalized, uniform threat coming from the whole of the society, as evident in the account by Jakob Perelman (AYV O3/1790). After returning to Parczew from Germany, where he had worked as a forced laborer and had to hide his Jewishness from other Poles, Perelman continued to hide his identity out of fear of his own companions, who, "as soon as they learn that we are Jews, will kill us." In the section of his account titled "Our Lives after the War," Perelman relates:

> In Parczew, there were up to a hundred Jews then who survived in the camps and forests. Not all of them came from Parczew itself: there were some from surrounding towns and villages; they were afraid to live where there were few Jews. Our lives were temporary because we saw that we were still being persecuted by the Poles; here and there, a fact happened of a murder of a Jew. All of us wanted only to liquidate our property, to get back what was possible, and to leave the town, which was a cemetery for us in any case. . . . All Jews living presently in Parczew kept very friendly relationships among themselves; we kept together in this hostile world.

Perelman also describes the survivors' self-defense and all-night watches:

> The Jews were afraid to take trains; they were afraid to go outside the town; everywhere there were murderers lying in wait for us. One night during February 1946, a great danger threatened us, and I am able to say that I saved everyone. That night all of us were gathered at the home of the Szczupak family, which was leaving Parczew the following day. It was a custom that everyone who was leaving would arrange an evening, [after which we would] say good-bye, and all would see them to a train.

I had just left the neighbor's home when I saw two Polish soldiers and heard one say, "Fix him!" And the other one said: "Don't make any noise because they just entered the town!" I understood the situation immediately: that in front of every Jewish house there stood murderers, that the Poles showed them where the Jews were living, that far greater forces were about to come, [and] that a great danger was approaching. I immediately returned home, ran to the attic, jumped out into the other yard, [and] ran to the Szczupaks', where they were all gathered. I ran again into the two bandits, but they didn't stop me, but I saw that they caught another Jew and told him to stand under a pole. Then I heard a shot, and I didn't know what happened to that Jew. I managed to run to the Szczupaks' with a cry: "Save yourselves, there is a band in town!" They all scattered into the meadows, cellars, [and] niches. My sister and I were sheltered by a Pole; we were lying there the whole night, we were looking out the window frequently, and we saw a lot with our own eyes. The partisans' club was mostly surrounded by the bandits, but they didn't enter as they knew that all the Jews had weapons. They stood and waited for them to come out, and then the first victim fell. A Jew named Mojsze Kowal[5] came out of the club because he was so strong and large, as smiths usually are. The bandits shouted: "Hands up!" The other Jew who was with Mojsze didn't lose his cool, fired a shot, and ran away. That strong Mojsze Kowal raised his hands, [though, and] the bandits took out his revolver from his pocket and shot him.

Perelman describes three other murders that night by the bandits who were "running amok till four o'clock in the morning. They plundered Jewish apartments, tore bed sheets, [and] broke furniture in every house. Our neighbors, the Poles, were leading them from one Jewish apartment to another and were helping in the act of destruction."

Subsequently, the band, which Perelman identified as "NSZ-*owcy*" (NSZ people), tried to force a militiaman to order the Jews to leave their apartments. Surprisingly, the militiaman instead warned the Jews, urging them to shoot back at the band. After that pogrom, local authorities established a curfew because "a lot of Poles from Parczew collaborated with the AK and the NSZ." The survivors received reinforced weapons (principally grenades) for their self-defense. With satisfaction, Perelman reports also how he managed to take revenge on an "NSZ bandit" who was about to threaten another Jewish survivor. Not surprisingly, after experiencing these deadly encounters, Perelman left Parczew for Wrocław. When he later returned one more time to Parczew to arrange for some papers, his train was stopped in Radzyń Podlaski by another band that was checking to see whether any Jews were on it. After that, Perelman and his sister "left [their] hometown forever." Joining some Germans who were leaving the "recovered lands" in western Poland, he spent four years in the DP camp in Lampertheim and then immigrated to Israel in 1949.

Perelman's account, written fifteen years after the events, shows that he retained a vivid memory of the physical and emotional horrors that the survivors experienced after the war was over. Their isolation from the rest of the Polish population, their constant need to be armed and vigilant, the collaboration of Polish neighbors in helping the "bands" identify and harass them—all paint a picture of a fearful, besieged, "posthumous" community, desperately clinging together and searching for the same means of survival that they had used when they had been hunted by the Nazis (for example, hiding at the homes of "good" Poles). We also learn about a ritual of throwing farewell parties for those who were able to manage to leave, one by one, family by family. Perelman succeeded in fleeing these horrors with a feeling of satisfaction that—to some extent—he helped defend other survivors and even managed to take revenge on one killer.

Fayge Ozer's testimony (AYV O3/3025) mentions good Christian rescuers who warned her about murders committed by the AK. Her account is also a concise illustration of a broad spectrum of the ethnic Poles' behaviors, so I quote a longer passage from it:

> INTERVIEWER: What were relationships with the Poles like?
> OZER: At the beginning, the attitude of the Poles was not bad, but it soon changed: we were forced to leave town. We believed that we would know how to organize ourselves. Jews lived a collective life; we shared everything. One evening, when I . . . slept on a carriage, for I was afraid to stay in my room because of the goyim, the bandits, I had not yet lain down when a Christian came— Janek Kubacki—and asked me to come to his place. When I came

there, he locked the door and told me: "You have to disappear from town, because my cousin has told me that the AK has placed a death sentence on you. . . . As we have been friends since childhood, I will save you." Soon a Russian soldier came with a car and took me away. I went away to Częstochowa [and] from there, after a few days, to Kraków. Proszowice is thirty kilometers from Kraków; there I learned what happened in the town and also heard the news about my family.

INTERVIEWER: Were there Poles with you when the AK was murdering Jews in the town, or were they in the neighborhood?

OZER: After my escape from the town, the AK murdered two of my friends, Abraham Les and Wolff Les. I kept telling them not to go to the village. They didn't listen. They were in the village at the home of the same goy they had been hiding with during the war for twenty-eight months. They were sleeping there with the Christians. The AK came at night, took them out on the street, and shot them. I want to add that in our neighborhood the AK have murdered many of those who survived the Gehenna of war.

INTERVIEWER: Apart from the murders, did the Poles with you in the town help the Jews after the liberation?

OZER: There were goyim with whom the Jews kept their valuables, who returned them after the war. There were also goyim who helped send their known Jews to KZs [*Konzentrationslager*, concentration camps]. There was a Christian among us, named Kozoba, who was a believer. Every Sunday he used to dress himself in a silk coat (*kapote*) of the Jews who were in his house and so go to the church to pray. It was all a remembrance and a proof that there were Jews in his house.

In certain respects, this account could have been written in Poland in 1946 and not twenty years later in Israel. The detailing of the survivors' situation ("One evening, when I . . . slept on a carriage, for I was afraid to stay in my room because of the goyim, the bandits") and the short expressions providing such basic facts could well be found in early Polish testimonies. In the YV accounts, however, there seems to be a greater emphasis on establishing a continuous exodus narrative (in the case of this particular narrative, emphasizing a uniform change in the behavior of Poles toward the Jews), which is evoked, at least in part, by interviewer questions (which are absent in the Polish documents) such as "What were relationships with the Poles like?" or "Were there Poles with you when the AK was murdering the Jews?"

2. Direct Threats or Attacks against One's Person

About 15 percent of the YV sample accounts mention direct threats or attacks on the persons giving testimony. In more than half of these cases, the threats resulted in actual violence. As in the ŻIH testimonies, if the rumors of the killings of Jews are added to actual personal threats and attacks, the YV testimonies indicate that the memory of violence—direct or indirect—is the predominant memory recorded in one-third of the sample. Sixty-six percent of the testimonies that mention threats or attacks were recorded in Polish, 31 percent in Yiddish, and 3 percent in Hebrew.

The YV testimonies recall physical violence in a variety of ways. Attackers often persisted through a longer period of time and employed means of harassing Jews that were straight out of wartime practices. Ester Kaminska (AYV O3/3029) returned to Dęblin after the liberation, where, she says, "I again had a fuss because the Poles thought that they would get all this. When they saw those few Jews, they carried out a fresh massacre. They did not want the Jews to return at all."

A Pole who had been given the Kaminska family bakery by the Nazis was unhappy that Ester had returned and tried to get a group of Soviet soldiers (who resided in the town) drunk to incite them to kill her. These drunks caused a scandal one night, bringing Kaminska to the verge of despair: "There were no doors, no key, nothing to lock with. We were crying all night; there was nobody to turn to and nowhere to go. It was worse than the camp."

Finally, Kaminska's distressed daughter intervened, notifying the Soviet People's Commissariat for Internal Affairs (NKVD), which arrested the soldiers and forced the Poles to move out. Although Kaminska managed to recover part of her apartment, she continued to be harassed by extortionists (referred to as "Poles" or "bands" in the testimony), who, in a gruesome repetition of wartime actions, demanded a "ransom" to leave her alone. She did not have enough money to pay it, so she departed for Palestine through Lower Silesia.

Chana Nusenblatt (AYV O3/2881) experienced the effects of antisemitic attitudes for the first time after the war from the new Soviet regime in Proskurov (now Khmielnicky) in Ukraine. When in 1944 she applied for her new identification papers, she realized that she would be charged a higher price "as a Jew," and so she retained her Polish nationality instead. When she moved to Poland, she heard about the Kielce Pogrom and about the "NSZ killing everyone," even former rescuers of the Jews. She reports that they were after her when she traveled from Kraków to Nowy Targ. Nusenblatt's testimony mentions two underground organizations: the AK and the NSZ. Her estimation of their attitudes toward Jews is more in concert with the general opinion held by historians: "The AK was much more liberal, [it] didn't hit the Jews," whereas the NSZ were "fascist," murdering not only Jews but also members of the AK in the forest near Kraków in April 1946.

3. Various Negative Societal Reactions

The second image that survivors in Israel clung to most in their memories, following violence that they had heard about or their direct experience of violence, was that of a generalized hostility on the part of the Polish population. Negative reactions were mentioned in 28 percent of the "active" sample, and most of these testimonies were given in Polish (83 percent versus 13 percent in Yiddish and 4 percent in Hebrew).

The negative attitudes that the survivors perceived ranged from the well-known reactions of surprise, bordering on dismay, that a returning Jewish neighbor had actually survived to the administrative and legal hurdles that now formed part of the new regime's daily routine and the comments heard in public places about the undesirability of Jews in postwar Poland. Additional context is supplied by the fear experienced by the rescuers of the survivors, who, frequently intimidated and even beaten for hiding Jews, carried their own sad message to the survivors that "the war, for the Jews, is not yet over." Sometimes, in an ironic twist of history, rescuers were "saved" by fleeing Jews, who took the rescuers with them when they escaped.

In Avigdor Mandelbaum's account (AYV O3/2289), one encounters a general silence as to why, soon after liberation, he decided to leave Poland for Germany. One lone intimation about his rescuer exists to help us reconstruct Mandelbaum's impressions of the welcome he received: "She [the rescuer] wanted me to survive to live, but she was also afraid for herself." After being provided with care until he recovered his health and being given some gold, Mandelbaum left, probably before the Kielce Pogrom occurred in July 1946. His file contains very affectionate and caring letters from his rescuers.

Many negative memories are barely signaled by vague expressions. According to Irena Lisikiewiczowa (AYV O3/2657), survivors could experience a greater sense of threat from hostile looks and silence than from a wartime law that had condemned their very existence: "When I came out [of hiding]," writes Lisikiewiczowa, "I was more afraid than during the German times. Nobody welcomed us; the atmosphere was very unfriendly."

Other testimonies contain explicit memories that leave no doubt as to why survivors felt compelled to leave Poland: Dr. Henryka Rakocz (AYV O3/2342) was in the Lublin area when it was liberated in August 1944. She had continued to hide her identity, though, because "relations were everywhere dangerous." Trying to support herself as a dental aid (she was a dentist by profession), she quickly learned that exposing her origins would cause both her medical partner and her patients to be afraid. Upon learning that Dr. Rakocz was Jewish, the doctor for whom she worked slammed the door in her face; meanwhile, her landlord sent her a threatening letter. When Dr. Rakocz returned to Radom, her hometown, her apartment appeared to have been taken over by a Pole. As she narrated, "He would not even let me spend a night there. I knew I could not make it in my hometown, so I quickly left for Lublin. . . . I started my [medical] practice there, still hiding my identity, because in Lublin there were cases of murders of Jews who were coming out from hiding. I stayed in Lublin from March 1945 until the end of 1949. Then I left for Paris on the way to Israel, truly liberated only then."

With respect to living in Israel, in spite of the difficulties connected with living in a new state as well as "the threat of war with the Arabs," Dr. Rakocz insists at the end of her account that she is "happy to be in [her] Fatherland": "If today they promised me a fortune and the best positions in Poland, I would not return to the strangers."

The testimony of Romuald Paporisz (AYV O33/651) evokes a feeling of being hunted and of being blamed—as a Jew—for "starting up" the war as well as for causing the postwar situation. Paporisz wrote a moving diary as well as an extraordinary letter to his son over the span of ten years. In the letter, the father explained his wartime circumstances as well as his reasons for eventually leaving Poland. He confessed that when they were in hiding, he had sometimes considered killing his son, merely an infant at the time, so as not to endanger a group in hiding. He reported on the "remorse" that their angry rescuers expressed after the war for having rescued them. He also mentioned that after the war their maid had tried to discourage the son from visiting a swimming pool with the dictum that it was "full of Jews." The event that precipitated Paporisz's emigration appears to have come during the Polish October[6] because he most likely left Poland soon after that.

4. Postwar Hiding

Another memory retained in some of the testimonies adds to the sense of fear that many "active" accounts report: the phenomenon of hiding after the war, either physically (for example, not showing up in town) or legally (continuing to live under an assumed Christian identity). Mania Brudner and her twin sister, Ida Pechter (AYV O3/2673), after coming out of their hiding place, preferred to pretend to have traveled from Germany rather than admit to being Jewish. Dr. Rakocz's testimony, discussed earlier, likewise paints a vivid image of the possible result of disclosing one's Jewish identity and why even medical professionals, although they were in extreme demand after the war, had better not "be Jewish."

Almost all of the testimonies that speak of postwar hiding link hiding to the threat of violence. Adding such cases to those considered in this analysis strengthens the basic finding that the most frequently expressed emotion accompanying the first interactions of Jewish survivors with non-Jewish Poles was fear of being hurt by the Poles.

Positive Memories

Only about 16 percent of the testimonies in the "active" YV sample (with 71 percent of this portion in Polish, 29 percent in Yiddish) contain reports of positive memories of first interactions with Poles, although in almost all cases the good experiences are mixed with the bad. Sometimes the "positive memory" consists of nothing more than a neighbor's warning of a threat coming from "forest bands."

For Chawa Fink (AYV O3/2544), whose family survived thanks to several brave individuals as well as to a convent of nuns and the protection provided by Archbishop Andrzej Szeptycki, help from Poles extended beyond the war: her principal rescuer warned her not leave her cellar because "the Soviets haven't entered yet, and one must be careful, as one Jew was shot on the street because he left his hiding place too early."

The same rescuer provided the Fink family with a sewing machine so that its members would be able to work and earn a living; other Poles also provided incidental help. The Finks remained in Poland until 1950; we do not have any indication of why they decided to leave then or whether they had tried to leave earlier.

Ester Seibald (AYV O3/3066) survived the war in hiding at the home of a Polish peasant and was protected by a local priest. After the liberation, she reports, she was afraid of being recognized as a Jew. In spite of that fear, she was received and cared for by her Polish friends, who asked why she had not come earlier. Like many other survivors, Seibald decided to move to the western part of Poland, where Jewish survivors had managed to rebuild some structures of former Jewish communities; she relates that after a year, however, she "fled" or "escaped" Poland. We do not know what exactly precipitated that decision, although the year, 1946, may indicate the Kielce Pogrom as a possible final blow.

In several testimonies, the positive reaction was noted but vague and unexplained. Adam Zomper (AYV O3/1821) writes positively about Poland after the war but does not provide any details: in contrast to a majority of the survivors, Zomper managed, after returning to Poland, to locate some of his relatives; he also got married and started to work. At the same time, in 1947, he organized a youth group to join the Haganah, a Jewish paramilitary organization in Palestine, and so he tried to acquire a permit to leave for himself, which he finally succeeded in obtaining in 1956. Before he left, he was apparently satisfied with his life in Poland, at least with his career. As he explained, "I was an appreciated and respected employee, and I did not experience antisemitism. I moved up in my work, for which I received various awards and bonuses."

In Zomper's case, it may have been his Zionist political leanings that caused him to persevere in applying for the exit visa. His account does not testify to any discriminatory treatment but mentions rather positive impressions of his environment.

"Silent" Memories

Although we must acknowledge the problem of declaring certain accounts "silent" on the subject of interactions with Gentile Poles (as suggested in chapter 3), the muteness on the topic in Israeli depositions is more puzzling than it is in the Polish ones. Altogether, 39 percent of the preselected YV accounts contain no recollections of such interactions (with 74 percent of these "silent" accounts in Polish, 20 percent in Yiddish, 3 percent each in Hebrew and German).

To attempt to divine reasons for a survivor's *not* mentioning a subject in a narrative would be a matter of speculation, a rather futile speculation at that. The format of a testimony, whether it was given in replies to a questionnaire or as part of a personal interview, whether the deposition was a "free-flowing" narrative of what the survivors decided to reveal or part of an application to grant a rescuer the title of "Righteous among the Nations"—all affected the content of a testimony, yet specific motives for gathering each testimony were not a subject of categorization in the YV efforts, so we cannot legitimately impose such distinctions ex post facto.

The silence about postwar interactions with Poles is most "vocal" when present in otherwise eloquent and detailed testimonies left by quite literary survivors. In the seventeen-page testimony of Dr. Dovid Kindler (AYV O3/2560), for example, his prewar life and the Sokal Jewish community are well depicted, as is his survival in Sokal, together with fourteen other Jews, in the house of Franciszka Halamajowa. In Kindler's account, the Polish woman-rescuer announces the liberation on July 25, 1944, with an exclamation in country-style Polish even though the testimony is otherwise written entirely in Yiddish: "Matka Boska was uratowała!" (The Blessed Mother has saved you!). This religious proclamation is immediately followed by Dr. Kindler's anticlimactic reference to the arrival of "the first Bolshevik in town." Dr. Kindler then describes the fear of the Ukrainians, who frightened the Poles as much as they frightened the Jews, as well as the threat of returning Germans. At the first opportunity, Dr. Kindler returned to work at a hospital and later, with Soviet officers, moved to work in Lviv. There, he rescued eighteen old copies of the Torah. After his transfer to Poland with other repatriates (against the wishes of the "Soviet officers," who did not want to let him go), Dr. Kindler settled first in Kraków and then soon in Warsaw to consult with Emil Sommerstein (a lawyer, Zionist activist, and prewar Jewish politician who became a minister in the new Communist Polish government). Sommerstein recommended that Dr. Kindler move to Silesia, which was becoming famous for Jewish settlers, but Dr. Kindler preferred to emigrate. Nothing in the testimony explains his reasons for his decision. Dr. Kindler arrived in the Land of Israel two years before the Zionist dream of statehood was fulfilled. Were there some other encounters with Poles, unmentioned in the testimony, that "helped" him decide to leave the country—to "abandon . . . Poland," as the introductory comments by the interviewer put it? From the coincidence of dates—Dr. Kindler's arrival in Palestine at the end of the summer of 1946—one might suppose that the Kielce Pogrom was the most obvious reason to leave. Or could it have been "just" a maturing of a Zionist longing, not necessarily the result of his immediate circumstances? Although the lack of motive appears intriguing, it is not possible, in this or in other instances, to know all of the particular reasons why individual Jews fled Poland.

Cemetery Syndrome

In my reading of the Israeli testimonies, as in my reading of the Polish testimonies, I found that "cemetery syndrome" does not feature prominently as an explicit memory of the survivors. Only 5 percent of YV testimonies (all of them in Polish) in the selected sample signal reactions stemming from "cemetery syndrome" as a memory, either following a return home or in providing an important reason to leave Poland.

Like various other negative memories, "cemetery syndrome" was usually one reason among many that propelled a survivor to leave. Alta Weber (AYV O3/1317) recalls certain painful impressions of the Polish countryside, on top of the impossibility of living on the graveyard of her past:

> The Polish population was hostile to the Jews who survived. On Lubelska Street one could hear shouts: "Are you still alive, you scab?" "Hasn't Hitler finished you all off yet?" "So we haven't gotten rid of them yet?" In little towns, villages, the Jews were being murdered; in the whole country one could hear, "Beat the Jew!"
>
> Was there room for joy under such conditions? Nothing changed for me yet. I continued to live as during the German times. I continued to work for the peasants. . . . I was afraid of the peasants; I kept hearing about murders of Jews. I was in Lublin, and I went to my old apartment. What pain pierced my heart when I saw the door of my apartment! My little son, who used to run up these steps, is not there, my husband is not there! I did not enter the apartment; I ran away quickly. I could not live there, even if I were to manage to recover it.
>
> I felt I had to leave Lublin, that I would not be able to endure it in this city, in which every street, every house would remind me of my past.
>
> At the beginning of April 1945, I took my bundle and left for Warsaw.

Jakob Perelman, whose testimony is quoted earlier and who likewise had many reasons to feel hunted by hostile Polish Gentiles, adds in his account: "Our lives were temporary because we saw that we were still being persecuted by the Poles; here and there, a fact happened of a murder of a Jew. All of us wanted only to liquidate our property, to get back what was possible, and to leave the town, which was a cemetery for us in any case."

On occasion, "cemetery syndrome" turns out to be the only impression of postwar Poland that is spelled out in a testimony. Jakub Grubner (AYV O3/2500) ends his testimony with these haunting words:

> At the end of April, having been released from the hospital as an invalid, . . . I arrived in Tarnów; at the place where my mother-in-law had lived with my wife and child, I encountered growing grass. From a Catholic friend of my mother-in-law, the owner of a bakery, Mrs. Malińska, I learned about the tragedy of my dearest ones. From there I went to the home of W. near Kraków, my hometown. I did not find anyone; the house was taken apart, the earth dug up.
>
> And during the whole time of my misery, there was not a minute when I wasn't thinking about my dear ones—and I am alive.

Grubner's former life, family, and home literally disappeared, leaving him with an empty life and a nonexistent space. This lack of a proper cemetery where he could have mourned his family and past left him and possibly other survivors with a "phantom mourning"—analogous to phantom pain—in which there apparently was nothing physical to mourn, and the whole geographic and political area became an unbearable, uninhabitable "cemetery."

Remarks on Language

The majority of the "active" testimonies selected from the YV archives were given in Polish (71 percent), with one-fourth of them in Yiddish (24 percent) and only 3 percent in Hebrew. (See chapter 6 for a more thorough linguistic analysis.) Although such a distribution of languages across the depositions cannot be strictly compared to the general distribution of languages among Jewish Polish survivors, one coincidence is worth mentioning. In Irena Hurwic-Nowakowska's sociological study of Polish postwar Jewry, conducted from 1947 to 1950, almost 60 percent of the respondents used Polish every day, and only 28 percent knew and used Yiddish.[7]

With respect to the style in which the Israeli testimonies were written, the survivors in Israel tended to speak about encounters with Poles in an open and even emotionally revealing way that was rare among the accounts in the Polish ŻIH collection. For example, Dr. Symcha Hampel (AYV O33/950) describes a range of Polish attitudes. During the war, he worked as a supervisor on an estate; after the war, the workers wanted to keep him, even as they also wanted at the same time to get rid of a Polish supervisor, who apparently was a mean person and, in fact, eventually had to flee the "people's justice." After Dr. Hampel returned to his hometown, Radomsko, his wife wanted to leave, but he joined the Citizens Militia to finish off any German bands in the area. Dr. Hampel relates two antisemitic encounters in Radomsko: first, upon attempting to regain his house, he found that it had been taken over by a certain Kaleciński, who refused even to share it, saying that "he would not live with some little Jew." Later, when Dr. Hampel managed to get an apartment in a Jewish home, he met a colleague, known for his prewar anti-Jewish opinions, who welcomed him with the caustic statement, "Colleague, you are alive!"—to which Dr. Hampel adds, "Every Jew who survived the war was a real thorn in his [the colleague's] side, but he sat quietly because of the Soviets." The testimony also mentions administrative discrimination in the fact that the color of Jewish registry cards differed from the color of the cards issued to ethnic Poles. Dr. Hampel most felt their growing social isolation as Jewish survivors when his wife gave birth: "It was when lying in bed that my wife finally felt the lack of her mother. Nobody would visit us, and who was to help the woman who had just been in labor?" He then reports:

> The murders of Jews already began by the beginning of April. We heard that in the Lublin area and other provinces Jews were being murdered. Initially, we did not want to believe it ourselves, but the facts spoke for themselves. A great tragedy began. . . . Living two and a half years as Poles, we knew well that nobody liked us, but nobody can be forced to do that. Yet I had counted on our lives not to be threatened. It turned

out to be just the opposite. After several months, the murders of Jews began.... Over the course of five years, the Poles had learned to finish off the Jews. They don't want us, and therefore they murder us.

After giving several examples of the murders of Jewish survivors (including seven employees of a kindergarten), and upon encountering another legal obstacle (with respect to his medical degree, which he had obtained in France before the war owing to a *numerus clausus* policy at Polish universities), Dr. Hampel finally decided to leave with his family for France. They first went to Czechoslovakia, where he obtained a French visa, and then he returned once more to Radomsko—only to learn that in the meantime a Jewish mother and daughter had been murdered. The character of this crime was so obvious that a Soviet officer had remarked to the doctor conducting the autopsy: "You yourselves murdered them. Have we brought you freedom so that you would murder your own citizens? You are not worth liberty." Apparently, no ethnic Poles were present at the funeral, nor did the daughter's school send a delegation. Poles standing on the street, however, were heard saying, "There will be two Jews fewer!" Dr. Hampel left Poland on July 11, 1946, just one week after the Kielce Pogrom.

Dr. Hampel's testimony represents a kind of narrative that seems to be more easily, if not typically, found in the YV collection. The accounts in this collection tend to emphasize the continuity of Polish antisemitism, which adds to the arguments in favor of a decision to leave Poland.

6
Comparative Analysis of the Data
Memory on a Curve

> When the nations will have concluded peace
> and their peoples will come trampling over
> the unmarked graves of our slain, in the towns and villages,
> then I shall certainly go insane.
> —Yitzhak Katznelson, "Vittel Diary"

The analysis of selected sources from the collections of the Jewish Historical Institute and Yad Vashem with respect to Holocaust survivors' memories of their postwar reception by the Polish population seems to confirm an initial suspicion that the survivors would be more likely to speak of their postwar encounters with the Gentile population once they were safe in Israel. In the two preselected samples, 61 percent of YV testimonies raised the subject as opposed to 17 percent of the ŻIH testimonies.

Several reasons for such a disproportion have been suggested in previous chapters. In the case of Poland, the first reason is practical: the survivors had just barely returned to their hometowns and were not yet sure how their attempts to find surviving relatives and to reestablish themselves would work out. Some, in fact, even deposited their testimonies on the way to their hometowns, thus before having experienced any kind of reception from their neighbors. A second reason is ideological: the Central Jewish Historical Commission (CŻKH) was interested primarily in recovering from the survivors an image of what had been lost—in terms of the whole people—and then only secondarily in how the person had managed and was continuing to manage to survive. The CŻKH historians were also gathering information on specific means of Jewish annihilation—on how the Germans executed their Endlösung, Final Solution, and on whether they did so with a special cruelty (such information could become potential evidence in future court proceedings). In the general questionnaire prepared by the CŻKH, the only reference to postwar interaction with the Gentile population was included obliquely with three questions placed at the end of one of sixteen sections, "Personal Experiences and Specific Facts the Witness Observed":

1. How did the witness survive ("Aryan" papers, bunkers, partisan groups)?
2. When and under what circumstances was the witness freed?
3. Did the Jewish survivors lose anything after liberation (material losses, human losses)?[1]

The whole interaction between the returning survivors and the Polish population, therefore, was framed in terms of objective losses (physical property appropriated or lives lost), without considering the social attitudes that formed part of the typical experience of returning home. The questionnaire's ideological tendency may have been due to the CŻKH's dependence on the Communist authorities, who were pursuing their own agenda of legitimization. Societal reactions to returning Jews, therefore, although often known to be hostile, were not considered part of that agenda.

In contrast to the approach taken by Jewish historians in postwar Poland concerning the recent catastrophe, Israeli historiography was following Zionist premises and so was interested in exploiting the postwar hostilities and violence occurring in the survivors' surroundings. This is not to imply that the antisemitic persecutions were in any way less real, only that the Zionism dominating the Israeli political and social life of the period fostered the emergence of a narrative of exodus and return, which encouraged both the collectors of the testimonies and the survivors themselves to dwell on the experiences of the return home. In fact, because the questionnaires contained questions about the survivors' postwar situation, it is surprising that 39 percent of the sample testimonies do not comment at all on relations with the Gentiles (see table A1 in the appendix).

In this chapter, I analyze several testimonies from the collections under investigation to create a more in-depth picture of the survivors' expressions of their experiences. To achieve this, I compare significant testimonies from each archive as representative of several styles of recounting the survivors' experiences. I use elements of narrative analysis to form an understanding of how the memory of the first encounters with the Poles was transformed in Israel. In addition, I consider the different paths that the survivors' lives took in Poland and abroad.

Methodologically, I aim here to provide a qualitative analysis of the collective memory. Words such as *many*, *most*, *some*, *predominantly*, and *a few* give an estimate of the frequency of occurrence of a style; however, more precise estimates are neither possible nor relevant here. I give general descriptions of the kinds of rhetoric employed to recount the memories; they are meant to deepen an "understanding interpretation" that complements "objectified" methods of source criticism.[2]

Poland in the Postwar Period

The Police Report, or On the Banality of Language

The most frequent style of the ŻIH testimonies utilizes ordinary, common language to describe uncommon suffering. Such testimonies read like police reports or court depositions, which was often the perceived goal of the testimony. Even when the survivors were being interviewed for explicitly unofficial reasons (with the assumption that the goal of the deposition was to aid historical research), the testimonies very often applied an officious, unemotional, and impersonal style to record the war and postwar experiences.

Pesla Pencyna (AŻIH 301/1525), for example, whose husband was murdered seventeen days before liberation, visited her husband's hometown immediately after the war and reported on the violence there in one quick sentence: "I reached the [day of my] liberation in the manor. I stayed there for one month because I didn't know that [my husband] had died.

He died seventeen days before the liberation. I went to my husband's family in Klementów. *I was there until the Reaction* [a Communist name for the opposing Underground forces] *began to murder the Jews*. Two days before the murder of the Jews, I left" (emphasis added).

Squeezed in, so to speak, between Pencyna's report on how several of her friends were denounced or killed in hiding and her story of recovering a niece from a Gentile unwilling to return her, the laconic statement about the murder of Jews testifies to just one more "inconvenience" that the surrounding world had to offer to the survivors. Such plain, almost detached language may signify that the fact of such murder was simply too common to require any unusual stylistic emphasis or emotional comment. The survivor, who had endured a series of hiding places, who had been frequently robbed and mistreated by her rescuers and by blackmailers, and who was in constant fear for the lives of her husband and daughter, confessed that when she met her husband in December 1944, he had reassured her that she should remain calm because the village where she hid was under the partisans' control, and the Germans would not come there. "I left [the village] in a [state of] complete mental balance," she intimated; "I was deluding myself that we would survive." Her self-confessed regret that *she* did not survive (i.e., in her role as a wife, for her husband was dead) leaves her with only a short, factual, common style in which to report on more dead Jews in an alleged time of peace. In her testimony, in her language, and possibly even in her life, Pencyna appears to have run out of tears with which to tell about the continuation of the violence against her people.

In a similar vein, Lieba Tiefenbrun (AŻIH 301/1182), who lost all of her family and was moved from camp to camp, including Auschwitz, Płaszów, and Stutthof, reported on her experiences in simple, ordinary language. When she occasionally quotes crude concentration camp songs, however, her testimony gains a bizarre hue of ribaldry verging on the grotesque, which paradoxically elevates it to a more sophisticated literariness. When describing her return home, though, Tiefenbrun resorts again to plain, straightforward language: "On train stops we were cared for by the Red Cross. That's how I got to Tarnów. There, my first question to the train conductor was, 'Are there any Jews in the town?' He told me that there were a few, but that they had to hide because they were afraid. I became afraid. I went downtown. I was weak; I was barely holding up on my legs. That's how I got to our house's door keeper; she alone told me about this committee [the local branch of the CKŻP]."

The Jews again "had to hide because they were afraid. I became afraid." After Tiefenbrun had suffered through the deaths of her parents and siblings and endured continual death-camp selections, beatings, starvation, disease, and the like, was there really anything else that she should have been "afraid" of? For us, the readers of Tiefenbrun's testimony, the word *afraid* seems pathetically inadequate. It is an attempt at a catch-all term, a groping in the dark for a linguistic approximation that falls miserably short of conveying her true feelings upon her return home after experiencing hell on earth. She confesses that she was "afraid" and "scared" of the Poles around her, of people who had known her and her family since long before the war—people who were occupied and, to some degree, enslaved by the Germans, although not, like the Jews, destined for total annihilation. These Poles had been her compatriots and neighbors. Based solely on her testimony, it is hard to divine what the twenty-five-year-old Tiefenbrun felt when she was told that the few Jews who had managed to survive the Shoah and return were "afraid." One may suspect, however, that the feeling she describes was infinitely more like terror, shaking, and devastation.

Dry, unemotional language is somehow less jarring when those pogroms that have a well-established historiography are described: Rzeszów (June 12, 1945), Kraków (August 11, 1945), and Kielce (July 4, 1946). The few witnesses who gave these accounts were probably well aware of the historical significance of their testimonies and of the expectation that their narrative be "objective" so as to aid the pursuit of justice. Ida Gerstman (AŻIH 301/4567) left a detailed account of her sojourn in Kielce between July 2 and July 5, 1946, reporting on the beginning of the greatest postwar pogrom in Poland as well as on how it metastasized to the transiting trains. Her deposition opens up like a proper police report of an event: "I arrived in Kielce on the second of July in the evening. Until Wednesday 9 a.m., it was completely peaceful. At 9 a.m. I heard at the mortgage office from a Jew I knew that a crowd has surrounded the house at Planty 7, where the Jewish Committee, the Kibbutz, and the repatriates returning from Russia resided." Gerstman and other Jews gathered in the office to beg the officials to let them stay there, but the officials harshly refused, and the Jews were forced out onto the street. Between descriptions of events, Gerstman mentions her emotions ("I was very afraid to go out on the street because I heard that they attack and murder Jews. But I had no other choice. I saw on the streets how they were beating and kicking Jews"), but such mentions are only a quick hint—said in passing—meant to explain her actions (of delaying to leave the office) as well as to indict the callous officials who "might have, with some good will, locked us up in the office, and then they would have saved many Jews." Once on the street, Gerstman's companion and a Pole who offered to protect him were attacked by a hostile mob, and Gerstman ran away and hid for two nights and a day in a field of wheat. When she thought that the worst was over, she walked to the next train stop after Kielce. What makes Gerstman's testimony more palpable than other semiofficial narratives is that she was attuned to what people said, and she quotes these statements as well as the cries of the mob *in extenso*:

> Near the station I heard one of the country women say, "I'm going on a journey, I'm taking a knife. If I catch a Jew or a Jewess, I will cut pieces of them and will salt them." I bought my ticket and got on the train, happy that nobody had recognized me.
>
> On the train I noticed that they observed me. One of the women pointed at me: "This is a lousy kike; throw her under the train." And another one: "We'll turn her over to the militia at the next station; let them shoot her." At the next stop the women grabbed me by the feet and by the head and pulled me onto the tracks to throw me under the train. I begged them to spare my life, but they said I was a Jewess, and so I must die. Children started to throw stones at me. I begged a railwayman to shoot me because I could not suffer any longer, but he answered: "You want to die an easy death; slowly, you can suffer for a little longer." Fortunately a militiaman was walking across the tracks; he ordered them to let me go but [said] that he would take care of me himself. They let me go, and the militiaman demanded that I give him some drink money. I gave him my last five hundred zloty. He let

> me go. I boarded a train once again, and again women recognized me and turned me over to the militia, shouting, "Kill the kike." The train militiaman led me to a detention room at the railway station. This was in Jędrzejów. They led me to a cell, where they also brought another Jew, whom they had likewise removed from the train once they had identified him as a Jew. Before my eyes the militiaman kicked him, and a man in civilian clothes in the office hit him in his face. A group of children threw stones at us through an open window, shouting that they want to stone us. A young girl in a school uniform shouted, "Get out from under the bed so that we can stone you. Your good times are over; now you must all die in return for our blood. We will put up a golden monument to Hitler, and we keep asking God that a new Hitler arise."

Thus, while struggling to provide an "objective," detached account of the "events in Kielce," Gerstman unwittingly reaches to and highlights a set of deep-seated anti-Jewish convictions held by some segments of the postwar Polish population.[3]

The common ascetic quality of the language of most of the ŻIH testimonies, which nearly invariably describe horrifying instances of murder and torture, suggests a twofold limit: the well-noted exhaustion of the language (the inability to express in an available linguistic canon the true nature of the trauma that the survivors went through[4]) and the exhaustion of the soul's ability to absorb the continuation of violence (the dulling of the mind that already existed during the war as the cup of suffering ran over even then). With respect to the former, words fail to express the terror of the soul; with respect to the latter, the very repetition of tales of terror, quotidian and therefore mundane, becomes banal. It is significant, therefore, to notice that the language of the testimonies does not change when the postwar period is described; its persistent monotony testifies, rather, to the fact that certain traumas that originated during the war continued after the war in the experiences with Poles and as a result did not require a new pattern of expression.

Dry, simple language is also used when positive memories are being reported, but this use requires a different explanation. Diana Mackiewicz-Rotberg (AŻIH 301/3076) describes her return home in the following words: "After the liberation, when I returned to Warsaw, Kifar was the first man who helped me. He lived in the undestroyed house at 43a Sienna Street; he was the chairman of the House Committee. He gave me a good apartment in this house, but I left Warsaw after six weeks. I left this apartment to Mrs. Guzek."

Mackiewicz-Rotberg was able to survive thanks to few heroic individuals, and she does not seem to have gone through the more gruesome experiences of the ghetto, deportations, executions, and the camps. Gratitude to her rescuers appears as a dominant theme in her account, but she narrates her neighbors' helpful deeds in a simple, factual manner as deeds to be commended, even rewarded.

Somewhat similarly, Miriam Koryska (AŻIH 301/2065), although a survivor of harrowing experiences in the Vilna Ghetto, focuses her account on the goodness of her rescuers: some who provided her long-term help with a place to hide, other anonymous helpers who provided her with short-term needs such as food and water or a way out of a house from which other Jews had been liquidated. She thus concludes her testimony: "After the Red Army entered Wilno [Vilna], while the bombardment was still going on, [our rescuer] took us to his shelter because in that situation he was no longer afraid that we would get anything unpleasant from his neighbors. We stayed with him for a whole month after the liberation. Mr. Cielecki, his wife, and his children showed us such care that we returned to our strength in a short time. At present, Mr. Cielecki lives with his family in Bydgoszcz, where he works at the head office of the railway company."

A perusal of the testimonies indicates that memories of such good experiences were rare among the survivors. Such memories are recorded in the simplest possible manner, using plain words to describe the actions of those who helped them.

This reliance on the simplest, commonest language corresponds to Berel Lang's assertion that the language of chronicles—mundane, dry, and factual—serves most accurately for describing the events and experiences of the Holocaust.[5] It is a linguistic canon to which traumatized individuals resort with frequency.

Rachel Weeping: A Lament

> A voice is heard in Ramah,
> lamentation, and bitter weeping,
> Rachel weeping for her children;
> she refuses to be comforted for her children,
> because they are not.
> —Jeremiah 31:14

Lamentation has been a traditional mode of prayerful response to catastrophes throughout the Jewish Diaspora.[6] Although it has been suggested that the lament as a literary form can no longer serve as a response to an event of such magnitude as the Holocaust,[7] it does appear to be one of the predominant styles the survivors employ in their testimonies.

The account given by Rachel Kosower (AŻIH 301/4418, reviewed in chapter 3) is quite unique among the testimonies as a whole and appears unequaled among other testimonies by women, which, in general, already seem more emotionally revealing than those deposited by men.[8] As Kosower's testimony attests, the women tended to pay more attention to noticing and naming their feelings and likewise tended to judge their surroundings by whether people around them were inclined to show them sympathy.

Felicja Markiewicz (AŻIH 301/4470), who with her son was held by a "rescuer" against their will, describes the period after the liberation:

> We couldn't walk at all. Lying in the attic for over two years, we [had] lost the habit of walking. This state lasted for three months. I took the child to the doctor. We were in a state of total exhaustion. I already knew that, apart from my husband, I [had] lost my parents, two brothers, and [my] whole extended family.
>
> I described here only in brief how we survived. And yet *this is only a little particle of what we have experienced.* Our Gehenna lasted three years: each day was a century, each day seemed [likely] to be [our] last. *It is impossible to give expression to these sufferings, this despair, this hopelessness experienced throughout the years. It is impossible to describe the continuous fear, the inhuman humiliation, the existence worthy of an animal. Still, today, I reflect during the nights on what I went through. It is difficult for me*

to believe that my little son, whom I fed with little seeds and ice and warmed with my own frozen body through three horrible winters, survived this. (emphasis added)

In the face of Markiewicz's declaration that it was "impossible to give expression to these sufferings," one may only attempt to imagine the extent of the solitude and human abandonment that were her daily bread by the war's end. Her hints at the despair, humiliation, and everything else she suffered depict a survivor who struggles to formulate expressions adequate to her sufferings and who revisits them nightly. The improbability of her son's survival—its absurd, almost surreal occurrence against all odds—and the fact that she herself finds it nearly unbelievable are emphasized by the paradox that it was her "frozen body" that "warmed" him. Markiewicz still mourns all the pains and transgressions visited upon her, her son, and her whole family; she attempts to name these transgressions, even while the one good thing remaining in her life, the survival of her son, appears unfathomable to her.

Although women in general were more open than men to expressing emotions in their testimonies, men sometimes also resorted to emotional, mournful language in telling their tales of hardship. It was most probably a man ("Jeremiah") who composed Rachel's lament (Jeremiah 31:15), a passage often cited as an expression of the universal human need to mourn the loss of loved ones, and it is often in the men's accounts that one may find the most moving laments in the survivor collections. Moszek Pantofel (AŻIH 301/2195, mentioned in chapter 3) creates a sort of historiosophical tractate in his testimony, deliberating on and assessing the "reasons" for the war and the persecution of the Jews. When he describes the end of the war, his tone renders this event nearly apocalyptic:

> Joy fills us, our hearts beat livelier. We are the witnesses of the defeat of our enemies, our oppressors. A battle takes place nearby. An hour of happiness is approaching; the madness of joy embraces us all. . . . Three days pass; the fighting goes around us. Three days of awe, three days of fighting, of joyful anticipation. The awaited moment arrives, the moment we have been waiting for almost six years: the moment we

are to regain our freedom. The words of the contemporary Nero have not been fulfilled—we are alive. The brave Soviet Army has liberated us from a heavy barbaric yoke, from a cursed slavery. It has pulled us from the mouth of a lion, [which] did not have time to swallow all of its victims. Twelve o'clock has struck for us—we remain, alive. I am returning to the [enjoyment of] the old human rights. To regain freedom after such resignation! At the last moment before the annihilation, to gain freedom, to be saved through justice! For our sufferings, for our pain, for our miserable life, we are receiving, unfortunately, too late a reward. The hunger [and] poverty are over; the thugs no longer can reach us. Now another question arises: Does our life still have any value for us without our closest, dearest creatures, without those who died for Jewishness?! Our life is and will be hard on the thresholds of our hometowns. *No one will welcome us; no one will lend us a hand. Ruins everywhere; our homes are destroyed. We are strangers in our hometowns.* Our wounds are incurable. Our tragedy continues.

Yet, in spite of all that, time will heal our pain; [it] will cure our wounds. We will live, we will work—that is what our destiny desires. We have remained yet a handful of witnesses of all that has happened here. (emphasis added)

Pantofel's testimony depicts the joy that the survivors felt at the anticipation of the end of the war, but he also describes how that joy would soon become tainted by the realization that no one would "welcome" them, that life as they knew it, including the entire Jewish world in which they had lived, had been "destroyed," and that no one appeared to care about their tragedy. Such ambivalent emotions surrounding the moment of liberation and its aftermath appear quite common among the survivors once they realized the extent of the destruction and of the non-Jewish population's general indifference and hostility toward them.[9] The lament "we have remained yet a handful of witnesses of all that has happened here" mourns for those who have been lost and reminds its hearers of the obligation to remember them and to teach about the destruction. The last paragraph of Pantofel's testimony, not translated here, speaks of a need to take revenge on the Germans and to bring about a new democratic order that will eliminate racism.

Another notable lament for the murdered Jews is found in the diary of "Dr. Michał Goldfein, Castaway." This diary is a unique document that merits separate treatment in comparison with another diary deposited in YV, so I discuss both more fully later in this chapter.

Silence and Absence

Most of the testimonies in the ŻIH collection (83 percent), as noted, are silent about the postwar reception of Jews by the local population. This silence is occasionally a deliberate choice that emphasizes what has *not* been said. Benedykt Münz (AŻIH 301/476), a sixty-five-year-old optician from Lviv who submitted his testimony on the official stationery of the Łódź Ghetto (bearing the header "Der Oberbürgermeister von Litzmanstadt")—thus inscribing his survival story under his oppressors' own letterhead—describes traveling to Warsaw after the liberation. The train trip from Kielce through Częstochowa was a horrendous experience for him; workers on the train tried to suffocate him and a few Jewish women with whom he was traveling. He ends his account with pregnant words that suggest a continuation, perhaps even an escalation, of such violence once he reached the capital: "On this I finish the description of my survival during the war occupation, not wanting to report further events in the very area of Warsaw."

Even more disturbing is the testimony of Feiwel Pistrąg (AŻIH 301/693), which, although it ends with the conventional statement "We remained in hiding until the liberation by the Red Army," is accompanied by an unusual and horrifying editorial addition: "A remark of the President of the Historical Commission: The witness Feiwel Pistrąg was, a short time after depositing the above account, murdered in his house by bandits!!" Thus, what appears to be a "standard" story of a survivor who *experienced the liberation* turns out to be both a witness's account of the war and an informal obituary announcing how he was "murdered . . . by bandits"—that is, by persons who were continuing a private war on Jews after the war ended.

One meaningful topic in the survivors' descriptions of the disappearance and absence of Jews after the war is the masking of one's Jewish identity in the postwar context. A strategy of social survival that many apparently adopted so they could start a new life after the war was to retain a Polish surname and to refrain from reaching out to the Jewish community. Such "borrowed" identities would occasionally be "returned," but eventually, in 1968, the Polish government took those borrowed identities away by stripping the Polish citizenship of those who elected to leave Poland in the wake of the antisemitic campaign.

Eugenia Ordower (AŻIH 301/3511) was nineteen years old when she deposited her testimony. She had spent the last years of the war in forced labor in Germany, where she had repeatedly attempted escape, with occasional, temporary success. Because she was underage at the war's end, she was placed in a Jewish children's home, but, as her account bears out, she was not happy with this arrangement:

> After a year [of working and living in Germany], I decided to go back to Poland and look for my relatives. I came to Koźle, to the Children's Home, which was distributing children to other centers. From there a transport of children was sent to Pawłów, and I was among them as one underage. I was in Pawłów three months, and I wasn't doing anything; my teeth, heart, [and] nerves were all sick. They were treating me. They sent me to Wisła for a rest. I went to the Amborski family because I had learned by letter from the teacher I was in correspondence with that my aunt was alive and staying in Bergen Belsen. I was nicely received by them [the Amborskis], so I started to visit them often. From them, also, I received the address of the aunt, and I started corresponding with her by letter. *I was not coming back to the Jews. I did not have the courage to admit it to my girlfriends because they were very open with me, and they talked badly about the Jews. I was going to school, studying bookkeeping. I still go there and play comedy in front of my friends; I haven't dropped the mask yet.* (emphasis added)

Trying to find her aunt and writing letters to the Department of Education to request help in leaving Poland to visit her aunt so that she would not be alone, Ordower kept her Jewish identity hidden from her "friends." This constant effort to be on her guard, to plan and to scheme, to invent stories that would match her assumed identity is as admirable as it is pitiful in the case of this young girl after the war. Surprisingly, she does not perceive her own resourcefulness: "Yet I am a Jew. I have lost completely my old independence—because I am not doomed to rely only on myself. I don't know—is it good? I have become inert." The hard work of bearing the suffering of hiding—this time more spiritual than physical—evokes a certain passivity, a kind of inertia, that leaves the survivor in an in-between state, waiting for change. In spite of her self-assessment, Ordower certainly did not appear "inert"; she appeared, rather, to be active in playing out a personal drama—a "comedy"—that she had to sustain in order not to suffer, not to lose "friends" who "talk badly about the Jews." The word *comedy* is suggestive of the tragic irony of her situation: she hid from her "friends" the very fact that she had to be hiding from her—*and their*—enemies, the Germans. To drop her mask during the war would likely have cost her life; now, after the war, it would cost her "only" her way of life and her "friends."

Zelman Baum (AŻIH 301/2425) describes in his testimony another intricate game of hiding that follows the pernicious forced marches of inmates from camp to camp in Germany and Czechoslovakia prior to the Soviets' arrival. At that time, while boarding a train bound for Poland, Baum attempted to learn something about his dear ones:

> Riding from Dziedzice to Sandomierz, I was inquiring in conversations with the Poles from central Poland about the situation of the Jews in Poland. . . . [In Sandomierz,] I stopped an inhabitant of Tarnobrzeg to [ask him to let me] ride with him. During our conversation, I told him that I was returning from a camp and I was from a village in the Sandomierz County. I told him that, nearer the border with Germany, one can still meet many Jews, but that I haven't yet seen one here. He answered me that there had been a small bunch of Jews here, but they all were finished off. He told me about a fact that took place in Klementów, where they had killed four Jews, even after the liberation. After that, I learned that in Klementów my cousin, his wife, and two acquaintances whom we had helped to hide during the German occupation had been killed by Poles.
>
> In Sandomierz, I got into the Hospital of the Holy Spirit as a Pole. Here I met a girl who was serving the sick, and I asked her whether there were any Sandomierz Jews left. I told her that I had been in a lager

with a Sandomierz Jew, who stayed in the hospital in Terezienstadt: he had asked me to write to him if anyone from his family remained. The girl told me that there was a Jewish Committee in Sandomierz, consisting of eight Jews; she told me their names. I pretended not to know any of them, and I asked her to let the Jewish Committee know that I have a message from a Jew (I invented a name there), and I asked for somebody to come to me in regards to that question. That same day somebody from the committee came to me. A nun let me go out with him to the garden near the hospital, where I talked with him. I learned from him that there was a partisan officer named Janek who would come here about the properties left by him in Sandomierz County and that he also knew that his [Janek's] two sisters, who had survived on Aryan papers in Germany, were back. I understood that these were my sisters and that Janek is my cousin. He didn't know their exact address because they had escaped from Rzeszów during the pogrom that took place there after the liberation. He was consoling me that he was expecting the arrival of Janek any day now in Sandomierz. The third day, my cousin came to me to the hospital. He took me, and together we went to Zabrze in Upper Silesia, where I met my whole family.

Baum's poignant, elaborate attempts to hide his identity and at the same time to extract some information about his people are indicative of the young man's impressive assessment of the dangers he was exposed to: he learned very quickly that he could not reveal his Jewishness in any circumstances at all, even those that appeared deceptively safe, such as a one-on-one encounter with a peasant or in the company of Catholic nuns. The narrative appears to withhold a collection of experiences that from the first moment Baum crossed the border to Poland and rode on a Polish train apparently taught him the necessity of covering up his Jewish tracks. Thus, we learn about Baum's unspoken experiences only by inference from his tortuous efforts to protect himself from coming to harm as a Jewish survivor.

Another gripping testimony, deposited by Gizela Pregerowa (AŻIH 301/2056), suggests the extent of the postwar continuation of the need to hide one's Jewish identity. Pregerowa's survival during the war was relatively unusual because of its uneventfulness: she managed to hide on the "Aryan" side, apparently without any threat of blackmail ("I managed to do quite well during the occupation," she writes). Only when she experienced sickness and became afraid of being buried with a Catholic rite did her fear move her to reassert her Jewish identity and to deposit her testimony: "Because I was still on Aryan papers, I was haunted by the ghost of Roman Catholic observance. I was afraid they would bury me as a Christian. During this sickness, I decided to stop that double life as soon as possible, and, still recovering, I came to Kraków, where the Jewish Committee took care of me very eagerly. I feel free here, and I am happy that I am finally among my own."

Pregerowa could have been one among countless Jews who chose to remain living under an "Aryan" identity and to keep their war experiences, their losses and traumas, to themselves. A testimony like hers allows us to catch a glimpse of the mind of a person who has finally decided to cross back over to her people and tell her story. Her testimony is suggestive of the possible existence of others who likewise chose not to reveal themselves as Jewish and would thus live out their lives without ever reconnecting to or even acknowledging their Jewish background and heritage.

A Tale of Two Doctors

I. "Dr. Michał Goldfein: Castaway"—a Lament

> It is as reasonable to represent
> one kind of imprisonment by another,
> as it is to represent anything
> that really exists by that which exists not.
> —Daniel Defoe, quoted in
> Albert Camus, *The Plague*

The diary of Dr. Michał Goldfein has been generally ignored in the literature. It records a fascinating odyssey that adds another layer of mystery to the story of Dr. Goldfein's life. This physician from Tarnów (a city forty-five miles east of Kraków), who apparently liked to put his mind at ease by writing in a notebook, began to write what would survive as his diary during Passover in 1939 and continued to write it throughout the war, with occasional interruptions that became progressively longer as the war dragged on. Throughout his travails, he managed to carry and protect this diary, even in the most dire circumstances encountered in the German camps. The diary was apparently found on him at his death in Paris in 1948 and was taken up by another Pole, the lawyer Dr. Jakub Herzig, who edited it and provided an introduction and explanatory final chapter, after which he deposited it in Yad Vashem under the Polish title "Rozbitek: Dr Goldfein—Wojenne dzieje lekarza" (Castaway: Dr. Goldfein—the War Story of a Physician) (AYV O33/195).[10] By discussing it here, I hope to present a deeply symbolic text of a "victim become survivor become victim," where certain crucial experiences of Polish Jews found an extraordinary exposition. I also juxtapose Dr. Goldfein's diary with that of another Polish Jewish physician, Dr. Julian Aleksandrowicz, whose war and postwar experiences encapsulate dimensions diametrically opposed to Dr. Goldfein's.

Dr. Goldfein began writing his war diary on April 4, 1939, the first day of Passover. He was at the time a well-known and well-established internist, with a loving family that included a wife, two young sons, and a small daughter. Already in his fifties, he looked back with pride on his service in the First World War, fighting on the Austrian side. He opened the diary with this sentence: "The last evening was very pleasant; for the sake of my occupation, however, I had to break the traditional ceremony unexpectedly."

His diary begins, then, with a tender recollection of the preceding evening, when his wife prepared the Passover dinner and he shared with his family a traditional Seder. Three elements that are typical for the whole diary appear already on the first page: first, Dr. Goldfein's loving attachment and devotion to his family, expressed in tender and at times sentimental language; second, his admiration of his Jewish heritage, with religious holidays understood not only in spiritual terms but also in generally humanistic terms: "The feast of Easter, the feast of Passover, . . . the feast of springtime awakening to the most exuberant life of nature" (2); and third, his total commitment to the duty of his work: "an honorable service for the good of humanity" (3) of which he is proud as a value found in Western civilization, to which Germans, as history proves, will have belonged only for a time.

The peaceful family Seder, during which Dr. Goldfein reads the Hagada and explains Jewish history to his children, is interrupted by the sudden sound of a doorbell. His little daughter asks with a smile, "Perhaps it is the prophet Elijah?" Marysia, the house maid, announces that someone needs Dr. Goldfein's assistance: it is Mrs. Larouge, the daughter of the attorney Rawski, his good friend. Mrs. Larouge, who lives permanently in Paris, is visiting her father, who has suddenly been taken ill. The appearance of these two women—Marysia and Mrs. Larouge—at the very beginning of the diary is of great symbolic and dramatic significance: they will play important roles in Dr. Goldfein's life after the war and even in the manner of his death.

The diary is frequently interspersed with didactic passages about the nobility of work and one's usefulness to society, observations that typically display the prewar Polish work ethic practiced by professionals and intelligentsia. On the occasion of the interrupted Seder, for example, Dr. Goldfein writes: "It is my habit to instill in my children healthy principles. . . . In the first place, one must fulfill one's own obligations, while family, relaxation, and holidays must take second place. . . . I noticed that my family and I became used to such surprises, and I praise God, in the first place, through my honest work" (3).

Dr. Goldfein recorded only three entries in the diary before the outbreak of the war. In the second one, the doctor reports with great pride that his oldest son, Józek, has passed his final high school examinations with distinction; in the third, he reports on an ominous episode that took place on August 15, 1939, in front of the old synagogue, where Jews were praying at the beginning of the new moon (Rosh Chodesh Elul). Apparently, a poor young Pole, whom Dr. Goldfein used to treat for free, looked at the Jews, who had just finished crying, "Shalom aleichem! Shalom aleichem!" (Peace be with you!), and admonished them facetiously, "Perhaps your prayers are honest, but you are praying badly. Your next new moon will be welcomed not by peace but by the fire of war!" An old Jew wagged his finger at the youngster and said, "Oy! You evil prophet!" and others who were gathered there called out, "Shaddai ishmereinu!" (Lord, protect us!). This sour incident left the doctor pensive and worried for hours: Perhaps, he mused, this young uneducated Pole has prophesied correctly?

The first diary entry after the outbreak of the war introduces a lamenting, wailing voice that will predominate from that point on in Dr. Goldfein's description of his family's misfortunes: "October 3, 1939. My head is heavy, my hand is trembling, and my brain is bursting when I am to describe my family's and my experiences during these last few weeks. Yet, I want to describe them, as it already relieved me, in my childhood, to spill out my thoughts on paper in difficult moments" (6). Here, as in other Holocaust diaries, the author begins to be aware of the disproportion between his need to record an experience and the insufficiency of language to serve that purpose. In the progression of Dr. Goldfein's life, this disproportion widens into an unbridgeable chasm.

Reporting on the development of the war and on the increasing German persecutions of the Jews, Dr. Goldfein also records facts and impressions that are common to other Polish Holocaust diaries: the bombardment of the town, the shock of German cruelty directed at Polish and Jewish civilians, and the writer's disappointment at the irrelevance of his or her own perceived contribution to the German culture (in his case as a physician on the Austrian side during the First World War). Observing the random killings of civilian Polish women, Dr. Goldfein quickly loses faith in what he had once admired in the German nation: "It's an illustration of the whole culture," he tells his wife, before adding, "Once I had trust in German culture, but the deeds of Hitler and his National Socialist band give little hope for illusion, very little hope, and our peaceful life has apparently passed away" (9). After such despairing statements, Dr. Goldfein would yet often find solace in religious expressions: "Everything is in the hands of God!" (9).

In September 1939, Dr. Goldfein records a dream in which a little, grotesque figure of a devil with Hitler's face dances menacingly around all the members of the family before finally kidnapping Dr. Goldfein's eldest son. The dream is so vivid and disturbing that the doctor goes to check to see that everyone is safe. Unfortunately, this dream proves prophetic: a few weeks later, while the Jews are gathered in the synagogue, the

Germans defile and destroy the holy scrolls, beat and humiliate the praying Jews, and separate the young males from the rest of the community before taking them out to be shot on the outskirts of the town. In spite of the Polish municipal authorities' attempts to intervene with the German command, the young boys are killed and left to be buried by their fathers. Dr. Goldfein describes the shock of the community on hearing the news, the people's cries, and the tearing out of their hair, and so he concludes the first part of his diary: "My ominous dream from the night came true: the devil prepared for us a true Judgment Day" (12).

From that moment forward, Dr. Goldfein's reflections turn to himself, to undeserved punishments, and to the rhetorical, unanswerable question "*Why*?" "On that day I lost my firstborn. Happiness and peace have gone out of my house forever. That day, I asked myself the question for the very first time, the question has been coming back to me since, more and more often, and with more and more strength: Why? Why has this happened? And why has it been happening, that which, since that day, has been dealing us a death blow? A question thrown into the vacuum. Neither can I find an explanation for it, nor can anyone else ever answer it for me" (13).

After that first blow, Dr. Goldfein's narrative describes the declining situation of his family in more bitter and desperate ways. We learn about his discussions with other local Polish intelligentsia, discussions that cannot change anything but provide a semblance of normal participation in developing events. We read about the growing terror directed at Jews in town and the community leaders' hopeless attempts to stave off the persecutions. We encounter Dr. Goldfein losing his comfortable apartment and medical office to a spiteful Nazi physician. We find his Polish maid, legally forced to leave his family, taking with her three suitcases filled with family treasures for safekeeping. We note the family's move to the ghetto. Finally, we witness the doctor's excruciating separation from his wife and daughter when they are forced onto trucks and sent to their death at Belzec and his anguish concerning his younger son, who disappears, taken for "labor," until he is murdered in Auschwitz. With each incident, the tone of Dr. Goldfein's reflection descends lower and lower, circling frantically around his inability to think himself out of his cycle of despair: "It is better not to think, not to analyze. But can we overcome the intrusive thoughts that thrust themselves upon us, that thrust upon us our pain and our sense of wrong?" (23).

As the Nazi noose tightens, the entries in the diary become sporadic. After two and a half years of silence, Dr. Goldfein writes in April 1942: "I am falling down with my family lower and lower. I am trying to think as little as possible, to remember as little as I can—and therefore my notes in the diary are becoming rarer. The present day shook me deeply, and therefore I feel the need to describe it, although I do not know whether anyone will ever read this description" (23).

What moves Dr. Goldfein to write again is one more case of superfluous violence in the Tarnów ghetto and the death of a fellow physician as part of one of the Germans' murderous feasts. After Dr. Goldfein loses his family, his reflections continually question the meaning of his further existence—the theme that will dominate his thoughts from this point forward. After another long silence, lasting about fifteen months, he resumes his diary, in November 1943, with a description of his experiences in the camps at Szebnia and Buchenwald. There he manages to survive in spite of his defiant, careless attitude toward his oppressors, in part because he fortuitously cures the camp commandant's daughter of an illness (he is called in to treat her as a last resort, after her German doctors have pronounced her case to be hopeless). His war account ends with the news of the death of his younger son, Marek, in Auschwitz; upon hearing of it, Dr. Goldfein faints.

What follows, then, is Dr. Herzig's report of another physician, a camp inmate, "Dr. S.," who tells him about finding Dr. Goldfein upon the liberation of Buchenwald. Dr. Goldfein is apparently found lying in bed mute, motionless, barely responsive, looking like a skeleton staring off into space. He weighs eighty-three pounds. The American delegation is shocked; Dr. Goldfein, whom his liberators have by this time learned was once a famous internist, will be paraded around as an example of the most horrid biological and mental degradation that the German war effort imposed upon human beings. After two months of gradual recovery by intravenous feeding, Dr. Goldfein is ready to leave the camp. "Dr. S." completes his report: "It is unbelievable! Dr. Goldfein has recovered over two months; he has put on some weight and some strength, has taken on some work, and has become the chief doctor from the end of June, helping inmates—now freed—in a very active way. He left the camp at the beginning of August, with the intention of returning to Poland" (49).

On August 30, 1945, Dr. Goldfein begins the third part of his diary, titled "Again in Tarnów." In this section—most relevant to my research—he describes his journey in a Soviet truck, which drops him off one day in the center of his hometown:

> My nervousness, caused by the fact of being in Tarnów for the first time after the war, took all my strength. I therefore had to lean strongly on my cane. I was walking slowly and as if dimmed. I was moving as if in a daze, not quite realizing what was happening to me.
>
> When I cast my eyes at some shop window, and when I saw my figure there, I became frightened of myself. Dressed in some old military coat, . . . I looked like a walking embodiment of misery.
>
> Not paying attention to my surroundings, I passed an elegantly dressed, young, blond girl standing in front of a book store, busy in a conversation with a soldier.
>
> Soon she ran after me, and, having stopped me, she threw out her arms in desperation, wailing over my looks.
>
> I could not recognize that woman, and I said that she must be mistaken, taking me for someone else.
>
> In reply, my conversant expressed astonishment that I did not recognize our Marysia. I looked at her more closely, and only then did I recognize her. In fact, it was difficult to recognize her. Once a brunette, she is now a blond; once, she used to dress up very modestly, and here I had in front of me an elegant person in silks and a hat. (52–53)

Marysia, formerly his family's Polish maid, becomes his guardian angel, helping him to settle in Tarnów and providing all sorts of useful information as well as material resources, including the contents of the three suitcases left to her during the war for safekeeping. Her grip on the Jews' situation ironically turns out to be even sharper than Dr. Goldfein's. She strongly encourages him to move to Silesia, where it is relatively easy to find an apartment and office space and where the surroundings are safer for returning Jews. She likely has her own family's concerns at heart when she offers to move there with him and help him settle. Although Dr. Goldfein feels "used up" and "useless," Marysia keeps telling him that he "might still be useful to the world, only he should forget the past" (55). Of course, the past cannot be forgotten, as Dr. Goldfein reports in the diary: "The losses I have gone through one can never forget. There is a fire burning in my head, sorrow and pain are weighing heavily on my heart—and this emptiness around—all this is a state I cannot stand, and I would rather die" (55).

Marysia does not give up; her energetic faith in the doctor, combined with her practical sense and abilities to deal with people and business, finally convince Dr. Goldfein to allow himself to experience a new beginning: "This whole meeting with Marysia and her plans surprised me so suddenly and unexpectedly that I could not concentrate my thoughts. It has been a long time since I have met someone who would show me so much warmth, and that touched me."

This resourceful young woman represents in Dr. Goldfein's narrative a true light of hope and renewed life that very few Jewish survivors appear to have encountered upon returning home. Being quite independent and helping her former employer for what appear to be completely honorable reasons (there is no insinuation of anything romantic or improper about their relationship), she assists Dr. Goldfein in his "return to life" simply out of gratitude and inherent goodness: "She reminded me that she came to our house as a nearly illiterate peasant girl, and she didn't know anything, and she was treated by us like our own child, and she grew up to be a human being" (55).

Having discussed the matter with his colleague and with his diary—"What connects me today with Tarnów? Probably only memories that awaken pain and bitterness" (57), Dr. Goldfein decides to move to Katowice, a city in Silesia. He concludes his decision with an ominous remark, which closes the third part of his diary:

> And if the experiment fails, if I don't manage to create for myself a minimum of peace, then it will probably be time to finish with oneself.

> After the return to Tarnów, limitless desperation took over me; the nightmare of memories burns me, but I will try. Perhaps I will manage to overcome myself, and not to give up.
>
> To be sure, I doubt it very much if I manage to go with the living ones. I cannot escape from Tarnów, but to forget about all that I have survived, about what once was, and to throw a curtain on blows dealt me by fate, by evil beasts, by Germans—No! That I cannot do!
>
> That is certain for me.
>
> My thoughts, my memories will go with me! (57)

Immediately following the third part of the diary, Dr. Herzig interjects a longer comment. He writes about Dr. Goldfein's virtues, his fame as an internist, and his great personal humility. He points out that this diary, although not having much literary value, might be of therapeutic value—continuing the professional work of the physician and curing "the most fashionable modern disease: the coma of the human conscience." This diary "goes out into the world as a voice of an ordinary mortal, a little man, but as a voice of man to man in the most noble sense of the word" (57a).

The fourth part of the diary, titled "In Katowice," begins on February 5, 1946. It describes Dr. Goldfein as a well-established and widely respected physician living in a large, comfortable apartment with Marysia, who makes all of the practical arrangements. He finds himself so well occupied with his professional affairs that he is able to "think less about the past" (59). Things seem to be going well for Dr. Goldfein to the extent possible: he has a growing group of grateful and adoring patients, who even publish an article about him in the local daily out of gratitude for his services, which he often renders without charge to the poor. Nevertheless, darker moments approach. On one occasion, a youth barges into his waiting room and berates his patients for using the services of "Kike doctors." Although the patients defend him, Dr. Goldfein experiences a flashback to the war, which deeply shakes him. Suddenly all the disappointments in human nature and all of the anger at human stupidity revealed again after the catastrophe erupt. In the subsequent entries, Dr. Goldfein reports with bitterness on the return of anti-Jewish violence, on the murder of a

Jewish colleague in Katowice, and on miraculously avoiding a killer right there in his office. Even Marysia is terrified and helpless. The only thing she is capable of recommending to him is that he flee abroad. Realizing that she might also otherwise be exposed to violence, Dr. Goldfein agrees to escape in a truck that will take him to France. The last passage written while the doctor is still in Poland reads,

> And so I am going into the unknown, but somehow, instinctively, I feel that my end is already coming. After all of my experiences, I am no longer capable of life's struggle. I feel it! And this, my present journey, will be—it seems—yet a failed attempt to start again a new life.
> No!! To tie again the broken thread of my life, I have no strength! But what can one do? One has to go on. I have nothing left to lose. So the will of God is happening! (65).

The returning use of an expression of resignation bordering on fatalism, the "will of God," ties this passage to Dr. Goldfein's first disappointments during the war. The language of the account seems inconsistent but in some ways may be biblical (reminiscent of Psalm 22). After exhausting an emotional range running from despair to anger to disappointment, the author returns to resignation and even consolation in the hands of God in such an easy, conventional way that it may not appear convincing to the reader.

The fifth and final part of the diary, titled "The End of the Journey: Paris," begins on June 2, 1946. Dr. Goldfein describes his futile attempts at starting a new life: "I have been in Paris for a week now. I cannot say that I live anywhere. I am roving" (67). His affairs are unraveling; he lacks sufficient money to exist, especially after being robbed, and the experiences he has of the survivors' support agencies are disappointing. He has little or no strength to fight the French bureaucracy, and begging for the means of subsistence fills him with self-loathing. It appears fundamentally transparent that he misses the care of someone loving, someone like Marysia, who takes an interest in his own survival. He appears to feel lost within an endless stream of survivors, calling to mind Hieronymus Bosch's sad depiction of a wounded humanity:

A true Tower of Babel! And everyone embittered, nervous, and unhappy.

Jews and Jewesses, men and women, juveniles and fledglings, children, children's carriages, pregnant women and cripples, and everywhere a crowd, a throng, squeezes and rambles. In a word: a kaleidoscope of Jewish poverty and the misery of homeless pariahs.

Each of them wants finally to stand in front of the officials giving the handouts, and everyone is impatient. (68)[11]

Dr. Goldfein also appears angry at what he perceives as the excessive and misplaced care of those Germans who have been afflicted by the effects of their own war: "And today's world? It, with some exceptions, has today one large collective care: properly to aid and feed the poor Germans, the innocent poor, who were seduced by Hitler! What irony! They receive a bonus for murdering, or for causing the death of 33 million people!" (68).

In his diary, Dr. Goldfein feels mostly incapacitated by being unable to practice his profession: his Polish medical degree is useless in France, and it would take him years to get it notarized, whether in France or in the United States, where some of the refugees have headed. He does not believe in the possibility of moving to Palestine—"The British government is looking for more and more hurdles to prevent us from going there" (69)—or to South America—"There they receive Catholics, mostly, and I don't want to leave under a false mask" (69). Finally, he observes,

> I have lost everything but honor, my character and good name. I will go to my grave with them.
>
> Coming here, I was under the illusion that maybe I could find work and some peace here, but I am slowly losing my illusions. I am losing the rest of my will to live.
>
> I used to be known as a good diagnostician. Now I am giving myself the diagnosis: it is time to finish this wretched life. My end has come. This is my diagnosis!
>
> I will put off my final decision for several days, but I doubt in any possibility of a positive change. But I am not thinking of vegetating here as a beggar. That has been decided. (69)

Dr. Goldfein makes his final diary entry on June 6, 1946. It is on this day that in an unusual encounter he comes across Mrs. Larouge, whom he last saw on that memorable Passover day in 1939. She does not recognize him at first. She is living comfortably with her architect husband in a beautiful apartment in the center of Paris. She shows him a letter from her father, Mr. Rawski, written before his death during the war, in which he expressed that he still missed Dr. Goldfein's friendship and therapeutic abilities. Dr. Goldfein records in his diary that "Dr. Rawski was a noble man, and his daughter is like him" (70). A strange twist of fate has given Dr. Goldfein another angel and another chance: Mrs. Larouge offers him a room in her apartment, and she is willing to help him procure his emigration papers. Dr. Goldfein, however, does not wish to be a burden on anyone. In this final entry, he finalizes his credo. He had formerly been an optimist; he had never given up on patients who had received deadly diagnoses. He would countermand the judgments of other physicians and return his patients to active, healthy lives. Then the German bandits murdered his family and robbed him of all his possessions. Just when he was beginning to recover a normal life again, another set of bandits, this time Poles, threatened his life and robbed him of his peace. He still has his diploma and his profession, but he cannot use them in his current situation:

> The result: I have no reason for being. It is a very clear and simple calculation!
>
> I am a realist, and I judge a situation without embellishment, as it truly is, as it is in reality.
>
> I think I have already drunk my cup of bitterness to the full, to the last drop. Such a cup of bitterness, drunk to the full, is a deadly poison. Still, a thought is coming over me that my life is, as if, a trace after a candle, of which the flame has gone out forever.
>
> I have lost all will, and I have no strength to overcome difficulties. And, in fact: What do I have from life? What does the world have from me, and what do I have from the world and life?
>
> I am ending. To express myself more strictly: I have reached the conclusion that I have to finish myself off! (71)

Thus ends Dr. Goldfein's diary, written in his own hand.

What follows in the archived manuscript is the account of several witnesses of his extraordinary death, compiled by Dr. Herzig. The account begins with a curious statement given by a graphologist "beyond a shadow of a doubt" that the writing of the last entry testifies to a decisive will to end one's life: "Some letters resemble a grasp of a revolver, while others a posture of a corpse" (71). Next comes the account by Mrs. Larouge, whom Dr. Goldfein visited on Friday afternoon, June 7, 1946, the day after he wrote his last diary entry. According to Mrs. Larouge, he was very upset and nervous, apparently on account of being mistreated by some young official in a relief agency. Mrs. Larouge again offered him a room in her apartment, but he did not want to hear about it, and so he decided to leave. Mrs. Larouge wanted him to stay longer because her husband was about to come home, and she hoped that the three of them could come up with a plan for Dr. Goldfein's future. After some hesitation, Dr. Goldfein sat down again. "Some evil spirit, apparently—as Mrs. Larouge expressed herself—inspired her to ask Dr. Goldfein if he would like to listen to the radio. Dr. Goldfein, in an apathetic state, nodded his head in agreement" (72).

Unfortunately, Mrs. Larouge's good intentions proved futile: during this "fatal broadcast," as she would later call it, the song "Mein Judische Mame" came on. Although performed in French, it brought painful memories to Dr. Goldfein. Listening, he

> broke off from his chair, caught his head in his hands, and, shaking it, said hollowly: "I also had such good Jewish mother once, and my wife was also such a good Jewish mother. How beautifully Ordonka used to sing it in Polish before the war"—and looking far away, as if in the far future, spoke softly, getting out his voice with difficulty—"We used to admire that song and when it was broadcast, my wife would sit near the radio, the children would stand near her, and all of the company would listen to the transmission in a state of concentration."
>
> Dr. Goldfein was trembling all over. Yet the broadcast that day was still persecuting him. After "Mein Judische Mame," the speaker announced a new song by a famous artist, called "Life's Castaway." (72)

This song, "Life's Castaway," tells of a man returning to his hometown to find his dear ones dead. It curiously embodies the sorrowful emotions of the survivors in Poland, for whom "nobody waits any longer" and to whom "nobody sends letters." The last stanza goes:

> There is no you, no you, oh!
> I look and search for nothing.
> You will not come, I will not see you.
> who has died, does not come back, oh no!

After this song finished playing, a strange change came over Dr. Goldfein. He shrank into himself, and his face took on a painful grimace. His eyes wandered, and he sputtered disjointed words: "Oh! Oh! This is my song! . . . This is—I, this is—I who is this castaway! Yes, this is I! I! . . ." Mrs. Larouge tried to calm him down, but he nervously tread the room and wanted to leave to get some fresh air. In spite of her admonitions to wait, he left.

Later, Mrs. Larouge read about his death in a newspaper.

In the next account added to the diary, a man witnessed the strange behavior of an individual he later learned was Dr. Goldfein. Dr. Goldfein stepped into a street busy with speeding cars, carrying a leather briefcase. According to the witness, when a policeman brought Dr. Goldfein to the sidewalk and asked what he was doing, Dr. Goldfein muttered words such as "I wanted . . . I had. . . ." The witness offered his help. Dr. Goldfein agreed, and so the man accompanied him on a bus ride, after which he observed him from a distance. Dr. Goldfein's last moments were on another busy street: he hesitatingly approached the street, threw his briefcase aside, and jumped in between the speeding cars, causing his death. A policeman and another older gentleman, who identified himself as a doctor, confirmed Dr. Goldfein's death. The contents of the briefcase included several papers, among them a letter to the prefecture in Polish, which the witness (either the man who helped him on a bus or the doctor—it is not clear in the testimony) translated. The letter reiterated Dr. Goldfein's desperate situation of being robbed of his family, his home, his possessions, and his profession; it complained of the world's callous attitude toward the Jewish survivors and of the British restrictions on efforts to regain a Jewish homeland. It ended: "I have nothing to live for, and, therefore, I die as one more victim for the glory of the world and the pride of twentieth-century culture. Michał Goldfein, once a doctor."

This extraordinary document seems to be an example of a diary that assumes high literary value without aspiring to it consciously. Lawrence Langer, in his influential work on the kinds of memories revealed in Holocaust testimonies, juxtaposes written narrative and oral narrative: the former "is finished when we begin to read it, its opening, middle, and end already established between the covers of the book. This *appearance* of form is reassuring (even though the experience of reading may prove an unsettling challenge). Oral testimony steers a less certain course, like a fragile craft veering through turbulent water unsure where a safe harbor lies—or whether one exists at all!"[12]

Langer's perceptive conclusion may refer to postwar documents through which the survivors attempted to make sense of their lives and reinterpreted their wartime experiences to create a relatively continuous narrative (even while, as Langer proves in his analysis, the deep, anguished, humiliated, tainted, and unheroic memories continuously threaten a more wholesome and consoling reintegration of the survivors to society). The situation of a diarist is unsettlingly different: he does not create a reassuring narrative; the unfolding events of his life create the narrative for him. Amos Goldberg calls such an incursion of "real life" and its shaping power into a diary "synecdochical writing." In such diaries, which are usually shorter (tens of pages) than the documentary ones, "the story is of the way the whole (historical catastrophe) operates on the small part (the writer and his immediate surroundings). In many ways the synecdochical view is the authentic one of the victim whose main interest is survival."[13]

Such diaries reflect, in their content as well as in their literary form, the crushing events of history, which the diarist tries futilely to describe and thus in some way to possess: "The importance of the excess expressed in these chaotic texts," states Goldberg, "increases precisely because something essential to the event of trauma is inscribed in that excess, namely an essence whose ungraspable character eludes any disciplined articulation."[14]

The life of Dr. Goldfein depicted in this diary exemplifies such excess: events encroach upon style and dictate the rhythm of its entries. The narrative resumes when the author regains his life fluency (in Katowice, for example, where he is able to work again) and breaks off in spasms when his situation truncates his ability to rebuild his existence. It is a living document that ends when the life itself ends.

The symbolic power of the events at the beginning of the diary reveals itself at the end: the document is framed by Dr. Goldfein's relationships with what one might refer to as two female "guardian angels" who open the war chapter of his life and close the postwar chapter. Marysia, an uneducated domestic, practically saves him from his own inertia as well as from those violent Poles who still hunt Jewish survivors. She inspires and practically arranges his move and sets up his new practice in Silesia. Under her pragmatic care, Dr. Goldfein is able again to find meaning in his life through his productive work—the only value still left to him after the loss of his family. Unfortunately, Marysia cannot rescue him from the Poland of his direct experience: this Poland does not want Jewish doctors anymore, and this Poland will get rid of them, whether they are needed and appreciated or not. Marysia cannot protect him from her own compatriots, with whom she had collaborated in the Underground against the Nazis. Her human care can go only so far. After that, this Poland—the antisemitic Poland—will banish Dr. Goldfein into the hostile world.

Whereas Marysia practically organizes Dr. Goldfein's return to life after the war, Mrs. Larouge encounters him probably too late and provides him with fewer resources. Although educated, relatively wealthy, and well established, she offers Dr. Goldfein merely a place to stay and the possibility of discussing his future with her husband. She does not act as his active rescuer, and she does not step in to arrange things for him, as Marysia is able to do. If we can imagine, for a moment, a French version of Marysia, we might envision a woman who knows her way around the refugee aid agencies, who might organize emigration papers for him to some other country or, at least, some semilegal way of regaining his medical practice. We must bow to the real Marysia, who truly saves Dr. Goldfein the first time around. Were he able to stay and work in Silesia, instead of being forced to leave it because of antisemitic attacks, his life and its meaning might to some degree have been saved.

The tragedy of Dr. Goldfein—and that of Poland—is that Marysia cannot save him the second time; she cannot save him from the murderous antisemitic seed that was planted in the Polish population during the war and then exploded in growth after it. Dr. Goldfein, who to some extent survived the Nazi Holocaust, is finally crushed, eliminated by the reception he receives in his home, Poland. He is the victim turned survivor turned victim again.

II. Separating Fiction from Fact

While researching this unusually poignant diary, I came across a publication by Dr. Herzig, who edited and submitted Dr. Goldfein's document to YV, entitled *The Wrecked Life: The War Story of a Physician*.[15] It turned out to be a version of Dr. Goldfein's diary beautifully translated into English but this time presented as a "novel" by Dr. Herzig. With that startling discovery and subsequent digging, I came to the conclusion that Dr. Goldfein's diary should be classified as a work of fiction. In fact, it was originally written in Polish by Dr. Herzig in 1947 while he was living in France and then forwarded by his wife to YV in 1959; she described it as "a drama written in Polish."[16] Dr. Goldfein's diary, then, was misplaced among a collection of "authentic" diaries. To confirm my impression, I corresponded with the YV archivists, who were apparently unaware of the fictitious character of "Dr. Goldfein's diary" until I alerted them to it. I also talked by telephone with Dr. Herzig's son, Adam H. Herzig.[17] It was indeed a mistake to include this manuscript—what is in fact a "novel" about "Dr. Goldfein" by Dr. Herzig—in the YV archival collection of "authentic" Holocaust diaries.

My initial disappointment about the apparent ineligibility of this source for research on Holocaust testimonies, however, eventually led me to formulate a challenging question concerning the heuristic value of interpreting "authentic" as opposed to "fictionalized" personal documents for the study of Holocaust experiences. Varying degrees of fictionalization take place in all documents, of course, including documents that consist of personal testimony. The latter type of documents may range from "true accounts" expressed in an author's natural voice to novelized but still authentic accounts, fictionalized diaries and memoirs, stories based on composite characters but authentic experiences, and, finally, utter hoaxes.

In fact, in one of the most famous controversies over the veracity of Holocaust literary fiction, it was debated in the 1980s whether Jerzy Kosinski's work *The Painted Bird* should be classified as a fictionalized memoir or outright fiction or even a plagiarized account.[18] The author's attitude and his claim of having written an autobiography produced an extremely controversial reception of the book. A comparison of the book with the known circumstances of Kosinski's childhood discloses that he could not have experienced hiding at the home of a Polish peasant in the way described in the text. With the establishment of that discrepancy, the book must be read as having a different truth-value from that of a literal account.

A separate issue is that of an author's willingness or unwillingness to admit definitively that a work is fictional. D. G. Myers elaborates on this issue in a review of a biography of Kosinski: "Although he backed away from this claim [to autobiography], Kosinski never wholly disavowed it. He described the book as an 'auto-fiction,' explaining that it 'draws upon a childhood spent, by the casual chances of war, in the remotest villages of Eastern Europe.' Although it is not 'easily justified,' he said, it is nonetheless 'convenient' to classify *The Painted Bird* as nonfiction."[19]

In contrast, we could situate in the "middle" of the range of veracity ascribed to Holocaust personal accounts Ida Fink's stories that describe the lives of composite characters who experienced real events of the Holocaust.[20] And then there are the fake Holocaust diaries. A most notorious example of this category is Bruno Dössekker's (Bruno Grosjean's) discredited work *Bruchstücke: Aus einer Kindheit*, published under the assumed identity Binjamin Wilkomirski.[21]

A subordinate question arises here: What defines an author's natural voice? When dealing with people of little literary training and limited language competency, it is relatively straightforward to determine whether their accounts represent what they have experienced. With authors of a more advanced educational and literary potential, the matter becomes more complex because such persons are capable of assuming, by choice, a symbolic but nonetheless adequate vocabulary and style for rendering their experiences. In the situation of an author of proven literary ability or of one who simply has time to write and rewrite his account, the matter is quite difficult: this person's account might be the most interesting and poignant but may also contain elements or aspects that are embellished, imagined, or otherwise fictionalized.[22]

In the case of the account written by Dr. Herzig, his son, Adam, confirmed to me that "Dr. Goldfein's" diary is in fact a fictionalized account based on what his father and his father's brother-in-law, a certain Dr. Goldman, experienced. The protagonist, "Dr. Goldfein," is therefore a composite character; the novel describes the author's (Dr. Herzig's) personal history as well as events experienced by his close relative, Dr. Goldman. One may further presume that the events from Dr. Goldman's life were relatively well known to Dr. Herzig.

Dr. Herzig wrote and eventually published "Dr. Goldfein's diary" as a novel. A mistaken assumption by an archivist—understandable considering that Mrs. Herzig sent the manuscript to YV without any explanation of the manuscript's provenance—seems to have created confusion in the document's categorization, allowing scholars to take the account at face value as an "authentic" diary. Further research, of course, could have revealed the truth, as it did for me, but a researcher can be excused for taking such a spurious document for an authentic one, at least initially. The presentation of what is really a novel as an autobiography—that is, as fact, not fiction—not only in its title but also in its archival designation can test the integrity of an entire system of scholarly inquiry. The dangers of such a situation are clear. Yet the ambiguity here can serve as an occasion for further reflection on the possible value of some fictionalized accounts.

Philippe Lejeune, in discussing differences between autobiographies and autobiographical novels, sustains that "if we remain on the level of analysis within the text, there is *no difference.*"[23] However, some literary scholars claim that a diary novel employs such distinct patterns and literary devices that it should be obvious to a skilled reader that he or she is dealing with an authentic or inauthentic autobiographical text. Trevor

Field, for example, defines a crucial difference between fictional and real diaries: real diaries are "dependent upon chronology and the events of the outside world for their ultimate effect, while . . . [fictional diaries] are shaped according to varying amounts of logic and aesthetics."[24] In other words, a novel has an organizing principle or plot, and to distinguish a fictional diary (novel) from a real diary means to reveal the former's pretense at artifice.

Here, however, we encounter something of the difficulty in categorizing the text in question. As demonstrated earlier, the "diary of Dr. Goldfein" follows its narrator's life trajectory. Symbolic elements, such as the two women framing the narrative, the "prophetic" dream, and the portentous interaction between Polish youth and elderly Jews might plausibly also be explained as fitting in the mysterious and unexplainable occurrences of an extraordinary life. If one takes into account the placement of the "diary of Dr. Goldfein" within a collection of diaries without any pertinent editorial comments, the conundrum experienced by an unsuspecting researcher becomes evident. The listing of Dr. Herzig as the one who collected and submitted all of the pages of the "diary" as well as the reports of the witnesses of the protagonist's death might also arouse some suspicion. However, such "editorial presence"—to use Field's term—in collecting the accounts of various witnesses to the death of "Dr. Goldfein" may likewise seem to lend credibility to the assessment of the document as indeed authentic.

The published version of the diary is presented as a diary novel, a work of fiction. Consistent with the genre of the diary novel, the "extended" editorial presence in the published document—for example, Dr. Herzig provides a preface to the work, which is conspicuously missing from the archival manuscript—manifests a more literary work and seems to be intended as a consciously mimetic tool. According to Field, "the tendency for real diaries to be prefaced by an introductory note of some kind means that such features naturally increase the level of mimetism."[25] The preface continues the game of deception that one is reading a "real" diary when it explains that the diary has been "somewhat edited and supplemented."[26] This comment furthers the conventional illusion that the author's name inscribed on the cover, "Dr. Jakub Herzig," is merely the one who discovered and salvaged the unique manuscript of a Holocaust victim, but the text itself is the work of "Dr. Goldfein."

In the diary novel, as the German tortures of the Jews intensify, the text presents "Dr. Goldfein" as succumbing to despair and eventually, in reaction to his postwar inability to find his place in life, to suicide. Several—presumably reliable—witnesses confirm his unbalanced state. The narrative as a whole is what Lorna Martens, discussing diary novel techniques, calls "the expressive mode" of writing. By an accumulation of anguished expressions, this mode evokes the reader's sympathy with the victim's plight.[27] The confirmation of the protagonist's victimhood does not disqualify him as an unreliable narrator; rather, it confirms the reasonableness of his suicidal response. This response is presented not as a pseudoexistentialist escape from absurdity but as a response to the psychological divestiture of any meaningful justification for continued existence—once enough points of reference (family, occupation, calling in life, friendly surroundings, country, city, sense of home, and, finally, the fundamental awareness of one's own dignity) have been called into question. The few positive turns in fortune that punctuate this perspective for "Dr. Goldfein" eventually add to his sense of futility at the deepening awareness of the systematic nature of a moral evil that continues to assault his life—destroying prospects, crushing hopes, and leaving him profoundly alone. If considered from this perspective, the diary appears to be a rather straightforward lament written in first person: a double tragedy of a man who survived hell on earth only to have his second chance at life brutally torn asunder. It is a reworking of the story of Job, a tale of cruel fate: a solitary man survives disaster; God inscrutably withdraws, ignores the biblical script, and scuttles the man's future along with his past.

In considering whether to ignore this document in my analysis or to include it, I concluded that it can be judiciously considered the approximation of an internal story written by a sympathetic individual who was also a survivor from Poland. Dr. Herzig knew the original protagonist, Dr. Goldman, well and combined the latter's experiences with his own. With that caveat, the use of this composite document in the present research may be justified, if only for its powerful expression of the plight of innumerable Jewish survivors who could not find a place to rest and live again in peace after the war and for its illumination of postwar Polish–Jewish interactions that did indeed occur. "Dr. Goldfein" represents those silent witnesses—embodied in Holocaust literature by Tadeusz Borowski, Jean Amery, Paul Celan, Primo Levi, and even Jerzy Kosinski—who could not recover from the loss of a world that formerly embraced them. The unique value of this diary is that it describes the emotional downfall of a survivor who was ultimately crushed not so much by the Holocaust itself as by his postwar reception by Poles. It is from this perspective that this "diary" may be considered Dr. Herzig's lament for all survivors whose spirit was broken by a postwar continuation of the murderous intent against Jews.

With these caveats in mind, such an account of a survivor who committed suicide after being expelled from Poland, where he had found some semblance of life's meaning in the performance of his work, may constitute a necessary contrast and background to other testimonies in which the authors chose different paths. In particular, such a contrast can be found in the experiences of another physician, whose account I describe in the next section.

III. Dr. Julian Aleksandrowicz—an Existential Manifesto

Dr. Julian Aleksandrowicz, prominent professor of medicine, scientist, and philosopher, is well known in Poland and internationally recognized among scholars, especially in the field of hematology. Among other achievements, he investigated the characteristics of the anticoagulant heparin, invented a substance that reinforces immunity in patients with blood disorders, and patented a mechanism for the extraction and conservation of blood, which popularized blood donation. He published several dozen important medical textbooks, several hundred scientific articles, and many popular books on ecology, ethics, and preventive medicine. During the war, he founded one of the three hospitals in the Kraków Ghetto; after the war, he founded several prestigious medical institutions, among them the world-class Kraków Clinic of Hematology. Through his mentoring of several generations of prominent Polish doctors, he is also considered the founder of a famous school of hematology.

Dr. Aleksandrowicz was a person ahead of his time. He promoted ecological preventive medicine before anyone else was demonstrating any awareness of it. For example, he initiated research on elements in soil and food and was the first to notice a connection between magnesium and leukemia. His active mind was constantly thinking of improving people's lives, and some of his ideas were simply early concepts of inventions that we now consider common: solar panels, bicycle lanes on city streets, and low-emission cars in cities, for example.

Dr. Aleksandrowicz is also known for having developed concepts of comprehensive psychotherapy that encourage the creativity of people suffering from somatic diseases. He urged his patients to write, paint, and express themselves in various art forms. Perhaps his most famous patient was Halina Poświatowska, a young woman suffering from heart disease, who continued writing and publishing poetry thanks to his encouragement and is now recognized as a significant poet of the twentieth-century Polish Parnassus.[28]

Born in 1908 to an assimilated family in Kraków, where he lived most of his life, Aleksandrowicz graduated from the Jagiellonian University in 1933 with a medical degree. During the Polish 1939 September campaign, he served in Poland's Seventy-Second Infantry Regiment and was later imprisoned in the Kraków Ghetto. Always concerned about his research, he managed to bury his research data and was able to retrieve them after the war. (The Pole Józef Adamski, who aided Dr. Aleksandrowicz in the ghetto, was eventually caught and beaten to death by a Polish policeman. He was posthumously awarded the title "Righteous among the Nations.") In 1943, Dr. Aleksandrowicz managed to cross over to the "Aryan" side, and he became a physician in the AK in the Kielce-Radom region under the Polish nom de guerre "Doktor Twardy" (Doctor Tough). Eventually becoming a platoon leader in the resistance, he would receive the highest Polish military award, the Virtuti Militari medal, as well as other awards, including the Cross of Merit with Swords and the Cross of Valor.

Dr. Aleksandrowicz writes in his testimony that he jotted down his diary fifteen years after the war and sent it in the same year to YV, asking whether YV might be interested in publishing the diary in a Hebrew translation—either as a booklet or as a series of newspaper articles. The diary was filed in the collection of memoirs and diaries (AYV O33/190). Although it was deposited in YV and is now included in that collection, I consider it a document that really belongs with the Polish collection, for it was created in Poland, and it concerns the experiences of a survivor who remained in Poland.

Dr. Aleksandrowicz's diary is entitled "Kartki z dziennika doktora Twardego" (Pages from the Diary of Doctor Tough); it was later published in Poland in 1962 as a book with the same title, which has been reprinted three times.[29] The title indicates that Dr. Aleksandrowicz meant to emphasize the most noble aspects of the Polish culture to which he belonged and that he felt he represented. It also suggests that his diary consists of a selection ("pages") of a larger quantity of notes taken during the war.

"Doktor Twardy's" deposition begins with a short note "From the Author" in which he assures his readers of the veracity of the described events: "The stories that I am placing in the hands of a reader constitute authentic events that were abundant in the life of a physician existing in Poland in the middle of the twentieth century." The author then continues, with the same clinical perspective,

> I looked at the people of this period with the eye of a naturalist. I observed how the period was shaping their characters. I saw the reactions of different individuals to similar impulses. I perceived a rich scope of their actions, from heroism to extreme degradation. Many reflections were born out of these memories. Today, after fifteen years, an overpowering need to write them down was created. They do not have any literary ambition; they merely constitute a nonpretentious registration of the facts and a naturalist's attempt to summarize the results of an observation.[30]

Dr. Aleksandrowicz places himself in the position of an outsider, an observer. He is the scientist researching human characters and "reactions." From his observations and reflections, he is able to distill a proper treatment. For man, the patient of the future, his prescription is rather moral and ethical:

We shall see how easy it is to make an evil man out of a *Homo sapiens*. Hitler's scientific educational method achieved it. We shall see also that in order to make a good man out of a human being, it is not enough to feed him on some humanistic philosophy or religion. Biological similarity, and not a declared idea, determines a man's attitude. I saw the most beautiful humanistic attitude in people of similar character, similar dynamic stereotype, therefore in people similar biologically, even though they differed in their opinions of the world. . . . Only based on the knowledge of this psychophysical essence may we realize that mutual kindness among people is a condition of a successful evolution of the species *Homo sapiens*. Kindness is a most powerful factor that prevents not only many nervous diseases of individuals, which destroy their hearts and brains, but most of all the tragic social disease, which is the mutual destruction of human beings, caught up in the passion of hate, which, as a consequence, leads to a collective psychosis: war. (intro., unpaginated)

Dr. Aleksandrowicz embraces the category "kindness," its simplicity and ability to be grasped by ordinary human beings, as the ultimate panacea for humanity's madness. It is rather characteristic that this view resonates with the moral precepts recommended by other great minds and unique personalities throughout history: Jesus of Nazareth, Albert Schweitzer, Janusz Korczak, Mahatma Gandhi, Tenzin Gyatso (the fourteenth Dalai Lama of Tibet), and many others.[31] It also bears resemblance to a school of ethics developed by another prominent Polish (Gentile) scholar, philosopher, and artist, Tadeusz Kotarbiński. Kotarbiński's ethics of reliability (*spolegliwość* in Polish) proposes "nobility" rather than "goodness" of behavior. Such a nobility draws one to care for other human beings, to work joyfully and disinterestedly for their moral development, and to provide help when it is needed. Kotarbiński called his system "independent ethics," for it was built independently from theological beliefs. Although he believed in the norms of Judeo-Christian ethics ("love of one's neighbor" was, for him, the ultimate expression of "reliability"), he concluded that once religion loses its binding power, so will religion-based ethics. He therefore strove to disassociate his ethics from religious grounding.[32]

In Dr. Aleksandrowicz's account of his wartime peregrinations, he depicts his imprisonment in the ghetto and his wanderings in search of shelter as the inevitable lot of a humiliated human being—a Jewish lot, deprived of the dignity of resistance against an inhuman ideology that refuses to acknowledge certain groups of persons as human. When he was in this humiliated state, there were people who helped him, and there were those who betrayed him. Dr. Aleksandrowicz professes his admiration for and faith in his family's rescuers, one of whom, Józef Adamski, a bricklayer, lost his life delivering packages of food to the imprisoned doctor. The members of the Adamski family risked their own lives to keep Dr. Aleksandrowicz, his wife, and his son alive during part of the war.[33] The doctor heaps praise on their heroism and so allows us to approximate the meanings of his otherwise rather elusive terms *biological similarity* and *kindness*:

> During the occupation, during the greatest degradation of the human species, I regained faith in man. Faith and conviction that if in our society only 15 percent of people think with the categories of the Adamskis, it is worthwhile to live and walk in their pathway, as much as the possibilities allow. It is worthwhile, and one should walk in the pathway of the true wise men—that is, the people who find the meaning of their lives in caring for other people. (68)

When circumstances allow Dr. Aleksandrowicz to join the partisans and to fight the Nazis, he experiences a fuller return of the humanity of which he felt robbed as a Jew. He presents this national-patriotic attitude as rescuing his dignity:

> The year 1944 comes along. I spent it in the Świętokrzyskie Forest in the service in the partisan divisions. A sad period for the nation arrives. The Uprising [Warsaw Uprising of August 1944] fell. . . . Although I do not know where will I put my head tonight, and I do not know if there will be enough food, *I have a good feeling. I have regained my abused dignity; I have fulfilled my duty; I live by the desires and problems of the nation. My maltreated image of the frightened, hunted man with wild eyes, who slips past under the walls, belongs to yesterday. Today I look into people's eyes*

with courage. I am no longer alone. I have my war companions. I have friends I can count on. For betrayal or blackmail—a shot in the head. I have my avengers. (68–69, emphasis added)

In this eloquent fragment, Dr. Aleksandrowicz juxtaposes his fearful and humiliated Jewish self of the past to the free man liberated by a Polish fighting ethos and military comradery. Nationally, he identifies himself as a Pole whose people have just lost the uprising. He is no longer like most of the few Jewish males who managed to survive until that year: "frightened, hunted [men] with wild eyes who slip past under the walls." His abused dignity has been redeemed through his service to save Poland. The doctor is surrounded by like-minded partisan companions, but, just in case some of them turn out to be less "like-minded," he is ready with "a shot in the head." The noble ethos of the Polish Underground, in which justice did finally catch up, in March 1943, with the blackmailers who would hunt and denounce Jews in hiding,[34] nevertheless becomes his own. Dr. Aleksandrowicz becomes the embodiment of this ethos as he leaves the darkness—and the humiliated ghosts of the Jews in hiding—and joins the light—the clandestine yet widely acknowledged and respected world of Underground Polish fighters. The passage from darkness to light is aided by the Adamskis and others like them—that "15 percent" of the Polish population that care about other human beings in danger and are even heroically willing to put their own and their families' lives at stake for a somewhat controversial moral value (as putting one's family in mortal danger to save another human being should be understood). Dr. Aleksandrowicz sides with the noblest Polish people, adopts their attitudes as a standard for his own behavior, and refuses to allow the ignoble or indifferent remainder—the 85 percent?—to affect his choice. He does not allow bitter feelings to change his evaluation of what people such as the Adamskis have offered to him and other Jewish Poles: the greatest sacrifice.

Dr. Aleksandrowicz's choice, however, comes at the cost of a rejection of something else. What he unwittingly leaves behind as he embraces the glorious life of a partisan is the way in which the Jews were dying: the dark, shameful way in which, like hunted game, they were being caught and pulled from hiding places; the massacres of nameless inhabitants, who are swallowed up in the uniformity of death in the ravines; the anonymous, suffocated bodies deprived of life and identity in gas chambers. This "Jewish death" is well described and contrasted to a "Polish partisan death" in Władysław Szlengel's poem *Two Deaths*:

> Your death is a death by bullets
> For something . . . for a country;
> Our death is stupid death
> In a garret or a basement.
> Our death is like a dog's
> In a corner of a street.
> Your death comes with decorations
> And communiqués;
> Our death is wholesale death.
> They bury you—and good-bye.
> Your death—face to face
> You meet in the open;
> Our death is hidden death
> Buried in a mask of fear;
> Your death an ordinary death
> Human and easy;
> Our death is a garbage death
> Jewish and—vile.[35]

Dr. Marek Edelman—the only surviving commander of the Warsaw Ghetto Uprising who remained in Poland—expressed a similar attitude in a book-length interview by Hanna Krall. He comments on the death of Krystyna Krahelska, a prewar poet and the model for the mermaid statue that has become a symbol of Warsaw, who died during the Warsaw Uprising of 1944 while running through sunflowers:

> What a beautiful life and a beautiful death! This is the only way a person should die. But this is the way beautiful and fair people live and die. The dark and ugly ones die in an unattractive way: in fear and darkness. . . . The dark and ugly ones, sapped by hunger, between humid sheets, wait for someone to bring them oats cooked with water or perhaps

something from the garbage can. . . . In the streets, their children tear packages right out of pedestrians' hands in the hope that they might find bread within; they devour everything immediately. In the hospital, children swollen with hunger receive half a powdered egg and one vitamin C tablet each day—this has to be distributed by the physicians because the ward attendant, who is also swollen, cannot handle the torture of the distribution. . . . At 18 Krochmalna Street a thirty-year-old woman, Rywka Urman, chewed off a piece of her child, Berek Urman, twelve years old, who had died of starvation the day before. . . . Death by starvation is as unaesthetical as is the hungry life.[36]

"Unaesthetical" and full of shame—that is the death that Dr. Aleksandrowicz is spared so that he can manage to redeem his fate by his own patriotic service for Poland.

"Doktor Twardy's" diary, then, appears to be a work of reconciliation with a better, brighter way of living and a better way of dying. The diary is his reassertion of the noble ideals of the Polish culture; one aspect of that culture might have failed man, but another aspect gave man hope. Science properly ordered and directed, a therapy of the whole human being that encourages that being's individual initiative and creativity, and, above all, human kindness are what Dr. Aleksandrowicz salvages from the shards of our civilization. Like Dr. Victor Frankl, who chose to respond to German violence with his own decision to find existential meaning in his sufferings and thus reasserted his dignity by an immanent act, and in a different way like Primo Levi, who revisited Homer and Dante on the way to fetch soup in Auschwitz and thus reclaimed his humanity, Dr. Aleksandrowicz draws new life from humanistic sources.

During the war, however, when "Doktor Twardy" redeemed his *abused dignity* by joining the partisans, his sacrifice and allegiance to the patriotic Polish Underground were constantly being threatened and called into question. His life, in fact, hung by a thin thread of deception. In testimony given by Salomon Reis (AŻIH 301/1791), Dr. Aleksandrowicz appears as Reis's rescuer when an Underground unit arrests Reis and his companion simply because they are Jews and threatens to take their lives. Thanks to the protection provided by the doctor and a lieutenant whose nom de guerre was "Huragan" (Hurricane), the two Jewish wanderers survived but were forced to leave the unit, as Reis describes in his testimony:

> The soldiers told us that we owe our lives only to Huragan and the doctor because if it weren't for them, we would have been dead a long time. At four o'clock, there was a meeting, the order was read, and we two Jews were commanded to leave. Then this doctor from Huragan's group went with me some five hundred meters into the forest and said good-bye to me; he kissed me, gave me a few thousand złoty, and said that I should know that his name is Dr. Aleksandrowicz and that he comes from Kraków. In case he fell, he asked me to tell his family. At the end, he told me: "My soll sich zejn in Erec Izrael." He also asked [me] not to tell anybody that he was a Jew because they would certainly kill him.

Dr. Aleksandrowicz spoke in Yiddish when he said, "My soll sich zejn in Erec Izrael": "We should see each other in the Land of Israel"—probably a version of "Next year in Jerusalem!" If that is, indeed, what Dr. Aleksandrowicz was wishing for in this statement made in a "secret language" (Yiddish), if he had to hide his Jewishness from his own comrades-in-arms in order to be able to survive, how tragic does his postwar statement sound, that he has "fulfilled his duty" and that he "lived by the desires and problems of the nation"? What a transformation, what a choice in identity, had to occur for him to pass from being a Jew hiding both with and *from* the Polish Underground, fulfilling his patriotic duty, to being a postwar Pole embracing that same Underground's patriotic ideals and excising those feelings that kept him in hiding, all the while wishing for life in Erec (Eretz) Israel.

After the failure of the Warsaw Uprising in 1944, the doctor returns to Kraków a changed man: "Thoughts are crowding under my skull: To whom am I going? What for? To endanger the living? With what will I go? . . . Who am I, finally? I have a different face today, a different psyche. My old style of thinking is lost irretrievably somewhere in the forest. Even my vulturous nose is upturned today" (71).

Dr. Aleksandrowicz goes into hiding again, this time as a member of the Underground capable of defending himself with a gun hidden smartly in a hat. From his hometown, he walks directly to Wieliczka, where his family is being hidden by the Stefanik family. He is able to join his wife, his son, and his grandmother, who for the sake of security, he notes, are "wonderfully trained. They manifest astonishment or joy only with gestures, like the mutes." However, after the joy of this short reunion, the doctor cannot remain in hiding any longer:

> What is to be done now? I will not stand it for long. A stuffy, small room. The old lady does not allow us to open the window. There will not be any room for a fourth person . . . possibly under the bed. Where are you, fresh forest air? I survived ten long days with my dear ones *in this unusual form of existence*. . . . It was uncomfortable, hard, and stuffy under the bed. *It was not the soft moss of my forest's bed.* . . . I held out until the tenth day. I ran out of the hiding place [*melina*] *the same way I got into it. The same day I reported* [for duty] *at the disposal of the commandant of Wieliczka and Lieutenant T. Hanula, four days before the order was issued.* (74, emphasis added)

Dr. Aleksandrowicz ends his memoir as a loyal Polish soldier. He cannot stand living in hiding ("in this unusual form of existence") in circumstances that, despite being uncomfortable, included an opportunity to stay with and defend his family and the safety of being able to count on reliable rescuers—circumstances that would have been relatively enviable for other Jews deprived of a hideout.

The doctor's diary, in the end, points to his identification with the patriotic ethos of Polish culture. He chooses to embrace the aspect of the culture through which he is able to work constructively and to be appreciated as a prominent specialist, and he does not mar this image with any uncomfortable memories of those who would have demanded that he leave the Polish Underground. His expressive silence on his return to Kraków after the war may indicate a will to eradicate any marginal recollections that could disturb his adherence to the representatives of the Polish crème de la crème.

Dr. Aleksandrowicz seemingly rejects the disturbing fact that his comrades-in-arms—the bearers of the ethos that he chooses as his identity—would just as soon be rid of him if they were to learn he is a Jew. The statement "My soll sich zejn in Erec Izrael"—a hushed-up, quickly whispered confession in Yiddish to another Jew on the run—leaves the impression of a nib of memory expressed in a secret language, moving against the current of a carefully built edifice of appreciated integration into the world of Polish culture. It is also a testimony to an unfulfilled dream to find rest in another reality, which Dr. Aleksandrowicz calls "Erec Izrael."

IV. Conclusion

The two doctors' diaries give expression to two kinds of survivors' experiences in postwar Poland. The first, represented in "Dr. Goldfein's diary," embodies the exit route of most of the survivors who either found themselves in Poland or returned there but then left again upon encountering violence or reports of violence. Many of these survivors managed to find meaning and relative integration in the societies to which they eventually moved, whether in western Europe, the Land of Israel, or the United States. Many, if not most, tried to do their best, often for the sake of their children (both those who survived the war and those who were born after the war), and so they lived outwardly well-adjusted and high-functioning lives, even while reliving the horrors in their interior lives. Relatively few of them could not cope with the traumatic memories and the impact of the past upon their present lives; these lost lives ought rightly be added to the list of the 6 million murdered during the war.

The second kind is represented by Dr. Aleksandrowicz, a case of successful integration into postwar non-Jewish society. Admittedly, there are some cracks in his narrative and even a rejection of disturbing memories (exhibiting what Langer might term a "humiliated" memory[37]) that might have been expected to make Dr. Aleksandrowicz realize that the society to which he belonged was willing to accept him only conditionally as a uniquely talented physician. His life was, at its most profound level, a donation, a free gift for the benefit of those who were in need of healing. By ignoring and even silencing his memories of those who lacked "kindness," while focusing instead on those who sacrificed their lives to save him (for example, Józef Adamski), Dr. Aleksandrowicz could transcend the small-mindedness of those who objected to his Jewishness, rising above their petty cruelty by performing a service for them and their compatriots. One might call such a return heroic; one might surmise that it was not typical for the majority of survivors, much less for the majority of people in general.

Both diaries were written by highly cultivated, literary men. "Dr. Goldfein" expresses himself in mournful, sometimes sentimental language that focuses on his emotional trauma and his inability to continue living. Dr. Aleksandrowicz offers a sage's reflection on human nature and describes a stoic perseverance in fulfilling his patriotic and humanitarian duty. "Dr. Goldfein's diary" is a lament written by a survivor about other survivors; Dr. Aleksandrowicz's diary is an existentialist manifesto that strives, as Albert Camus puts it concerning his character Dr. Rieux in *The Plague*,

> [to] state quite simply what we learn in a time of pestilence: that there are more things to admire in men than to despise.
>
> None the less, he knew that the tale he had to tell could not be one of a final victory. It could be only the record of what had had to be done, and what assuredly would have to be done again in the never ending fight against terror and its relentless onslaughts, despite their personal afflictions, by all who, while unable to be saints but refusing to bow down to pestilences, strive their utmost to be healers.[38]

Israel, Twenty Years Later

In Israel, the survivors' memory went through an evolution facilitated by the new state's ideological leanings. It was also influenced by the natural processes of time, aging, and the social character of Israel that affected the survivors' adaptation into its society. Individual memory assumes a unique shape that escapes social generalization. Communal memory that is shaped by an event, however—particularly by an event of catastrophically traumatic proportions—can be subject to a unifying change that forms part of a community's shared experience.

The questions asked by the researchers in the Yad Vashem Department of Testimonies imply an expected narrative. The YV questionnaire is almost identical to the ŻIH questionnaire, with two exceptions: the former asks more numerous and detailed questions concerning the survivor's prewar life and the prewar Jewish community in which he or she lived in as well as more questions referring to liberation and postwar life in Israel. An important part of the YV interview was devoted to the survivor's move to and arrival in Israel; the survivor was to describe extensively his or her life, family, and work in the Land of Israel. The end of the interview was reserved for the topic of rescuers in case there was a story to tell of an individual or individuals who had contributed to the survivor's rescue. This last section concerned possible contacts with these rescuers and testifies to one of the main purposes of collecting the testimonies beginning in 1963: to facilitate the conferral of the title "Righteous among the Nations" to deserving rescuers.

As in *yizkor bikher* (memorial books),[39] in testimonies collected in Israel the prewar period seems generally to be somewhat idealized, possibly providing a contrast to the fact of destruction; the testimonies frequently claim that Jewish and Polish communities lived like "one, big, happy family" before the war and that it was only the war that introduced social breakdown. Not surprisingly, the postwar period is treated in a vastly greater proportion of testimonies in the YV sample than in the Polish sample (61 percent versus 17 percent), but this proportion also indicates that nearly 40 percent of the accounts are silent on the issue of postwar contact with Poles. Considering that the theme of Polish hostility could have been exploited for the sake of a Zionist narrative, such a frequent silence may appear surprising and may suggest a need for further research. In this section, I present the typical narrative styles of the Israeli testimonies.

Story of Escape or Story of Arrival: Antisemitism and Zionism

A preponderance of the Israeli testimonies that form the data set for this research creates a narrative of exodus from Poland after the war. The characteristic feature of this narrative is the continuity of a patented prewar antisemitism that intensifies during the occupation and further explodes after the war, forcing survivors to flee Poland. Such accounts tend to summarize events into monolithic situations, often avoiding the details or focusing only on those details that support the exodus paradigm, before finishing with an expression of satisfaction upon arrival—that is, a version of "I am here, now." Most of the testimonies in this grouping share implicitly, at least to some extent, in the Zionist premise of the need to create one's own land for survival.

Rather atypical for a condensed Zionist narrative is the already quoted ending of the testimony submitted by Irena Lisikiewiczowa (AYV O3/2657): "When I came out, I was afraid, more than during the German times. Nobody welcomed us; the atmosphere was very unfriendly." In those two succinct sentences, Lisikiewiczowa gathers the world of emotions and experiences probably most common to other survivors from Poland: a new kind of fear of Poles in this postwar context—a fear of their indifference or potential hostility. Without factual details, the testimony communicated to other survivors what was already known to them and what therefore did not require much more than a hint.

More typical, however, are longer descriptions of postwar anti-Jewish hostilities and violence. Although these testimonies do not often contain particularly vivid details of the events, they do summarize their conclusions: the perceived need to react to the violence by moving away. In other words, they enumerate and multiply the reasons behind the escape, building a case against Poland, against eastern Europe, and against the Diaspora in general.

In Jakob Perelman's testimony (AYV O3/1790), for example, five pages—one-fourth of the entire deposition—are devoted to describing his postwar experiences of Polish antisemitism. Perelman's wartime actions were motivated by a fear of getting caught by the Germans, of course, but also increasingly by a fear of those overzealous Poles who chose to support the Germans in their policies of annihilation. In a wartime labor camp, Perelman managed to pass as a Pole among other Polish workers. He continued the deception when he joined the labor unit Stargard in Prussia, where he "befriended" other Poles: "All of them were antisemites; often they would say that they would like to catch a Jew; then they would show him."

At that point, a great danger loomed for Perelman: the appearance on the scene of a former school "friend," Szczepański, who tried to denounce him to the Germans. Mustering all of his resilience and talent for deception, Perelman managed to convince Szczepański—and everyone else—that Szczepański had made a mistake assuming that Perelman was a Jew. Perelman goes on to describe the denouement of this drama: "Szczepański and I became friends later, and he confessed to me that he had been helping the Germans to catch the Jews [and] that he had been searching for money and gold in the clothes of the murdered. . . . I knew enough about him to be able to get even with him, but before the Russians arrived, he disappeared." When the Russians finally did arrive, however, Perelman and his brother did not reveal themselves as Jews because "we were afraid of our friends, that when they learn that we are Jews, they would kill us."[40]

Back in Parczew, his hometown, Perelman experienced several attacks on the small community of survivors; he also reports on a generalized atmosphere of fear among them. Here it is helpful to return to a passage quoted in chapter 5:

> In Parczew, there were up to a hundred Jews then who survived in the camps and forests. Not all of them came from Parczew itself: there were some from surrounding towns and villages; they were afraid to live where there were few Jews. *Our lives were temporary because we saw that we were still being persecuted by the Poles; here and there, a fact happened of a murder of a Jew. All of us wanted only to liquidate our property, to get back what was possible, and to leave the town, which was a cemetery for us in any case.* . . . All Jews living presently in Parczew kept very friendly relationships among themselves; we kept together in this hostile world. (emphasis added)

After multiple, violent attacks against Jews by the Polish population and by members of the AK and NSZ (which Perelman describes in great detail, while also noting the behavior of the occasional, helpful Pole who was willing to defend the Jews), Perelman liquidated his property and left for Germany, where he stayed another three years in the DP camp in Lampertheim. In 1949, he arrived in Israel.

After such frequent brushes with death both during and after the war, Perelman's satisfaction at having arrived in Israel comes through emphatically in his telling of these experiences. His interviewer, Ida Gliksztajn, makes this satisfaction explicit in the comments she appends to the deposition, a procedure that was typical for those conducting survivors' interviews for Yad Vashem. Writing her addendum in a more dramatic present tense, she summarizes the postwar violence in Poland: "Jewish survivors want to liquidate their property, to take away what is possible, and go to Israel." In his testimony, however, Perelman does not state that the survivors intended to "go to Israel." According to him, the survivors returned to Parczew "only to liquidate our property, to get back what was possible, and to leave the town, which was a cemetery for us in any case."

Although it may appear obvious from Perelman's account that the survivors intended to leave Poland, the goal of their emigration is *not* specified. In a similar way, regarding Perelman's leaving Europe and coming to Israel, Gliksztajn, the interviewer, asserts: "Jakob Perelman stays three years in a camp in Lampartheim; after that he arrives on June 24, 1949, on the shores of the free fatherland." Once again, "the shores of the free fatherland" appears nowhere as the object of Perelman's longing: this expression and others like it represent the license taken by the interviewer to interpret the antisemitic reality of postwar Poland in a way that supports Zionist rhetoric.

In another example of an apparently implied Zionist narrative, Kopel Berman (AYV O3/2566) describes his life after the war:

> In this way, we awaited the end of the war, and on January 17, 1945, the Soviet troops liberated us. After the liberation, we returned to Wołomin. I started to work and to earn [money]. More Jews arrived—about thirty people, and we were thinking about rebuilding the Jewish community in Wołomin. After several months we received an anonymous letter from the AK that if we should wish to stay alive, we should move out immediately. We decided to leave Wołomin. All of the Jews, with the exception of two doctors, one of them a Dr. Frank, who had a Polish wife, and the other a Dr. Reznik, who had been baptized, left for Łódź.

I started to work there, and somehow I managed there. From the very beginning, I tried to leave Poland. In 1949, I received permission to go to Israel. We arrived in Israel at the end of October.

We settled down in Tel Aviv, where I work as a watchmaker in my own shop. My daughter married in Israel; her name is Lubochiński, and she already has two children.

Details of Berman's postwar existence—how exactly he returned to his hometown, whom he encountered, how he came to work, and the like— are apparently not important enough to be mentioned. The important memory in his testimony is the "anonymous letter from the AK" and his claim that "from the very beginning" he "tried to leave Poland." It is impossible to assess how accurate his memory of his wish to leave Poland was, although it is significant that he did try to rebuild "the Jewish community in Wołomin" and was able to settle twice in Poland—first in his hometown and again in Łódź. It seems questionable that he had indeed tried from the very beginning to leave Poland, but it does appear that when an opportunity presented itself, he did manage to go to Israel. What seems most important in the last paragraph quoted, as in many other Israeli testimonies, is an emphasis on the continuity of a family's life: although the daughter lost her family's name, she "married in Israel" and "already has two children."

Through such juxtapositions and addenda, the narrative of antisemitism in Poland, with its implication of a necessity to leave, is shaped into a narrative of arrival at the Land of Israel and of the Zionist rebirth of generations in Israel. In other words, although the testimonies are filled with believable descriptions of persecutions and murders, they do not, within the exodus narrative, necessarily point to the Land of Israel as a promised land. Israel was only one of the places the survivors went to, and there were many accidental reasons—sometimes as bare as the impossibility of immigrating to a European or US state of their choice— that aided or even determined the decision to migrate there. Once one was in the Land of Israel, however, the narrative was clearly transformed to emphasize that one saw Israel as the intended end from the very beginning. As exemplified, this kind of transformational work was done by both the interviewers of the YV Department of Testimonies and the interviewed survivors themselves.

Trying to Be "Happy through Tears," or On Loneliness

In some testimonies, what dominates is a need to "arrive" emotionally—that is, to present a relatively complete and healthy image of oneself. In such testimonies, which seem to belong exclusively to women, no matter what kind of neighborly reception the survivor may have received after the war, she attempts to overlook the experiences so as to start a new life, whether in Poland or in Israel. This style of ending a testimony is rather a complicated version of the first kind of narrative—that of the exodus toward Zion. It is a feature of these accounts that although striving to present a positive outcome of a survivor's postwar life in Poland and of the act of immigration to Israel, they appear unwittingly to reveal a greater sadness and solitude on the part of survivors who were making it on their own.

A typical example of such a narrative, Anna Sawicz's diary (AYV O33/639), written in Poland, ends in 1945 as follows: "At long last I lived to see the liberation. I became a free, liberated person, but what of this happiness to me if I am all alone in the wide world and all my dearest ones have died! Only now, after the liberation in 1945, I recognized my solitude; yet one needs to live!" After her immigration to Israel, Sawicz adds the following words to her testimony: "The year, 1949. I am already in Israel, and I live in Haifa in Bejt-Olim Bat-galim. It is hard to live here; perhaps I will describe this period one day. Yet I am happy to be already in our land, where I will wait to see a better life." It is almost impossible not to feel Sawicz's loneliness and even despair as she experiences them at the moment the war is over. Her apparently wishful thinking after the move to Israel, however—her naive hope that she will "see a better life" in her "own land"—sounds like a fearful exorcism of the prospect of the future unhappiness and solitude that many survivors continued to experience well after the end of the war.

In a similar though more complex, more elaborate manner, Ida Jarkoni (AYV O3/3060) tries to make sense of the atmosphere in Poland that induced her to leave a prestigious position as a teacher and move to Israel, where she was unable to find a proper place for herself. To put her memories in context, Jarkoni describes how a Jewish soldier in the Red Army warned her, when she was liberated, to be careful about revealing her identity: "I did not yet know that one should still play one's role as an Aryan, that the Polish population keeps persecuting the survivors who are coming back out of the forests and bunkers. I had to stay in Sławinek, for in Lublin I could have met someone who had known me before the war."

Jarkoni managed to rebuild her life: she took care of her daughter, remarried, worked part-time for the CŻKH, studied, and taught economics. Her years working in a technical high school, she writes, "were my best years after the war." In 1956, widowed for a second time, she visited her sister, who had lived in Israel since 1950. After one month in Israel, Jarkoni decided to move there with her two daughters and to start her life over. She makes no mention, as a possible reason for her decision, of the widespread antisemitic incidents in Poland before the Polish October (October 1956). Instead, she contrasts her professional status in Poland with the difficulties of being an unknown immigrant, a "nobody" in Israel: "The period of acclimatization was incredibly hard for me, on account of my not knowing Hebrew, and because of the completely different conditions in which I found myself. In Poland, I was independent. I was a person of status. I had a designated place in society." After a few failed attempts to find adequate work, Jarkoni became an interviewer for the YV Department of Testimonies. She ends her account by mentioning the achievements of her daughters, who were more successful than she in adapting to the difficult demands of life in the new state.

Although postwar Polish hostility certainly came to the fore in Jarkoni's testimony, she somehow managed to live under the protection of the Communist state and the state-sponsored school, to find fulfillment, and to be satisfied with her life in Poland. Something must have changed in 1956 that made the thought of emigration from Poland attractive to her. But her move to Israel was not undertaken without ambiguity, and she lived there in some respects against her will and ambition, continuing to miss the position she had held in Poland. Although Jarkoni is direct in speaking of her disappointment, it is clear that she takes pride in the achievements of her children, who, she implies, will be more able to achieve high positions in society and should not find themselves threatened by any discriminatory policies.

The Memory-Box, or What Is Happening

The most striking feature of survivors' memories of the time after the war, alongside many testimonies' silence on the postwar period, may be the unusually vivid detail and coloring of events, as though they had taken place in a very recent past.[41] Omer Bartov has coined the term *memory-boxes* to designate testimonies that "have all the freshness and vividness of a first account that one may find in some early postwar testimonies. This can be explained not least by the very fact that memory of the event was kept sealed inside the mind and never exposed to the light of day through telling and retelling."[42] Langer has termed the recollection of past events with unusual detail a narrative "in medias res"—as if the event is being recalled from the middle of its occurrence.[43]

Cwija Fuks (AYV O3/3782) narrated her postwar experiences in Poland in just such a vivid style, as if she were recording them immediately after the event, resorting to the occasional use of original Polish utterances transcribed in Hebrew characters in testimony written in Yiddish. After the liberation in August 1944, Fuks returned to her hometown, Sterdyń, where she remained with her brother. She received a friendly warning from a former classmate, who told her that "the war on the Jews was not over yet" and that she should not reveal the name of anyone who might have hurt her or stolen from her during the war. If she did, the AK might kill her. To this warning, Fuks responded: "Kruza, we will remain to live. God did this; he should take upon himself the grievances of the innocent blood that is being forgotten. I will not betray anybody." In her testimony, she then continues with her account of other Jews' return to the town:

> Someone has already let it be known, so that the whole town "was alive with the news," that the first two Jews were coming back.... My brother was a very well-known man, a sound member of society—strong, muscular ... so when he came to the *sztetl*, [they said]: "Haskel came from the

mill. . . . Haskel came from the mill. . . ." It was a great sensation in the *sztetl*; it got to the Russians. A Russian, who probably had the duty as the town commandant, said to my brother, "Brother, come here and tell me what the Poles have done here, whom they have killed."

"Oh," said my brother, "I was told that our war is yet not finished. I have so many troubles; there were so many death penalties; I looked in the eyes of death and remained alive. Why should I now leave the world? They should fall into other hands."

"No," says he, "You must tell: What has the commandant of the [Polish] police done here?"

The blue police had collaborated with the Germans, and they had murdered quite a few Jews. And he gave a few names. I don't remember the names, but I remember the Jews of the town. I had all of this written down. It got to the Christians, and it started; they wanted to kill us all over again. This time it was the Poles. At the time . . . the mayor of the town, Kryszak—he is a very fine man, he studied . . . and was not an antisemite; he was an egalitarian Christian—came to my father and told him: "Panie [Mr.] Rozenbaum, it is very hard to get the words of my mouth, but you have to leave the town, because there is conflict and a bloodbath coming."

I turned to my mother: "Mame, I want to go to the Christian Goworek, to whom we gave all of our goods." I wanted at least to get our pillows; we had forgotten how to sleep on pillows because we slept on straw like pigs. Why, we don't deserve this! I sleep in the open; while we are sleeping in the open, we should at least sleep on our pillows. I ran to the Christian woman, who was living with her son and daughter; they had taken the stuff from us willingly, agreeing that if we all survive, we will share it between us. I went to the house of this woman, Goworek; I see all of those beautiful things, with the beautiful embroidered lace covers on the bed (Goworek was a bricklayer) and the drapery. I tell her: "I would like you to give me our pillow[s]." She sees all of those things that her family had; the Christian son comes . . . and says, "Czy wy myślicie, że wojna już jest skończona? Jeśli będziecie tu jeszcze jedną minutę to wasza śmierć" [Do you think that the war is already over? If you stay here another minute, it is your death].

I didn't take anything. . . . I was alone in the house; there were still things that had not been burned, and all the Jews who had survived—some from Treblinka, a few from the forests, a few from the fields—were living together. There were sixteen of us, and my mother was a *mame* to everyone. The young people, they were picking up carrots and potatoes from the fields.

We were not living in Sterdyń for long, perhaps for two weeks, when we went away to Kosów Lacki. Kosów is a town in which my grandpa lived with [my] grandma. We stayed in Kosów a short time. It was then that we heard that in Mordyń, the neighboring town, thirteen Jews had been murdered for no reason, but only because they were Jews. I didn't know what to think; we went to Łódź, that is—where there was the greatest community of the Jews.

After two years, Fuks moved to Wrocław and from there to Israel in 1950. In her testimony, she supplies a report on one of her rescuers, who ironically looked to her for help after the war: "After the war, the AK members came into [Rozek's] house with two revolvers in hand and threatened to shoot him together with his wife and child for hiding and supporting Jews. We saved him. We took him with us to Lower Silesia, where he lives to this day with his wife and four kids."

Fuks's testimony is unique for its signs of urgency and a "frozen memory," so to speak, that does not process the original events. In certain intense moments, her narrative moves from the past to the present tense, creating an impromptu narrative that brings the reader *right there*. She does not paraphrase people's utterances; to the contrary, she quotes them raw, in a sometimes awkward, rural Polish (transcribed into Hebrew characters), which strike readers with a stunning and disturbing realization that they are unwillingly drawn to a scene of ethnic violence that really took place. One is tempted to ask: For whom was Fuks supplying these original Polish expressions? Did they matter to the listeners, to the collectors of the testimonies? Did they matter to other survivors from Poland? Might they have constituted a shared memory of vocabulary or phrases that the Jews in Poland had heard again and again? Finally, why was she narrating her memories in such an intense manner, as if she were *right there*?

It is possible that postwar experiences, having accumulated together with even more traumatic wartime experiences, became static, frozen, because memory could not access them other than in an original, raw form. Thus, frozen moments of anguish might betray a double narrative that tells stories of life and death.[44] Such an explanation would coincide with the nature of the trauma that the memory seeks to revisit time and again but that cannot really be lived through.[45] Although the postwar trauma of a hostile Polish reception, when not violent and life threatening, might seem relatively minor in comparison with the wartime experiences, it was likely that the accumulation, the unceasing nature, of multiple, serial traumas made it practically impossible for the survivors to deal with the postwar situation as a separate event. For the majority of those who survived, the return to deserted *shtetlech*, the realization of the extent of physical and spiritual destruction, and the population's hostile attitude created another trauma on top of the already horrendous wartime experiences. The memory of this postwar trauma might, therefore, be recollected in the same way as the previous wartime trauma.

Where Is the Shtetl, Where Am I? Absent Matsevot

Lamentation is found in some Israeli testimonies written from a perspective of the passage of time. Although not a frequent occurrence, such lamentation testimonies do exist. Their style evolved into a more nostalgic perspective and solidified into a sort of literary *matseva* (gravestone). In it, the survivor mourns either the death of a community or the death of oneself.[46]

Yaakov Abramowicz (AYV O3/3149) closes his account with a mournful recollection of the absence of the Jews: "Everything in place, only the people are no more," he writes. Upon encountering a Christian named Sadurski who welcomed him with that infamous question "Are you still alive?!" Abramowicz maintained his composure and wit and replied, "Yes . . . we live, and we want to survive you! We are looking for Korelicze Jews." Sadurski, in fact, turned out to be rather helpful in providing information on other Jews in the area, and so Abramowicz and a friend went together to this friend's house, although they remained outside, for they already knew "what was awaiting [them]." Finally, Abramowicz joined some other Jews who lived together, but even then he soon had to leave the town. He ended his testimony with this sorrowful passage: "Each of us walked the same road. With broken hearts we have turned back to Naliboki. We gave our little shtetl a good look and blessed ourselves with it. Who knows whether we will ever be in Korelicze [again]."

Whether Abramowicz ever returned to Korelicze, we do not know. It is clear, however, that he and other survivors felt banished from their own shtetl and that their last look at it constituted a way of erecting in their memory a *matseva*—a true *memorial* of the heart where one from stone could not be erected.

Anna Sznajd (AYV O3/1609), in contrast, suggested in her testimony that she herself in some way died together with the shtetl. In the last part of her testimony, entitled "The Liberation Did Not Free Me from Suffering," Sznajd describes her liberation while living in a church tower, protected by an Armenian priest. At one point, after futilely searching for any survivors of her family, she realized that "all have died. I remained alone in the world." She continues:

> One day I was sitting in Wały Hetmańskie [one of the main promenades of Lviv], and I noticed among the passers-by the Jews who have only just come out from cellars and hiding places, from forests. They were walking corpses. Seeing them, I started to cry. Next to me were seated two Russians from the NKVD. "You are crying," they said, "but were we in the place of Hitler, we would finish them all off; not one would be left." How their words hurt me! So [even] after such experiences, I still cannot raise my head up! What has my Jewishness given me? Only suffering. I thought of not coming back, maybe of continuing to live as a Pole. The priest told me that if God has saved me, and if I have survived so much oppression, I should remain with my Jewishness.

Sznajd began to work in an orphanage, but she was soon arrested by the new Soviet authorities on suspicion of espionage and membership in the AK. She was released with the help of some people who knew her, but she admits, "I left the prison broken in spirit and body, infested with lice, unable to live." The work in the orphanage was a great trial for her in these conditions. With bitter words, she described how Ukrainian children were attacking and persecuting Jewish children and how the Jewish children were reenacting their war traumas through violent games, screams at night, and attempts to escape. This is how she ends her testimony:

> Once I saw an event that filled me with bitterness. I came into the room with preschool children and that is what I saw: Jewish children were standing against the wall, and in front of them Polish and Ukrainian children were pointing sticks at them. They were pretending to shoot Jewish children. I could not look at that; I could not work there or be there or see it. The director of the orphanage was afraid of his responsibility and tried to cover up this nightly attack. The situation was really difficult to control. These children were no longer children.
>
> Will I manage to tell everything that I saw during the war? I saw the Ukrainians drowning Jews in the canals. They held a man by his legs, they put the head to the water, then they took him out, then [they put him] again into the water, until he died in torment. Can I even remember now how many times was I running away from persecutions, how many times was I seeing death in front of my eyes, how many times was I standing in front of the revolver?
>
> Now I am surprised: that I came through all that, at how I have gone through it, at how I have survived this.
>
> In 1957, I arrived in Israel.

Describing the continuation of violence both against other Jews and against herself, pointing out the cruelty of subjugating children to this continuation, Sznajd could not live in a place that, although liberated, did not end her suffering—or that of other Jews, for that matter. She wept upon seeing the prevalence of the anti-Jewish hostilities, and she considered for a moment her own escape from the condemned identity. One of her rescuers, the priest, saved her from this amputation of her roots—the loss of her Jewish identity. Although broken, lonely, and seemingly hopeless, she finally "arrived in Israel" in 1957 (we do not know whether she had tried to leave Poland earlier), and through this act she finally managed to sustain her Jewishness.

Silence: Does Everybody Know?

Silence—that is, a failure to mention postwar Polish–Jewish encounters—is much more rare in the selection of Israeli testimonies under consideration than in the Polish testimonies, so it is surprising when it occurs. The reasons for this silence might be as numerous as the survivors in whose testimonies such silence occurs. Nevertheless, taking into account a Zionist perspective, can one find more general reasons for it?

One explanation might be the pervasiveness of Zionism and the Israeli society's generally negative perception of the Diaspora and its political bankruptcy following the annihilation during the Holocaust. Such an attitude might be detected behind the interviewers' questions. One might reasonably assume that such a consensus was so clear and expressive that some survivors, including, perhaps, those who might otherwise have had positive or at least neutral experiences after the war, might not have seen a need to confirm or deny it. Orna Kenan's suggestion that the survivors created their own counternarrative against the Zionist neglect of survivors who were not ghetto fighters or partisans might also indicate that such a counternarrative was on occasion expressed by silence.[47]

Adam Zomper (AYV O3/1821), for example, does not provide any information about the Polish reception of him on his return home, even though he goes into detail about his general situation:

> We were driving to Częstochowa. I was looking for [the members of] my family, and I found them at [the home of] my aunt, who survived. Ewa's child was not there. My brother-in-law and my sister survived. We all started to come back into balance—to normal life. In search of bread and clothes, I started to work at several places to earn money. I lived that way until the year 1947, and after that I was organizing a youth group to [join the] Haganah, and I left together with them for a kibbutz in Lower Silesia in Mieroszów. People were gathering there before leaving for Erec [Israel]. I became ill, and that is why I didn't leave. After that I worked in a little metal factory until the year 1950. Although I tried to leave for Israel, I did not leave because I did not receive a permit to leave. I stayed in Poland until 1957.

In 1952, I married Noemi Centnerschwer, a ward of the Children's Home in Bielsko. She had been graduated from the pedagogical lyceum, and she was working at the time in a preschool.

In 1953, my son Jurek was born. I was working as a main metal mechanic in a state factory in Częstochowa. I earned little there, and I lived modestly. Still, I was a valued and respected worker there, and I did not experience antisemitism. I rose from the ranks, for which I received several medals and bonuses. I also worked in the cultural department of the factory—I was organizing various trips for our employees—to the sea, to the mountains—and cultural events, and I felt well there.

In 1956, when they announced the aliyah to Israel, we decided to leave as well. My wife and I were also present at the reunion of the Children's Home, which took place in Kraków. My wife's friends and the youth [there] said, "We are going to Israel!"

The arrival in Israel in June 1957 was sad because we felt suddenly homeless, even though during the first weeks we lived with my uncle in Tel Aviv.

From there, Zomper's comparison of Israeli society to Polish society proves to be a negative one.

> I never felt class differences so painfully as here, in Israel. I was like a machine, which has to make up these few hours to earn bread for itself and the wife. Our child was deprived of care because there is no free daycare for children under five. We did not want our child to join other children who are brought up in the street, in front of their home. My wife started to work hard, too, so we employed somebody to take care of our child. The boss I worked for treated me like a slave. With difficulty, I received a different job in a factory where they treat me well; nevertheless, I see and hear as our workers are being persecuted and treated at work as people "of an inferior kind." At each step we feel these class differences, which we didn't know in Poland. . . . Our child is free in Israel, and that is a source of joy for us. His childhood is carefree, although it is deprived of much of the cultural entertainment that children in Poland have. We live with him in our fatherland, and we want to create a life of a healthy generation equal to the children of Israel.

Zomper's testimony is quite unique for its very existence: this survivor seems to have been well integrated into Polish socialist society and satisfied with his job as well as with the class structure of the "workers' paradise." His immigration to Israel does not appear to be a necessary move following dissatisfaction with his situation in Poland. Although he was a Zionist, recruiting youth to Hagana, he clearly became disappointed with social relations in Israel and felt nostalgia for what he perceived to be the comparative equality of Polish society. The only positive outcomes of the move to Israel for him were a relatively free life for his son as well as the opportunity to participate in the building of the Jewish state. In his account, one is allowed to witness the evolution of a Zionist who failed in his first attempt to come to Israel; who found a certain fulfillment in his work and social surroundings in Poland; who likely felt impelled to emigrate during the intensification of antisemitic incidents following the Polish October in 1956; who finally arrived in Israel; and who then began to feel ambivalent, if not disappointed, about the difficulties that he faced there as a new immigrant. Although we do not learn anything specific from his testimony about Polish–Jewish interactions immediately after the war, the fact that he remained in Poland at that time, coupled with his claim that he "did not experience antisemitism," could signal either a positive social encounter immediately after the war or a negative encounter that did not need to be named in the context of his criticism of Israeli work relations.

Another equally paradoxical reason for the silence could be the same strong focus on Zionist values that encouraged survivors quickly to "get to the point" of their testimonies—that is, to emphasize the fact of immigration to Israel (the narrative of arrival) rather than to focus on reasons for leaving that were inherent in the Diaspora (the narrative of exodus).

In Samuel Kostman's testimony (AYV O3/1619), for example, one finds no mention of any postwar Polish encounter, although he describes his remaining years in Poland in some detail. His narrative has a strong, linear Zionist structure: he documents his attachment to the Land of Israel from before the war, including his commitment to purchasing stamps and cards to support the "Struggle for Palestine"; he was actively involved in organizing immigration to the Land of Israel; and he attempted to leave for Israel in 1948, received a "written refusal," and so waited for another opportunity, which finally arrived in 1958. Kostman elaborates on his difficulties in receiving the exit visa and on an opportunity to have his war experiences published when he befriended the director of a publishing house (an opportunity lost, however, when the director died). Although his testimony could belong to the Zionist category, his explicit silence on postwar Polish–Jewish relations as well as on the immediate postwar period complicates this interpretation and may suggest that, as in Zomper's testimony, this survivor might have some recollections—positive or negative—that may have either called into question his Zionist narrative or supported it but might have been redundant in the social context of Israel—or in the context of the interview itself.

In some testimonies, the silence regarding what survivors encountered upon their return home after the war seems to signal a lack of importance of that particular moment in the survivors' lives. They might mention something that came up later as a reason for moving (whether personal or political), but the very moments of their arrival home and of the first encounters with their neighbors apparently did not etch themselves strongly enough in their memories to be considered worthy of being recounted.

Conclusions
Toward Building a Collective Memory

The close reading of the survivors' testimonies from Poland and Israel on these pages reveals several relationships between the recorded memories of their postwar encounters with Polish Gentiles and the place and time of their recalling of those memories. The development of the memory of these interactions was such that both the passage of time and the move from Poland to Israel resulted in a much more frequent mention of such encounters as well as in a slight but vocal shift in emphasis on the quality of these contacts.

Memories of the first postwar Polish–Jewish encounters are relatively rarely recounted in the ŻIH testimonies given in Poland, and when they do appear, they tend to record a verdict of shock at the violence that continued after the war. The end of the war brought the Polish Jews scarcely anything that the word *liberation* promised: in fact, the great expectation of peace and unification with one's family was often immediately crushed in a tragically anticlimactic realization that one was the sole survivor of an entire family or even of an entire Jewish community. The inconceivable hostility of one's former neighbors to those who had been singled out for destruction during the war and whose relatives and friends had been murdered brought a depressing awareness that there was not much to look forward to even once the wartime violence was "officially" over. Langer observes, in this context, that for "many Holocaust survivors, liberation meant a new and unexpected (hence unprepared for) form of imprisonment. Survival was synonymous with the recognition of *deprival*."[1]

After the war, the survivors were for the most part unsure of whether they would remain in Poland or flee, and although the general atmosphere supported such flight from Poland, possible destinations as well as the timing of one's departure were precarious propositions. The remaining Polish Jews could not have predicted such a development of events. This additional postwar trauma clearly remained unabsorbed by the time testimony was given because it was typically manifested in the use of common, dry, and unemotional language and rhetoric.

Through my research, I have found that in Poland, where the early testimonies were being collected, the "discourse" of memory (i.e., a reasonably coherent sort of narrative that would suggest a collective memory) had not yet been created. It was apparently too early to do so, and the survivors first had to deal with the shock of the occurrence of violence and to come to grips with the fact that their entire culture, their language, and the majority of the Jewish population had been annihilated.

It appears, then, a necessary conclusion that in the immediate postwar period in Poland the Jewish survivors did not manage to develop a collective memory; such a development remained, for them, a process in construction. The surviving Jews, in shock at what was happening to them, were only slowly able to absorb their experiences and to build from them what would *later* become their collective memory, either in Poland or abroad.

In contrast, by the time survivors recalled their individual memories for Yad Vashem, they had already closed a chapter of their lives. They had made their decision to move to the Jewish homeland; they were convinced of the continuity of antisemitism in Poland (as evidenced by the postwar pogroms and by the antisemitic incidents of 1956); they were more vocal about their postwar encounters with their Polish neighbors (more of which, in proportion to positive memories, they also negatively characterized); and they employed explicitly Zionist vocabulary and imagery in their narratives, perhaps to prove that they belonged to the Israeli society. Indeed, Zionism often appears as an explicit value that gives meaning to the survivors' recounted experiences, at the same time that on occasion it may also appear to be a mere subtext of certain narratives.

From the "narrative" point of view, although the deep memory in the Israeli testimonies occasionally reveals a focus on an unabsorbed war and postwar events, the collective memory of the survivors from Poland aligned itself to Israel's national agenda, thus tending, in Friedländer's description, to "establish coherence, closure, and possibly a redemptive stance, notwithstanding the resistance of deep memory at the individual level."[2] In the context of postwar events, this deep memory helplessly revisited the hostile landscape, oscillating among the realization of the totality of Jewish destruction, the surrounding society's indifference to the extent of this destruction, and the continuation of deadly threats that must have seemed surreal once the Nazi annihilation was officially at an end.

Silence concerning Jewish interaction with Poles after the war, which is much less frequent but more expressive when it occurs in the Israeli testimonies than in the Polish documents, can be explained in various ways. In many "silent" narratives, an emphasis is immediately placed on life in Israel and its problems, and the Polish postwar context simply does not appear important enough to be included in the testimony. In place of the matter-of-fact or "reporting" style very common among the Polish testimonies, the survivors interviewed by YV constructed narratives of exodus or arrival to the Land of Israel. The almost total absence of such a "reporting" style in Israeli testimonies can be partially explained by different perceptions of the goals for which testimonies were to be collected. Although the survivors in Poland may have hoped, through the testimonies that they deposited with the ŻIH, to speed up the execution of justice toward the perpetrators of the crimes against them during the war, the principle reasons for collecting testimonies in Israel was to establish grounds for awarding the title "Righteous among the Nations" to non-Jewish individuals and to aid historical research.

Through the lens of the survivors' move to the Israeli state, one can identify the social factors of collective memory that shaped the survivors' testimonies in their postwar aspect. The expectation that the survivors had finally arrived to their own homeland—which, to be sure, they would have to defend but from which nobody would have a right to expel them—is reflected in the testimonies' emphasis on the survivors' generally negative reception by the Gentile population after the war and by sweeping statements that are often less descriptive of specific events and more a general summary of a survivor's impressions.

It is striking, finally, that on occasion a YV interviewer's zeal to highlight a Zionist theme in completing a narrative appears to backfire or at least to be subverted by a survivor's pregnant silence or neutral statements concerning Polish–Jewish interactions. The existence of a heroic narrative was a strong pressure with which the survivors attempted to grapple in various ways. Some testimonies created a counternarrative in the Israeli collective memory of the postwar reception of the survivors by their Polish neighbors. This counternarrative, frequently running silently beneath a survivor's actual statements, should be further investigated to understand the nuances of Israeli Holocaust memory.

It was in Israel, then, that a collective memory was created against the background of the Zionist enterprise. The most obvious and straightforward collective memory—of Polish hostility experienced on one's return home—should have been an easy piece to fit into the puzzle of a new Zionist identity, but it was not. Perhaps Zionist assumptions may have been too strong and too straightforward to go unchallenged. The dominating discourse evoked a "push back" from survivors who did not identify with the memory of heroic struggle and resistance that was the basis of the new sabra (native-born Israeli) identity. That "push back" might have resulted either in critical remarks regarding the experiences of the survivors in Israel or in silence concerning possible negative experiences in postwar Poland—or even in positive remarks on that postwar period.

In my reading of testimonies, I have considered the possible formation of a collective memory among the returning Holocaust survivors both at the time and place of their return and after a subsequent translation—in time and space—from life in a traumatized Poland to life in a reborn Israel. I have categorized the survivors' memories into groups, noting that although in Poland they tended to align "naturally" into similar narratives of the shock they experienced after being "liberated," in Israel they rather manifested more diverse and even subversive qualities that attempted to undermine the discourse of the heroic ghetto fighters. The collective memory of the survivors, therefore, appears to be more operational—both as something asserted and as something resisted—in the moment in which the testimonies were recollected in Israel.

APPENDIX

NOTES

BIBLIOGRAPHY

INDEX

Appendix
On the Value of Quantitative Analysis

Apart from qualitative analysis, my study also contains a limited amount of quantitative research on a sample of sources that I preselected based on indications that they were likely to contain information about postwar Polish–Jewish encounters. By computing these data, I attempt to provide a framework for understanding which memories occur most frequently *in relation to other memories* more than to indicate any exact representational value that they might express of a collective memory belonging to a specific group of survivors.

Researching narratives does not render the same kind of data as research in the hard sciences, where repeated experiments can be conducted to test a hypothesis. In the analysis of personal testimonies in historical research, several complications may arise from the data themselves: (1) Some self-selection is already implied in the survivors' choice to provide the interviewers with their testimonies. (2) The nature of these written testimonies is such that they represent what was allowed to be revealed in their interviews—that is, what the interviewers were willing or able to hear and record, but not necessarily all that the survivors may have wanted to reveal. (3) The accounts are also limited to certain periods of time; many of them deal with the period before the Kielce Pogrom on July 4, 1946 (a watershed moment for Polish Jews with respect to whether they would choose to stay in Poland or to go elsewhere) and were recorded before it, thus providing us with a perspective that was predictably less burdened by the violence directed at Jews.

Out of nearly 1,000 accounts preselected for this research based on clues given in catalog descriptions, I focused on several hundred that provided me with specific data on the central issue I analyze. I have labeled these documents "active" to indicate either that they do refer to postwar interactions with Poles or that although discussing other postwar matters, they are significantly silent about such interactions. Specifically, out of the 588 documents in ŻIH Collections 301 and 302 that I could minimally expect, based on their catalog descriptions as well as on other clues, to refer to the postwar situation, 98 (close to 17 percent) make reference to the Polish population (the proportion is much higher in testimonies than in memoirs and diaries: 20 percent versus 5 percent). Analogically, out of the 142 testimonies in YV Collections O3 and O33 that could have referred to postwar interactions with Poles, I chose 87 "active" testimonies that actually did or "should have" referred to such interactions based on their discussion of postwar events.

Although the results of this comparison are not as strict as the results of a rigorously conducted statistical analysis of a random sociological sample (an analysis that would be relatively useless in reference to the scarce mention of postwar events in the testimonies from Poland), they may reasonably provide an indicative value of the relationships between and frequencies of various themes occurring in the collective memory of the survivors in two different social contexts. Following grounded theory, therefore, they demonstrate the presence of real (social) phenomena expressed in a collective memory.

Table A1
Comparison of Jewish Historical Institute Collections 301 and 302 and Yad Vashem Testimonies regarding References to Postwar Polish–Jewish Interactions

Category	ŻIH 301 and 302 Testimonies, Poland, 1944–50	Yad Vashem Testimonies, Israel, 1955–70
"Active" sample of documents (as a percentage of the preselected sample)	17%	61%
Proportion of negative and positive memories within the "active" sample		
Negative memories	80%	49%
Positive or neutral memories	28%	16%
Categories Analyzed		
1 Rumors or news of the murder of nearby Jews	40%	30%
2 Direct threats or attacks against one's person	22%	15%
Total Memories of Violence (1 + 2)	**54%**	**33%**
3 Various nonviolent negative societal reactions	41%	28%
4 Postwar hiding	18%	8%
Total Negative Memories (1 + 2 + 3 + 4)	**80%**	**49%**
5 Positive memories	23%	16%
6 Cemetery syndrome	3%	5%

Table A2
Linguistic Comparison of Yad Vashem Testimonies by Categories of References to Postwar Polish–Jewish Interactions

Category	Polish	Yiddish	Hebrew	German
"Active" documents in preselected Yad Vashem testimonies	71%	24%	3%	1%
1 Rumors, news of murdered Jews	65%	30%	4%	–
2 Direct threats or attacks	62%	38%	–	–
3 General negative reactions from society	83%	13%	4%	–
4 Active hiding after the war	84%	14%	–	–
All Negative Memories	**70%**	**28%**	**5%**	–
5 Positive interactions	71%	29%	–	–
6 Cemetery syndrome	100%	–	–	–

Notes

Introduction: In Search of Postwar Memory

1. Chaim Wittelsohn, testimony, AŻIH 301/531, Żydowski Instytut Historyczny (ŻIH, Jewish Historical Institute), Warsaw. The ŻIH testimonies are subsequently cited parenthetically in the text. All testimony translations are mine unless otherwise noted.

2. The Warsaw Uprising of August 1944 should not be confused with the Warsaw Ghetto Uprising of April–May 1943.

3. Ita Koplowicz, testimony, AYV 03/1590, Yad Vashem (YV, Holocaust Martyrs' and Heroes' Remembrance Authority), Jerusalem. The YV testimonies are subsequently cited parenthetically in the text.

4. Jan Tomasz Gross, *Neighbors: The Destruction of the Jewish Community in Jedwabne, Poland* (Princeton, NJ: Princeton Univ. Press, 2001), and *Fear: Anti-Semitism in Poland after Auschwitz. An Essay in Historical Interpretation* (New York: Random House, 2006); Jan Tomasz Gross and Irena Grudzińska-Gross, *Golden Harvest: Events at the Periphery of the Holocaust* (New York: Oxford Univ. Press, 2012). In Polish: Jan Tomasz Gross, *Sąsiedzi: Historia zagłady żydowskiego miasteczka* (Sejny, Poland: Fundacja Pogranicze, 2000) and *Strach: Antysemityzm w Polsce tuż po wojnie: Historia moralnej zapaści* (Kraków: Znak, 2008); Jan Tomasz Gross and Irena Grudzińska-Gross, *Złote żniwa* (Kraków: Znak, 2011).

5. Maurice Halbwachs, *On Collective Memory* (Chicago: Univ. of Chicago Press, 1992), 40.

6. Ibid., 51.

7. Anna Green, "Individual Remembering and 'Collective Memory': Theoretical Presuppositions and Contemporary Debates," *Oral History* 32, no. 2 (Autumn 2004): 42, emphasis original.

8. See, for example, Pierre Nora, "Between Memory and History: Les lieux de mémoire," *Representations* 26 (Spring 1989): 7–24.

9. Jay Winter and Emmanuel Sivan, "Setting the Framework," in *War and Remembrance in the Twentieth Century*, ed. Jay Winter and Emmanuel Sivan (Cambridge: Cambridge Univ. Press, 1999), 30.

10. Boaz Cohen, *Israeli Holocaust Research: Birth and Evolution* (Abingdon, UK: Routledge, 2013), 276.

11. Jan Błoński, "Biedni Polacy patrzą na getto," *Togodnik Powszechny*, no. 2 (1987), at https://web.archive.org/web/20090214194707/http://tygodnik.onet.pl:80/21949,foto.html.

12. Michael C. Steinlauf, *Bondage to the Dead: Poland and the Memory of the Holocaust*, Modern Jewish History (Syracuse, NY: Syracuse Univ. Press, 1997), 60.

13. Barbara Engelking, *"Jest taki piękny słoneczny dzień": Losy Żydów szukających ratunku na wsi polskiej 1942–1945* (Warsaw: Stowarzyszenie Centrum Badań Nad Zagładą Żydów and Wydawnictwo Instytut Filozofii i Socjologii PAN, 2011), translated as *Such a Beautiful Sunny Day . . . : Jews Seeking Refuge in the Polish Countryside, 1942–1945* (Jerusalem: Yad Vashem, 2016).

14. Annette Wieviorka, *The Era of the Witness* (Ithaca, NY: Cornell Univ. Press, 2006).

15. David Boder published a selection of transcripts from his interviews in *I Did Not Interview the Dead* (Urbana: Univ. of Illinois Press, 1949).

16. Yehuda Bauer, *Rethinking the Holocaust* (New Haven, CT: Yale Univ. Press, 2001), 23, 24. See also Isaiah Trunk, *Jewish Responses to Nazi Persecution* (New York: Stein and Day, 1979).

17. See Saul Friedländer, *Nazi Germany and the Jews: The Years of Persecution, 1933–1939* (New York: Harper Collins, 1997), and *The Years of Extermination: Nazi Germany and the Jews, 1939–1945*, vol. 2 (New York: Harper Collins, 2007).

18. Christopher R. Browning, *Remembering Survival: Inside a Nazi Slave-Labor Camp* (New York: Norton, 2010).

19. Lawrence L. Langer, *Holocaust Testimonies: The Ruins of Memory* (New Haven, CT: Yale Univ. Press, 1991).

20. Shoshana Felman and Dori Laub, *Testimony: Crises of Witnessing in Literature, Psychoanalysis, and History* (New York: Routledge, 1992).

21. Ward Goodenough, *Description and Comparison in Cultural Anthropology* (Cambridge: Cambridge Univ. Press, 1970), 104–19.

22. Anselm Strauss and Juliet Corbin, *Basics of Qualitative Research: Grounded Theory Procedures and Techniques* (Newbury Park, CA: Sage, 1990), 24, emphasis in the original.

23. See, for example, Barney Glaser and Anselm Strauss, *The Discovery of Grounded Theory: Strategies for Qualitative Research* (Chicago: Aldine, 1967).

24. Strauss and Corbin, *Basics of Qualitative Research*, 23.

1. The Returning Survivors: Historical Context

1. Eugeniusz Duraczyński, *Wojna i okupacja, wrzesień 1939–kwiecień 1943* (Warsaw: Wiedza Powszechna, 1974) 58.

2. Tomasz Szarota, "Upowszechnienie kultury," in *Polska Ludowa 1944–1950: Przemiany społeczne*, ed. Hanna Jędruszczak, Krystyna Kersten, and Franciszek Ryszka (Wrocław, Poland: Zakład Narodowy im. Ossolińskich, 1974), 412.
3. Marcin Zaremba, *Wielka Trwoga: Polska 1944–1947* (Kraków: Znak, 2012), 96. All translations of non-English source material are mine unless otherwise noted.
4. Ibid., 17.
5. Andrzej Żbikowski, "Morderstwa popełniane na Żydach w pierwszych latach po wojnie," in *Następstwa zagłady Żydów: Polska 1944–2010*, ed. Feliks Tych and Monika Adamczyk-Garbowska (Lublin, Poland: Wydawnictwo Uniwersytetu Marii Curie-Skłodowskiej and Żydowski Instytut Historyczny im. Emanuela Ringelbluma, 2011), 78.
6. Albert Stankowski and Piotr Weiser, "Demograficzne skutki Holokaustu," in Tych and Adamczyk-Garbowska, eds., *Następstwa zagłady Żydów*, 15.
7. Czesław Łuczak, "Szanse i trudności bilansu demograficznego Polski w latach 1939–1945," *Dzieje Najnowsze* 26, no. 2 (1994): 12.
8. Józef Adelson, "W Polsce zwanej ludową," in *Najnowsze dzieje Żydów w Polsce: W zarysie (do 1950 roku)*, ed. Jerzy Tomaszewski, et al. (Warsaw: Wydawnictwo Naukowe PWN, 1993), 387.
9. Natalia Aleksiun, *Dokąd dalej? Ruch syjonistyczny w Polsce (1944–1950)* (Warsaw: Trio, 2002), 33.
10. Ibid., 46.
11. Yehuda Bauer, *Flight and Rescue: Brichah* (New York: Random House, 1970), 125.
12. Aleksiun, *Dokąd dalej?* 68.
13. Quoted in Ewa Koźmińska-Frejlak, "Asymilacja do polskości jako strategia adaptacyjna ocalałych z Zagłady polskich Żydów," *Kwartalnik Historii Żydów*, no. 2 (2013): 242.
14. Karen Auerbach, "Rodziny żydowskie z domu w Alejach Ujazdowskich 16 w powojennej Warszawie: Dylematy etyczne w badaniach nad asymilacją w Polsce Ludowej," in *Społeczność żydowska w PRL przed kampanią antysemicką lat 1967–1968 i po niej*, ed. Grzegorz Berendt (Warsaw: IPN, 2009), 151.
15. Małgorzata Melchior, *Zagłada a tożsamość: Polscy Żydzi ocaleni "na aryjskich papierach." Analiza doświadczenia biograficznego* (Warsaw: Wydawnictwo Instytut Filozofii i Socjologii PAN, 2004), 63.
16. Alina Skibińska, "Powroty ocalałych i stosunek do nich społeczeństwa polskiego," in Tych and Adamczyk-Garbowska, eds., *Następstwa zagłady Żydów*, 47.
17. Ibid., 48.
18. Ibid., 50.
19. Ewa Koźmińska-Frejlak, "Kondycja ocalałych: Adaptacja do rzeczywistości powojennej (1944–1949)," in Tych and Adamczyk-Garbowska, eds., *Następstwa zagłady Żydów*, 136.

20. Ibid., 143.

21. Irena Hurwic-Nowakowska, who conducted a unique study of Jewish attitudes immediately after the war, claims that "there are only a few cases of people who, having spent the occupation on 'Aryan papers,' reverted back to their old names." She called this continued use of an "Aryan" identity "a phenomenon of Jews abandoning Jewry," which reflects "an effort to free oneself from a state of humiliation." She observed this process among the Jewish intelligentsia, but not at all among Jewish workers (*A Social Analysis of Postwar Polish Jewry* [Jerusalem: Zalman Shazar Center for Jewish History, 1986], 126; see also Melchior, *Zagłada a tożsamość*).

22. See Yisrael Gutman and Shmuel Krakowski, *Unequal Victims: Poles and Jews during World War Two* (New York: Holocaust Library, 1986), 120–34.

23. Skibińska, "Powroty ocalałych i stosunek," 62.

24. Ibid.

25. Krystyna Kersten, *Repatriacja ludności polskiej po II wojnie światowej: Studium historyczne* (Wrocław, Poland: Zakład Narodowy im. Ossolińskich, 1974), 58–59.

26. Skibińska, "Powroty ocalałych i stosunek," 55.

27. Teresa Prekerowa estimated the origins of postwar survivors: between 30,000 and 60,000 came from hiding among the Polish population; between 20,000 and 40,000 returned from German camps; and between 10,000 and 15,000 came back from being partisans and from hideouts in forests ("Wojna i okupacja," in Tomaszewski, et al., ed., *Najnowsze dzieje Żydów w Polsce*, 384).

28. Skibińska, "Powroty ocalałych i stosunek," 56.

29. Ibid., 59.

30. Ibid., 46.

31. Adelson, "W Polsce zwanej ludową," 391.

32. Grzegorz Berendt, "Życie od nowa: Instytucje i organizacje żydowskie (1944–1950)," in Tych and Adamczyk-Garbowska, eds., *Następstwa zagłady Żydów*, 198.

33. Ibid., 199.

34. Aleksiun, *Dokąd dalej?* 73.

35. Żbikowski, "Morderstwa popełniane," 82.

36. Adelson, "W Polsce zwanej ludową," 397.

37. Skibińska, "Powroty ocalałych i stosunek," 63.

38. Quoted in Koźmińska-Frejlak, "Kondycja ocalałych," 143.

39. David Sfard, *Mit zich und mit andere* (Jerusalem: Farlag "Jeruszalaimer Almanach," 1984), 160, quoted in Joanna Nalewajko-Kulikov, "Pierwsze wrażenia: Żydowski intelektualista w rzeczywistości odradzającej się Polski (na przykładzie Dawida Sfarda)," in *Zagłada Żydów: Pamięć narodowa a pisanie historii w Polsce i we Francji*, ed. Barbara Engelking, Jacek Leociak, Dariusz Libionka, and Anna Ziębińska-Witek (Lublin, Poland: Wydawnictwo Uniwersytetu Marii Curie-Skłodowskiej, 2006), 229–33.

40. Skibińska, "Powroty ocalałych i stosunek," 64.

41. Quoted in Andrzej Tłomacki, "Życie społeczno-religijne ludności żydowskiej powiatu bialskiego w latach 1944–1947," *Kwartalnik Historii Żydów* 214, no. 2 (2005): 225–26.

42. Skibińska, "Powroty ocalałych i stosunek," 65.

43. Adam Penkalla, "Władze o obecności Żydów na terenie Kielecczyzny w okresie od wkroczenia Armii Czerwonej do pogromu kieleckiego," *Kwartalnik Historii Żydów* 208, no. 4 (2003): 557–77; Adam Penkalla, "Stosunki polsko-żydowskie w Radomiu (kwiecień 1945–luty 1946)," *Biuletyn Żydowskiego Instytutu Historycznego* 7, no. 3 (1995): 175–78, and 6, no. 2 (1996): 57–66.

44. Quoted in Skibińska, "Powroty ocalałych i stosunek," 49.

45. Ibid.; see also Koźmińska-Frejlak, "Kondycja ocalałych," 146–47.

46. Andrzej Rzepliński, "Ten jest z ojczyzny mojej? Sprawy karne oskarżonych o wymordowanie Żydów w Jedwabnem w świetle zasady rzetelnego procesu," in *Wokół Jedwabnego*, vol. 1, ed. Paweł Machcewicz and Krzysztof Persak (Warsaw: IPN, 2002), 355.

47. Żbikowski, "Morderstwa popełniane," 72.

48. Two major waves of famine occurred in postwar Poland: in the eastern regions during the process of liberation (summer 1944 to spring 1945) and during the winter and summer of 1946. Official data indicate that village inhabitants consumed 1,396 calories per day during 1945 and 1946. At least two and a half million people were in need of food aid during this time. Infant mortality, which stood at 20 to 25 percent across all of Poland, was 40 to 50 percent among the repatriates from the East. Deaths outnumbered births by 30 percent. The situation was catastrophic in the hospitals, which lacked basic medications, medical tools, bedsheets, and other necessary items (Zaremba, *Wielka Trwoga*, 514–34).

49. Roman Knoll, head of the Foreign Affairs Commission, Office of the Government Delegate for the Homeland, to Polish government in London, memorandum, August 1943, given in Emanuel Ringelblum, *Polish–Jewish Relations during the Second World War*, ed. Joseph Kermish and Shmuel Krakowski (Evanston, IL: Northwestern Univ. Press, 1992), 257.

50. The letter is included in Zofia Borzymińska, "*I ta propaganda zapuszcza coraz nowe korzenie* . . . (Listy z Polski pisane w 1946 roku)," *Kwartalnik Historii Żydów* 222, no. 2 (2007): 229–30. This letter was most likely written in the summer of 1946.

51. Some historians tend to see the murders that occurred at the time in the Suwałki area (the worst of which took place in Jedwabne, Radziłów, and Wąsosz) in the context of revenge for the alleged participation of Jews in the Red Army's terror campaign in September 1939 (see Zaremba, *Wielka Trwoga*, 85).

52. For example, in the fall of 1945 sixty-seven Jews among five hundred officials worked in managerial positions of the Ministry of Public Security (a rate of 13 percent as opposed to the 0.5 percent of Jews in the whole of society), but throughout the period 1944–54 Jews there held 36 percent of the highest positions (August Grabski,

"Żydzi a polskie życie polityczne [1944–1949]," in Tych and Adamczyk-Garbowska, eds., *Następstwa zagłady Żydów*, 171–73; see also Krystyna Kersten, *Polacy, Żydzi, komunizm: Anatomia półprawd 1939–68* [Warsaw: Niezależna Oficyna Wydawnicza, 1992], 83–84).

53. Kersten, *Polacy, Żydzi, komunizm*, 84.
54. This is one of the theses of Gross, *Fear*; see also Zaremba, *Wielka Trwoga*, 97.
55. Grabski, "Żydzi a polskie," 167.
56. Kersten, *Polacy, Żydzi, komunizm*, 133.
57. Żbikowski, "Morderstwa popełniane," 79.
58. Ibid., 80.
59. Ryszard Śmietanka-Kruszelnicki, "Podziemie antykomunistyczne wobec Żydów po 1945 roku—wstęp do problematyki (na przykładzie województwa kieleckiego)," in *Z przeszłości Żydów polskich: Polityka, gospodarka, kultura, społeczeństwo*, ed. Jacek Wijaczka and Grzegorz Miernik (Kraków: IPN, 2005), quoted in Skibińska, "Powroty ocalałych i stosunek," 67.
60. Skibińska, "Powroty ocalałych i stosunek," 65.
61. Żbikowski, "Morderstwa popełniane," 78.
62. For an anthropological analysis of the blood libel, see Joanna Tokarska-Bakir, *Legendy o krwi: Antropologia przesądu* (Warsaw: Wydawnictwo W.A.B., 2008).
63. The militia's involvement in spreading this dangerous legend was documented in Chełm in the spring of 1945 in an attack on a Jewish orphanage in Rabka in August 1945, in Kalisz in July 1946, and in the well-known pogroms in Rzeszów, Kraków, and Kielce (Zaremba, *Wielka Trwoga*, 589–615).
64. Danuta Brus-Węgrowska, "Atmosfera pogromowa," *Karta*, no. 18 (1996): 87–107.
65. Żbikowski, "Morderstwa popełniane," 72.
66. See Adelson, "W Polsce zwanej ludową," 401; Lucjan Dobroszycki, "Restoring Jewish Life in Post-war Poland," *Soviet Jewish Affairs* 3, no. 2 (1973): 66; Yisrael Gutman, *Hajehudim be-Polin acharei Milchemet Ha'olam Hashniya* (Jerusalem: Merkaz Zalman Shazar, 1985), 33, quoted in Aleksiun, *Dokąd dalej?* 96; Alina Cała, "Kształtowanie się polskiej i żydowskiej wizji martyrologicznej po II wojnie światowej," *Przegląd Socjologiczny* 169, no. 3 (2000): 167–80, quoted in Żbikowski, "Morderstwa popełniane," 85.
67. David Engel, "Patterns of Anti-Jewish Violence in Poland 1944–1946," *Yad Vashem Studies* 26 (1998): 60. Engel claims that Yisrael Gutman's estimates of at least 1,000 Jewish deaths after the war were high, whereas the recorded number of Jewish deaths between November 1944 and December 1945 was too low.
68. Żbikowski, "Morderstwa popełniane," 86.
69. Engel, "Patterns of Anti-Jewish Violence," 69–70.
70. Żbikowski, "Morderstwa popełniane," 88.
71. Zaremba, *Wielka Trwoga*, 117, 155, 211, 215, 217, 259, 269, 317, 463, 517.
72. Adelson, "W Polsce zwanej ludową," 393.
73. Koźmińska-Frejlak, "Kondycja ocalałych," 144.

74. Żbikowski, "Morderstwa popełniane," 92.
75. Ibid., 93.
76. Adelson, "W Polsce zwanej ludową," 417–18; Koźmińska-Frejlak, "Kondycja ocalałych," 127, 145.
77. Aleksiun, *Dokąd dalej?* 82–84.
78. David Engel, "Poland since 1939," in *The YIVO Encyclopedia of Jews in Eastern Europe* (New York: YIVO Institute for Jewish Research, 2010), at http://www.yivoencyclopedia.org/article.aspx/Poland/Poland_since_1939.
79. Jaff Schatz, *The Generation: The Rise and Fall of the Jewish Communists of Poland* (Berkeley: Univ. of California Press, 1991), 208.
80. Aleksiun, *Dokąd dalej?*; Bożena Szaynok, "Problem antysemityzmu w relacjach polsko-żydowskich w latach 1945–1954," in Engelking et al., eds., *Zagłada Żydów*, 235–46. Szaynok claims that the "cemetery syndrome" was the main reason for the Jewish exodus, at least until the Kielce Pogrom.
81. Hurwic-Nowakowska, *Social Analysis*, 10, 126.
82. Quoted in Żbikowski, "Morderstwa popełniane," 77.
83. Adelson, "W Polsce zwanej ludową," 424, 476.
84. Skibińska, "Powroty ocalałych i stosunek," 42.

2. The Central Jewish Historical Commission and Its Project of Documenting Survivors' Stories

1. Philip Friedman, "European Jewish Research on the Holocaust," in *Roads to Extinction: Essays on the Holocaust* (New York: Jewish Publication Society of America; Philadelphia: Conference on Jewish Social Studies, 1980), 500–524.
2. Laura Jockusch, "Chroniclers of Catastrophe: History Writing as a Jewish Response to Persecution before and after the Holocaust," in *Holocaust Historiography in Context: Emergence, Challenges, Polemics, and Achievements*, ed. David Bankier and Dan Michman (Jerusalem: Yad Vashem; New York: Berghahn Books, 2008), 136.
3. Laura Jockusch, *Collect and Record! Jewish Holocaust Documentation in Early Postwar Europe* (Oxford: Oxford Univ. Press, 2012), 228 n. 4.
4. Marian Fuks, "Z działalności Żydowskiego Instytutu Historycznego w Polsce," *Kwartalnik Historyczny* 88, no. 3 (1981): 905.
5. Rafał Żebrowski, "The Scholarly Tradition in Warsaw's Jewish Community in the Nineteenth Century," in *Jewish Historical Institute: The First Fifty Years 1947–1997. Conference Papers*, ed. Eleonora Bergman (Warsaw: Żydowski Instytut Historyczny Instytut Naukowo-Badawczy, 1996), 25.
6. Ibid., 23.
7. Marian Fuks, "The Institute for Jewish Studies in Warsaw (1928–1939)," in Bergman, ed., *Jewish Historical Institute*, 31.

8. Ibid., 34.

9. Ibid., 35.

10. Artur Eisenbach, "Jewish Historiography in Interwar Poland," in *The Jews of Poland between Two World Wars*, ed. Yisrael Gutman, Ezra Mendelsohn, Jehuda Reinharz, and Chone Shmeruk (Hanover, NH: Univ. Press of New England, 1989), 455.

11. Yisrael Gutman, "Emanuel Ringelblum: A Historian and His Time," in *Emanuel Ringelblum: The Man and the Historian*, ed. Yisrael Gutman (Jerusalem: Yad Vashem, 2010), 81.

12. Eisenbach, "Jewish Historiography," 460.

13. Ibid., 466.

14. Jockusch, "Chroniclers of Catastrophe," 137.

15. Simon Dubnow, "Let Us Search and Research: A Call to the Wise of Our People Who Volunteer to Collect Material on the Jews in Poland and Russia" (in Hebrew), *Pardes* 1 (1891): 221–42, quoted in Jockusch, "Chroniclers of Catastrophe," 142.

16. Jockusch, "Chroniclers of Catastrophe," 143.

17. Ibid.

18. David Engel, "Historical Writing as a National Mission: The Jews of Poland and Their Historiographic Tradition," in Gutman, ed., *Emanuel Ringelblum*, 127. See also Jockusch, "Chroniclers of Catastrophe," 138–39.

19. Engel, "Historical Writing," 128.

20. *Der Moment*, no. 291 (Dec. 31, 1914), 3, quoted in Jockusch, "Chroniclers of Catastrophe," 146.

21. Engel, "Historical Writing," 128.

22. Jockusch, "Chroniclers of Catastrophe," 154.

23. Samuel D. Kassow, *Who Will Write Our History? Emanuel Ringelblum, the Warsaw Ghetto, and the Oyneg Shabes Archive* (Bloomington: Indiana Univ. Press, 2007), 9.

24. Engel, "Historical Writing," 131–33.

25. Gutman, "Emanuel Ringelblum," 87.

26. Kassow, *Who Will Write Our History?* 90.

27. Gutman, "Emanuel Ringelblum," 100.

28. Jockusch, "Chroniclers of Catastrophe," 156.

29. Ibid.

30. Kassow, *Who Will Write Our History?* 213.

31. Gutman, "Emanuel Ringelblum," 101.

32. Kassow, *Who Will Write Our History?* 230–68.

33. Ibid., 2.

34. Jockusch, "Chroniclers of Catastrophe," 158.

35. Jockusch, *Collect and Record*, 89–90.

36. Natalia Aleksiun, "Rescuing a Memory and Constructing a History of Polish Jewry: Jews in Poland 1944–1950," *Jews in Russia and Eastern Europe* 1, no. 2 (2005): 11.

37. Jockusch, *Collect and Record*, 90.
38. Aleksiun, "Rescuing a Memory," 12–13.
39. Philip Friedman, "Polish Jewish Historiography between the Wars," in *Roads to Extinction*, 486.
40. Salo Wittmayer Baron, introduction to Friedman, *Roads to Extinction*, 1–8.
41. Roni Stauber, *Laying the Foundations for Holocaust Research: The Impact of the Historian Philip Friedman*, Search and Research no. 15 (Jerusalem: Yad Vashem, 2009), 10.
42. Raul Hilberg, *The Destruction of the European Jews* (New Haven, CT: Yale Univ. Press, 1961).
43. Friedman, "European Jewish Research," 503, 508, 505.
44. Philip Friedman, *Zagłada Żydów lwowskich*, vol. 4 (Łódź, Poland: Wydawnictwa Centralnej Żydowskiej Komisji Historycznej w Polsce, 1945), quoted in Natalia Aleksiun, "The Central Jewish Historical Commission in Poland, 1944–1947," *Polin: Studies in Polish Jewry* 20 (2008): 84.
45. Gutman, "Emanuel Ringelblum," 93.
46. Rachel Auerbach, *Oyf di felder fun Treblinke: Reportaszh* (Łódź, Poland: Tsenṭraler Yidisher Hisṭorisher Ḳomisye, 1947).
47. Kassow, *Who Will Write Our History?* 200.
48. Ibid., 205.
49. Aleksiun, "Central Jewish Historical Commission," 77.
50. Ibid.
51. Quoted in Aleksander Donat, *The Holocaust Kingdom: A Memoir* (New York: Holt, Rinehart and Winston, 1965), 210–11.
52. Aleksiun, "Central Jewish Historical Commission," 79.
53. Ibid., 83.
54. Stauber, *Laying the Foundations for Holocaust Research*, 20.
55. Aleksiun, "Central Jewish Historical Commission," 87.
56. Ibid., 81.
57. Josef Kermisz, *Instrukcje dla zbierania materiałów historycznych z okresu okupacji niemieckiej* (Łódź, Poland: Wydawnictwa Centralnej Żydowskiej Komisji Historycznej w Polsce, 1945). Here I use a forthcoming English translation: Josef Kermisz, *Instructions to Interview Jewish Survivors in Poland*, trans. Anna Purisch and Daniel Purisch, in *Early Jewish Texts on the Holocaust: The Collections of the Central Jewish Historical Commission in Poland*, ed. Laura Jockusch (Göttingen, Germany: Vandenhoeck & Rupprecht, forthcoming), quoted with permission from the editor.
58. Kermisz, *Instructions to Interview Jewish Survivors in Poland*, emphasis original.
59. David Graber, no title, Ringelblum Archive, part 1, no. 132, ŻIH; quoted in Kassow, *Who Will Write Our History?* 3.
60. Kermisz, *Instructions to Interview Jewish Survivors in Poland*.
61. Ibid.

62. Jockusch, *Collect and Record*, 92.
63. Kermisz, *Instructions to Interview Jewish Survivors in Poland*.
64. Jockusch, *Collect and Record*, 105.
65. Ibid.
66. Zelig Pacanowski to the CŻKH, statement, May 30, 1946, quoted in Jockusch, *Collect and Record*, 108.
67. Aleksiun, "Central Jewish Historical Commission," 82.
68. Friedman, "European Jewish Research," 510.
69. Maurycy Horn, "Działalność naukowa i wydawnicza Centralnej Żydowskiej Komisji Historycznej przy CKŻwP i Żydowskiego Instytutu Historycznego w Polsce w latach 1945–1950," *Biuletyn ŻIH*, nos. 133–34 (1985): 125. See also Philip Friedman, *To jest Oświęcim!* (Warsaw: Państwowe Wydawnictwo Literatury Politycznej, 1945), and Michał Borwicz, *Uniwersytet zbirów* (Kraków: Wydawnictwa Centralnej Żydowskiej Komisji Historycznej w Polsce, 1946).
70. Maurycy Horn, "Żydowski Instytut Historyczny w Polsce w latach 1944–1949," *Biuletyn ŻIH*, no. 109 (1979): 11.
71. Maurycy Horn, "Czterdzieści lat działalności w Warszawie Żydowskiego Instytutu Historycznego w Polsce," *Kalendarz żydowski*, 1987–88, 135.
72. Maurycy Horn, "Scholarly Activity of the Jewish Historical Institute in Poland, 1947–1996," in Bergman, ed., *Jewish Historical Institute*, 42.
73. Horn, "Czterdzieści lat działalności," 136.
74. Friedman, "Polish Jewish Historiography," 486.
75. Horn, "Scholarly Activity," 42–43.
76. Emanuel Ringelblum, *Notitsn fun varsher geto* (Warsaw: Farlag "Yidish Bukh," 1952).
77. Horn, "Scholarly Activity," 42–43.
78. Jockusch, *Collect and Record*, 9.

3. First Encounters with the Neighbors as Represented in the Jewish Historical Institute Collection

1. Returning survivors often identified themselves to one another with shibboleths. Zofia Dufman (AŻIH 302/261) depicts such a moment in her memoir: "On the streets of Lublin, a few Jews that survived were carefully observing the passers-by. When they seemed to recognize a Jew, they would approach him with a question—*Amchu?*—and if he smiled, happy, they would fall into each other's arms like brothers."
2. Henryk Shoshkes, *Poyln—1946* (Buenos Aires: Zentral-Farband fun Poylishe Yiden in Argentina, 1946), 72–81.
3. Translated by Karen Auerbach, Christina Manetti, and Michael Jacobs. I am grateful to Antony Polonsky for making this translation available to me.

4. Yad Vashem Testimonies in the Context of Israeli History

1. Gulie Ne'eman Arad, "Israel and the Shoah: A Tale of Multifarious Taboos," *New German Critique*, no. 90 (Autumn 2003): 7.

2. Hanna Yablonka, *Survivors of the Holocaust: Israel after the War* (New York: New York Univ. Press, 1999).

3. Orna Kenan, *Between Memory and History: The Evolution of Israeli Historiography of the Holocaust, 1945–1961* (New York: Peter Lang, 2003), 7.

4. Quoted in Arad, "Israel and the Shoah," 8.

5. S. Dobromil, "On Immigration and Absorption" (in Hebrew), *Tzor Michravi*, Ein Harod (Apr. 12, 1944), quoted in Kenan, *Between Memory and History*, 9.

6. Dina Porat, "With Forgiveness and Grace: The Encounter between Ruzka Korczak, the Yishuv, and Its Leaders, 1944–1946," *Journal of Israeli History* 16, no. 2 (1995): 101–32.

7. Kenan, *Between Memory and History*, 11.

8. See Cohen, *Israeli Holocaust Research*, 17.

9. Arad, "Israel and the Shoah," 10.

10. Kenan, *Between Memory and History*, 41.

11. These three proposals were (1) from the Zionist Left, which put an emphasis on heroism and conducted commemorative ceremonies on April 19, the date of the outbreak of the Warsaw Ghetto Uprising; (2) from the religious Zionists led by the chief rabbinate, who opposed the "ordinary" distinction between survivors and heroes and commemorated the memory of all the Jewish martyrs on the tenth of Tevet, the traditional date for the first siege of Jerusalem by the Babylonian king Nabuchadnezzar; and (3) from the revisionist Herut Party, which opted for a date unconnected to the uprising (Kenan, *Between Memory and History*, 15; see also Roni Stauber, *The Holocaust in Israeli Public Debate in the 1950's: Ideology and Memory* [London: Vallentine Mitchell, 2007], 40–44).

12. Quoted in Yitzhak Arad, *Ghetto in Flames: The Struggle and Destruction of the Jews in Vilna in the Holocaust* (Jerusalem: Yad Vashem, Martyrs' and Heroes' Remembrance Authority, 1980), 411–12.

13. Yael Zerubavel, *Recovered Roots: Collective Memory and the Making of Israeli National Tradition* (Chicago: Univ. of Chicago Press, 1995), 76.

14. Dalia Ofer, "The Past That Does Not Pass: Israelis and Holocaust Memory," *Israel Studies* 14, no. 1 (Spring 2009): 1–35, especially 4.

15. Cohen, *Israeli Holocaust Research*, 10–11.

16. Ibid.

17. Stauber, *The Holocaust in Israeli Public Debate*, 16.

18. Quoted in Kenan, *Between Memory and History*, 28.

19. Ibid., 19.

20. Yisrael Gutman and Yehuda Bauer later developed, still within the bounds of Zionist historiography, the trend of including in the notion of nonviolent resistance all

those who had previously been perceived as passive victims. See Yisrael Gutman, *The Jews of Warsaw, 1939–1943: Ghetto, Underground, Revolt* (Bloomington: Indiana Univ. Press, 1982), and Yehuda Bauer, *They Chose Life: Jewish Resistance in the Holocaust* (New York: American Jewish Committee, Institute of Human Relations, 1973).

21. On the concept of Kiddush ha-Shem, as applied and transformed by the Holocaust survivors, see Mark Dworzecki, "The Day-to-Day Stand of the Jews," in *Jewish Resistance during the Holocaust: Proceedings of the Conference on Manifestations of Jewish Resistance* (Jerusalem: Yad Vashem, 1971), 152–81.

22. Kenan, *Between Memory and History*, 27.

23. Quoted in ibid., 53.

24. Ibid., 24–25.

25. Cohen, *Israeli Holocaust Research*, 141.

26. Dalia Ofer, "The Strength of Remembrance: Commemorating the Holocaust during the First Decade of Israel," *Jewish Social Studies* 6, no. 2 (Winter 2000): 27.

27. Kenan, *Between Memory and History*, xxiii.

28. Ibid., xxv.

29. The name "Yad Vashem" comes from Isaiah 56:5, where all those who join the Lord are promised, "And to them I will give in my house and within my walls a memorial [Yad Vashem] better than sons or daughters: I will give them an everlasting name that shall not be cut off."

30. Cohen, *Israeli Holocaust Research*, 5.

31. Kenan, *Between Memory and History*, 44.

32. Ibid.

33. Ibid.

34. Stauber, *The Holocaust in Israeli Public Debate*, 49–50.

35. Protocols of the Executive Board of Yad Vashem, Apr. 29, 1958, 5–6, AYV, quoted in Kenan, *Between Memory and History*, 47.

36. Kenan, *Between Memory and History*, 48–50.

37. The appointment of Ber Mark as director of the Jewish Historical Institute (ŻIH in 1949), which had replaced the Central Jewish Historical Commission (CŻKH) in 1947, epitomized its takeover by Jewish Communists.

38. Boaz Cohen, "Rachel Auerbach, Yad Vashem, and Israeli Holocaust Memory," *Polin: Studies in Polish Jewry* 20 (2008): 199.

39. Ibid.

40. Rachel Auerbach, AYV P16/41, quoted in ibid.

41. Dalia Ofer, "The Community and the Individual: The Different Narratives of Early and Late Testimonies and Their Significance for Historians," in Banker and Michman, eds., *Holocaust Historiography in Context*, 519–535, 526.

42. Rachel Auerbach, "Testimonies: On the Margins of Yad Vashem's Activities" (in Hebrew), AYV P16/69, translated and quoted in Ofer, "Community and the Individual," 527.

43. Rachel Auerbach, AYV P16/41, quoted in Cohen, "Rachel Auerbach," 200.
44. Rachel Auerbach, AYV P16/77, quoted in Cohen, "Rachel Auerbach," 201.
45. Rachel Auerbach, AYV P16/41, quoted in Cohen, "Rachel Auerbach," 200.
46. Cohen, "Rachel Auerbach," 202.
47. Ibid.
48. Cohen, *Israeli Holocaust Research*, 79–85.
49. Philip Friedman, "Problems of Research on the Holocaust," in *Roads to Extinction*, 559.
50. Ibid., 563.
51. Kenan, *Between Memory and History*, 52.
52. Ibid., 57.
53. Ibid., 55–56.
54. Cohen, "Rachel Auerbach," 205.
55. Boaz Cohen, "Setting the Agenda of Holocaust Research: Discord at Yad Vashem in the 1950s," in Bankier and Michman, eds., *Holocaust Historiography in Context*, 255–92.
56. Quoted in Cohen, "Rachel Auerbach," 206.
57. "Protocols of the Executive Board of Yad Vashem," AYV, May 22, 1958, 7, quoted in Kenan, *Between Memory and History*, 59.
58. Rachel Auerbach, "What the Struggle within Yad Vashem Is All About," *Davar*, Oct. 7, 1958, quoted in Kenan, *Between Memory and History*, 60.
59. Ibid., quoted in Cohen, "Rachel Auerbach," 209.
60. Ibid., quoted in Cohen, "Rachel Auerbach," 209.
61. Kenan, *Between Memory and History*, 61.
62. Ibid.
63. Cohen, "Rachel Auerbach," 213.
64. Ibid., 210–11.
65. Ruth Bondi, *Lefetah Be-lev Ha-mizrah* (Hebrew) (Tel Aviv, 1975), 20, translated and quoted in Kenan, *Between Memory and History*, 67.
66. Nadav Davidovitch and Rakefet Zalashik, "Recalling the Survivors: Between Memory and Forgetfulness of Hospitalized Holocaust Survivors in Israel," *Israel Studies* 12, no. 2 (Summer 2007): 149.
67. Yablonka, *Survivors of the Holocaust*, 139–208.
68. Ibid.
69. Neima Barzel, "Dignity, Hatred, and Memory? Reparation from Germany: The Debate in the 1950s," *Yad Vashem Studies* 24 (1994): 266.
70. Kenan, *Between Memory and History*, 69.
71. Arad, "Israel and the Shoah," 10.
72. Quoted in Cohen, *Israeli Holocaust Research*, 13–14.
73. Dina Porat, *The Blue and Yellow Stars of David: The Zionist Leadership and the Holocaust 1939–1945* (Cambridge, MA: Harvard Univ. Press, 1990), esp. 239–62.

74. Kenan, *Between Memory and History*, 69.
75. Quote in ibid., 71.
76. Ibid., 73.
77. Stauber, *The Holocaust in Israeli Public Debate*, 149–66.
78. Haim Gouri, "Facing the Glass Booth," in *Holocaust Remembrance: The Shapes of Memory*, ed. Geoffrey H. Hartman (Oxford: Blackwell, 1994), 155.
79. Saul Friedländer, for example, emphasizes that "silence did not exist *within* the survivor community. It was maintained in relation to the outside world, and was often imposed by shame" ("Trauma, Memory, and Transference," in Hartman, ed., *Holocaust Remembrance*, 259, emphasis in the original; see also Anita Shapira, "The Holocaust: Private Memories, Public Memory," *Jewish Social Studies* 4, no. 2 [Winter 1998]: 40–58).
80. See Wieviorka, *Era of the Witness*.
81. Hanna Yablonka, *The State of Israel vs. Adolf Eichmann* (New York: Schocken Books, 2004), 233–34.
82. "Ka-tzetnik" is a well-known survivor and author of books on Auschwitz.
83. Quoted in Cohen, "Rachel Auerbach," 214.
84. Quoted in Kenan, *Between Memory and History*, 78.
85. Despite the doubt regarding the validity of the victims/heroes distinction, Diaspora Jews were still regularly subjected to the prosecution's question "Why did you not rebel?" See Hannah Arendt, *Eichmann in Jerusalem: A Report on the Banality of Evil* (New York: Penguin Books, 1994), 230.
86. Kenan, *Between Memory and History*, 78; see also Yablonka, *State of Israel vs. Adolf Eichmann* (New York: Schocken Books, 2004), 167.
87. Yablonka, *State of Israel*, 163.
88. Ibid., 164.
89. Bruno Bettelheim, *The Informed Heart: Autonomy in a Mass Age* (Glencoe, IL: Free Press, 1960); Hilberg, *Destruction of the European Jews*; Arendt, *Eichmann in Jerusalem*.
90. Kenan, *Between Memory and History*, 81.
91. Yablonka, *State of Israel*, 167.
92. Ibid., 225; Kesev Shabtai, *As Sheep to the Slaughter?* (Bet Dagan, Israel: Keshev Press, 1962).
93. This tendency began in 1967 with a colloquium at YIVO (Kenan, *Between Memory and History*, 82).
94. Ibid., 83.
95. Ibid.
96. Friedländer, "Trauma, Memory, and Transference," 260.
97. Dalia Ofer, "We Israelis Remember, but How? The Memory of the Holocaust and the Israeli Experience," *Israel Studies* 18, no. 2 (Summer 2013): 77.
98. Ibid.

99. The soldier's comment is included in Avraham Shapira, ed., *The Seventh Day: Soldiers' Talk about the Six-Day War*, recorded and edited by a group of young kibbutz members, trans. and ed. Henry Near (New York: Scribner's, 1971), 38, quoted in Kenan, *Between Memory and History*, 87.

100. Ofer, "We Israelis Remember," 78.

101. This soldier's statement is also given in Shapira, *Seventh Day*, 160–61, quoted in Arad, "Israel and the Shoah," 14.

5. Memories of the First Encounters as Represented in the Yad Vashem Collection

1. Cohen, "Setting the Agenda of Holocaust Research."
2. See Yablonka, *Survivors of the Holocaust*, 16.
3. Ofer, "Community and the Individual."
4. Some of the lopsidedness of this result might stem from confusion about which group was actually involved in a given incident. Such confusion may also have been exacerbated and taken advantage of by groups and individuals who would feign membership in one underground army rather than another and thus give that one a bad name. Another complication in interpreting these testimonies is that, as the accounts often say themselves, the Underground was frequently looking for Communists to kill, and one's Jewish identity might not always have been the primary reason for a death threat or actual attack.
5. The Polish word *kowal* means "smith."
6. The "Polish October" of 1956 was the Polish "thaw" following the death of Stalin and the revelations by Khrushchev, during which internal conflict within the Polska Zjednoczona Partia Robotnicza (Polish United Workers' Party) became a pretext to oust Jewish Communists from central positions.
7. Hurwic-Nowakowska, *Social Analysis*, table 4.

6. Comparative Analysis of the Data: Memory on a Curve

1. Kermisz, *Instructions to Interview Jewish Survivors in Poland*.
2. Jerzy Jedlicki, "Dzieje doświadczone i dzieje zaświadczone," in *Dzieło literackie jako źródło historyczne*, ed. Zofia Stefanowska and Janusz Sławiński (Warsaw: Czytelnik, 1978), 355.
3. Joanna Tokarska-Bakir conducted an anthropological analysis of mob shouts during the three postwar pogroms according to Victor Turner's performative theory; this research allowed her to verify the presence of the blood-libel myth in postwar society and not just among the "riffraff." See Joanna Tokarska-Bakir, "Cries of the Mob in the Pogroms in Rzeszów (June 1945), Cracow (August 1945), and Kielce (July 1946) as a

Source for the State of Mind of the Participants," *East European Politics and Societies* 25, no. 3 (Aug. 2011): 553–74.

4. Those who attempted to record the catastrophe as it was occurring were well aware of the insufficiency of language. Abraham Lewin, for example, wrote in his diary: "But perhaps the disaster is so great there is nothing to be gained by expressing in words everything that we feel.... Words are beyond us now. Our hearts are empty and made of stone" (*A Cup of Tears: A Diary of the Warsaw Ghetto* [Oxford: Blackwell, 1988], 97).

5. Berel Lang, "The Representation of Limits," in *Probing the Limits of Representation: Nazism and the "Final Solution,"* ed. Saul Friedländer (Cambridge, MA: Harvard Univ. Press, 1992), 300–317.

6. David G. Roskies, *Against the Apocalypse: Responses to Catastrophe in Modern Jewish Culture* (Cambridge, MA: Harvard Univ. Press, 1984).

7. Friedländer, "Trauma, Memory, and Transference," in *Holocaust Remembrance: The Shapes of Memory*, ed. Geoffrey H. Hartman (Oxford, UK: Blackwell, 1994), 255.

8. David Roskies claims that whereas in Holocaust literary works the contributions by women came rather late and in relatively small numbers (he considers Auerbach the first distinct female voice in that genre), in personal testimonies (i.e., works in which the primary goal is to record personal experience, without literary ambitions) women tended to share more of their interior lives and thus to give more expressions of their experiences than men, which is perhaps to be expected (introduction to *The Literature of Destruction: Jewish Responses to Catastrophe*, ed. David G. Roskies [Philadelphia: Jewish Publication Society, 1989], 12).

9. Studies on trauma often present what William G. Niederland terms survivors' "magical expectations" concerning life after the trauma. Such expectations appear paradoxically to increase a survivor's feelings of abandonment, solitude, and emptiness ("An Interpretation of the Psychological Stress and Defenses in Concentration-Camp Life and the Late Aftereffects," in *Massive Psychic Trauma*, ed. Henry Krystal [New York: International Universities Press, 1968], 66).

10. In citing and quoting from Dr. Goldfein's diary, I provide my own translation and give page numbers from the manuscript "Rozbitek: Dr Goldfein—Wojenne dzieje lekarza" (AYV 033/195) parenthetically in the text.

11. The use of archaic vocabulary in Polish makes this passage even more literarily dramatic:

> Istna wieża Babel! A każdy rozżalony, zdenerwowany i niezadowolony.
>
> Żydzi i Żydówki, mężczyźni i kobiety, wyrostki i podlotki, dzieci, wózki z dziećmi, kobiety w ciąży i kaleki, a wszędzie tłok, ścisk, ciżba i huki. Krótko mówiąc: Kalejdoskop żydowskiej biedoty i nędzy żydowskich pariasów.
>
> Każdy z nich chce wreszcie stanąć przed obliczem zapomodajnych urzędników i każdy jest niecierpliwy.

12. Langer, *Holocaust Testimonies*, 17, emphasis in original.

13. Amos Goldberg, "Jews' Diaries and Chronicles," in *The Oxford Handbook of Holocaust Studies*, ed. Peter Hayes and John K. Roth (New York: Oxford Univ. Press, 2010), 403.

14. Ibid., 405.

15. Jakub Herzig, *The Wrecked Life: The War Story of a Physician*, trans. Adam Gillon (New York: Vantage Press, 1963). As indicated in note 10, however, in quoting from Dr. Goldfein's diary, I have given my own translation of the original Polish manuscript "Rozbitek" (AYV 033/195).

16. Mrs. J. O. Herzig to Dr. J. Melkman, YV director general, Mar. 31, 1959, AYV O.3/1696. I owe thanks to Ms. Timorah Perel for providing me with information about this letter and some other relevant information about the depositions by Dr. Herzig in the YV collection.

17. The telephone conversations with Adam H. Herzig took place on August 29 and September 5, 2013.

18. Jerzy Kosinski, *The Painted Bird* (Boston: Houghton Mifflin, 1965).

19. D. G. Myers, "A Life beyond Repair: Review of James Park Sloan, *Jerzy Kosinski: A Biography*," *First Things* 66 (Oct. 1996): 58–64, at https://www.firstthings.com/article/1996/10/003-a-life-beyond-repair.

20. Ida Fink, *A Scrap of Time and Other Stories* (New York: Pantheon Books, 1987).

21. An English translation was published as Binjamin Wilkomirski, *Fragments: Memories of a Childhood, 1939–1948*, trans. Carol Brown Janeway (New York: Schocken, 1996).

22. Langer, for example, compares Barbara T.'s terse description of her camp experience in an oral testimony with her account published in a book, which contains a series of imaginative yet bizarre and inappropriate *similia* (*Holocaust Testimonies*, 18–19).

23. Philippe Lejeune and Paul John Eakin, *On Autobiography* (Minneapolis: Univ. of Minnesota Press, 1989), 13.

24. Trevor Field, *Form and Function in the Diary Novel* (London: MacMillan Press, 1989), 62–63.

25. Ibid., 60–61.

26. Herzig, *The Wrecked Life*, preface, unpaginated. By publishing the "diary" under his own name, Dr. Herzig confirmed what Lejeune and Eakin call a "fictional pact," which places a seal of certainty upon the fact of the published material's fictitiousness, in contrast to an "autobiographical pact," in which an author explicitly declares his identity as the narrator (*On Autobiography*, 17).

27. Lorna Martens, *The Diary Novel* (Cambridge: Cambridge Univ. Press, 1985), 49.

28. Grażyna Borkowska, *Nierozważna i nieromantyczna: O Halinie Poświatowskiej* (Kraków: Wydawnictwo Literackie, 2001).

29. Julian Aleksandrowicz, *Kartki z dziennika doktora Twardego* (1962; reprint, Kraków: Wydawnictwo Literackie, 2001).

30. In quotations from Dr. Aleksandrowicz's diary, I provide my translation of Julian Aleksandrowicz, "Kartki z dziennika doktora Twardego" (AYV O33/190), and give manuscript page numbers parenthetically in the text.

31. Historically, the simple ethics of "kindness" bears a stronger resemblance to the philosophy of Albert Schweitzer, another doctor-ethicist, and his "reverence for life." A direct influence would have to be established, of course, but it is possible to place this ethical notion within the broader European philosophical context of responding to the twentieth-century crisis of ethics, relevant to national catastrophes and genocides, with a basic, pragmatic return to respect for the needs of the human being known in a personal encounter—a philosophy expressed by thinkers as diverse as Emmanuel Levinas, Martin Buber, and Albert Camus. Another approach, from across the Atlantic, includes the simple notions of "goodness" and "hospitality," which Philip Paul Hallie detected in the rescuers of the Jewish inhabitants of the French village Le Chambon-sur-Lignon (*Lest Innocent Blood Be Shed: The Story of the Village of Le Chambon, and How Goodness Happened There* [New York: Harper and Row, 1979]).

32. There is evidence in a letter written by Halina Poświatowska that Dr. Aleksandrowicz read and valued the philosophy of Kotarbiński. See Halina Poświatowska, "Letter from Northampton, November 7, 1961," at http://www.koniczynka.art.pl/index.php?option=com_content&task=view&id=281&Itemid=108 (accessed Jan. 7, 2014).

33. Władysław Bartoszewski and Zofia Lewinówna, *Ten jest z ojczyzny mojej: Polacy z pomocą Żydom, 1939–1945* (Kraków: Znak, 1969), 545–51.

34. The announcement by the Kierownictwo Walki Cywilnej (Directorate of Civil Resistance), a section of the Polish government in exile in London, of a penalty for denouncing Jews was not issued until March 18, 1943, which was already after the liquidation of the Warsaw Ghetto.

35. Władysław Szlengel, *Dwie śmierci* (Two Deaths), in Władysław Szlengel, *Co czytałem umarłym: Wiersze getta warszawskiego*, ed. Irena Maciejewska (Warsaw: Państwowy Instytut Wydawniczy, 1977), 105, translated in Kassow, *Who Will Write Our History*, 320–21.

36. Hanna Krall and Marek Edelman, *Shielding the Flame: An Intimate Conversation with Dr. Marek Edelman, the Last Surviving Leader of the Warsaw Ghetto Uprising* (New York: Holt, 1986), 15–17.

37. Langer, *Holocaust Testimonies*, 77–120.

38. Albert Camus, *The Plague*, trans. Stuart Gilbert (New York: Vintage Books, 1991), 308.

39. Monika Adamczyk-Garbowska and Adam Kopciowski, "Zamiast macewy: Żydowskie księgi pamięci," in Tych and Adamczyk-Garbowska, eds., *Następstwa zagłady Żydów*, 466.

40. The frequent use of words such as *friend* and *befriend* in the context of betrayals by such "friends" makes one pause and search for the distortions of meaning that the reality of the war imposed on the language of those who tried to survive.

41. The psychology of trauma confirms the possibility of the storing of a life memory and the sudden triggering and eruption of that memory: "The memories from the past are revitalized as if occurring in the present, even after very long intervening delays. It is a common observation that the returning memory becomes traumatic in the face of new losses and new threats" (Haim Dasberg, "Late-Onset of Post-traumatic Reactions in Holocaust Survivors at Advanced Age," in *Das Schweigen brechen: Berliner Lektionen zu Spätfolgen der Schoa*, ed. Alexandra Rossberg and Johan Lansen [Frankfurt am Main: Peter Lang, 2003], 329).

42. Omer Bartov, "Wartime Lies and Jewish–Christian Relations in Buczacz, 1939–1944," *East European Politics and Societies* 25, no. 3 (2011): 488.

43. Langer, *Holocaust Testimonies*, 66.

44. Lawrence L. Langer, "Remembering Survival," in Hartman, ed., *Holocaust Remembrance*, 71.

45. Cathy Caruth describes trauma as the experience of having survived death without knowing it; thus, it appears as a kind of a "missed experience," which by the nature of being "missed" requires repetition and return. Traumatic disorder is in this context an apparent struggle to die (*Unclaimed Experience: Trauma, Narrative, and History* [Baltimore: Johns Hopkins Univ. Press, 1996], 60–64).

46. The psychology literature talks about the *missing monument syndrome*. This term was first used in Joost Abraham Maurits Meerloo, "Delayed Mourning in Victims of Extermination Camps," in Krystal, ed., *Massive Psychic Trauma*, 74. Jack Kugelmass and Jonathan Boyarin use it in reference to *yizkor bikher* in the introduction to their collected volume *From a Ruined Garden: The Memorial Books of Polish Jewry*, ed. Jack Kugelmass and Jonathan Boyarin (Bloomington: Indiana Univ. Press, 1998), 34.

47. Kenan, *Between Memory and History*, 5.

Conclusions: Toward Building a Collective Memory

1. Langer, "Remembering Survival," 70, emphasis in the original.
2. Friedländer, "Trauma, Memory, and Transference," 254.

Bibliography

Adamczyk-Garbowska, Monika. *Patterns of Return: Survivors' Postwar Journeys to Poland.* Washington, DC: United States Holocaust Memorial Museum, 2007.

Adamczyk-Garbowska, Monika, and Adam Kopciowski. "Zamiast macewy: Żydowskie księgi pamięci." In *Następstwa zagłady Żydów: Polska 1944–2010*, edited by Feliks Tych and Monika Adamczyk-Garbowska, 441–70. Lublin, Poland: Wydawnictwo Uniwersytetu Marii Curie-Skłodowskiej and Żydowski Instytut Historyczny im. Emanuela Ringelbluma, 2011.

Adelson, Józef. "W Polsce zwanej ludową." In *Najnowsze dzieje Żydów w Polsce: W zarysie (do 1950 roku)*, edited by Jerzy Tomaszewski, 387–477. Warsaw: Wydawnictwo Naukowe PWN, 1993.

Adorno, Theodor. *Negative Dialectic.* New York: Continuum, 1973.

Agamben, Giorgio. *Remnants of Auschwitz: The Witness and the Archive.* New York: Zone Books, 1999.

Aleksandrowicz, Julian. *Kartki z dziennika doktora Twardego.* 1962. Reprint. Kraków: Wydawnictwo Literackie, 2001.

Aleksiun, Natalia. "The Central Jewish Historical Commission in Poland, 1944–1947." *Polin: Studies in Polish Jewry* 20 (2008): 74–97.

———. *Dokąd dalej? Ruch syjonistyczny w Polsce (1944–1950).* Warsaw: Trio, 2002.

———. "Polish Historiography of the Holocaust—between Silence and Public Debate." *German History* 33, no. 3 (2004): 406–32.

———. "Rescuing a Memory and Constructing a History of Polish Jewry: Jews in Poland 1944–1950." *Jews in Russia and Eastern Europe* 1, no. 2 (2005): 5–27.

Arad, Gulie Ne'eman. "Israel and the Shoah: A Tale of Multifarious Taboos." *New German Critique*, no. 90 (Autumn 2003): 5–26.

Arad, Yitzhak. *Ghetto in Flames: The Struggle and Destruction of the Jews in Vilna in the Holocaust.* Jerusalem: Yad Vashem, Martyrs' and Heroes' Remembrance Authority, 1980.

Arendt, Hannah. *Eichmann in Jerusalem: A Report on the Banality of Evil.* 1963. Reprint. New York: Penguin Books, 1994.

Auerbach, Karen. "Rodziny żydowskie z domu w Alejach Ujazdowskich 16 w powojennej Warszawie: Dylematy etyczne w badaniach nad asymilacją w Polsce Ludowej." In *Społeczność żydowska w PRL przed kampanią antysemicką lat 1967–1968 i po niej,* edited by Grzegorz Berendt, 148–55. Warsaw: IPN, 2009.

Auerbach, Rachel. *Oyf di felder fun Ṭreblinḳe: Reportaszh.* Łódź, Poland: Tsenṭraler Yidisher Hisṭorisher Ḳomisye, 1947.

Bankier, David, and Dan Michman, eds. *Holocaust Historiography in Context: Emergences, Challenges, Polemics, and Achievements.* Jerusalem: Yad Yashem; New York: Berghahn Books, 2008.

Bańkowska, Aleksandra. "Partyzantka polska lat 1942–1944 w relacjach żydowskich." *Zagłada Żydów: Studia i Materiały,* no. 1 (2005): 148–64.

Bar, Doron. "Holocaust Commemoration in Israel during the 1950s: The Holocaust Cellar on Mount Zion." *Jewish Social Studies* 12, no. 1 (Autumn 2005): 16–38.

Baron, Salo Wittmayer. Introduction to Philip Friedman, *Roads to Extinction: Essays on the Holocaust,* 1–8. New York: Jewish Publication Society of America; Philadelphia: Conference on Jewish Social Studies, 1980.

Bartoszewski, Władysław, and Zofia Lewinówna. *Ten jest z ojczyzny mojej: Polacy z pomocą Żydom 1939–1945.* Kraków: Znak, 1969.

Bartov, Omer. "Wartime Lies and Jewish–Christian Relations in Buczacz, 1939–1944." *East European Politics and Societies* 25, no. 3 (2011): 486–511.

Barzel, Neima. "Dignity, Hatred, and Memory? Reparation from Germany: The Debate in the 1950s." *Yad Vashem Studies* 24 (1994): 247–80.

Bauer, Yehuda. *Flight and Rescue: Brichah.* New York: Random House, 1970.

———. *Rethinking the Holocaust.* New Haven, CT: Yale Univ. Press, 2001.

———. *They Chose Life: Jewish Resistance in the Holocaust.* New York: American Jewish Committee, Institute of Human Relations, 1973.

Bender, Sara. *The Jews of Białystok during World War II and the Holocaust.* Waltham, MA: Brandeis Univ. Press, 2008.

Berendt, Grzegorz. "Życie od nowa: Instytucje i organizacje żydowskie (1944–1950)." In *Następstwa zagłady Żydów: Polska 1944–2010,* edited by Feliks Tych and Monika Adamczyk-Garbowska, 191–214. Lublin, Poland: Wydawnictwo Uniwersytetu Marii Curie-Skłodowskiej and Żydowski Instytut Historyczny im. Emanuela Ringelbluma, 2011.

Bergman, Eleonora, ed. *Jewish Historical Institute: The First Fifty Years 1947–1997. Conference Papers.* Warsaw: Żydowski Instytut Historyczny Instytut Naukowo-Badawczy, 1996.

Bettelheim, Bruno. *The Informed Heart: Autonomy in a Mass Age.* Glencoe, IL: Free Press, 1960.

Błoński, Jan. "Biedni Polacy patrz ą na getto," *Togodnik Powszechny*, no. 2 (1987). At https://web.archive.org/web/20090214194707/http://tygodnik.onet.pl:80/21949,foto.html.

Blumental, Nachman. *Instrukcje dla badania przeżyć dzieci żydowskich.* Łódź, Poland: Wydawnictwa Centralnej Żydowskiej Komisji Historycznej w Polsce, 1945.

———. *Instrukcje dla zbierania materiałów etnograficznych z okresu okupacji niemieckiej.* Łódź, Poland: Wydawnictwa Centralnej Żydowskiej Komisji Historycznej w Polsce, 1945.

Boder, David. *I Did Not Interview the Dead.* Urbana: Univ. of Illinois Press, 1949.

Bogner, Nahum. *At the Mercy of Strangers: The Rescue of Jewish Children with Assumed Identities in Poland.* Jerusalem: Yad Vashem, 2009.

Borkowska, Grażyna. *Nierozważna i nieromantyczna: O Halinie Poświatowskiej.* Kraków: Wydawnictwo Literackie, 2001.

Borwicz, Michał. *Uniwersytet zbirów.* Kraków: Wydawnictwa Centralnej Żydowskiej Komisji Historycznej w Polsce, 1946.

Borwicz, Michał, Nella Rost, and Józef Wulf, eds. *Dokumenty zbrodni i męczeństwa.* Kraków: Wydawnictwa Centralnej Żydowskiej Komisji Historycznej w Polsce and Wojewódzka Żydowska Komisja, 1945.

Borzymińska, Zofia. "I ta propaganda zapuszcza coraz nowe korzenie . . . (Listy z Polski pisane w 1946 roku)." *Kwartalnik Historii Żydów* 222, no. 2 (2007): 227–34.

Brand, William, ed. *"Thou Shalt Not Kill": Poles on Jedwabne.* Warsaw: Tow. "Więź," 2001.

Brog, Mooli. "In Blessed Memory of a Dream: Mordechai Shenhavi and Initial Holocaust Commemoration Ideas in Palestine, 1942–1945." *Yad Vashem Studies* 30 (2002): 297–336.

Browning, Christopher. *Remembering Survival: Inside a Nazi Slave-Labor Camp.* New York: Norton, 2010.

Brus-Węgrowska, Danuta. "Atmosfera pogromowa." *Karta,* no. 18 (1996): 87–107.

Cała, Alina. "Kształtowanie się polskiej i żydowskiej wizji martyrologicznej po II wojnie światowej." *Przegląd Socjologiczny* 169, no. 3 (2000): 167–80.

Camus, Albert. *The Plague*. Translated by Stuart Gilbert. New York: Vintage Books, 1991.
Caruth, Cathy. *Unclaimed Experience: Trauma, Narrative, and History*. Baltimore: Johns Hopkins Univ. Press, 1996.
Cesarani, David, and Eric J. Sundquist, eds. *After the Holocaust: Challenging the Myth of Silence*. London: Routledge, 2012.
Cichopek, Anna. "The Cracow Pogrom of August 1945: A Narrative Reconstruction." In *Contested Memories: Poles and Jews during the Holocaust and Its Aftermath*, edited by Joshua D. Zimmerman, 221–38. New Brunswick, NJ: Rutgers Univ. Press, 2003.
——. *Pogrom Żydów w Krakowie, 11 sierpnia 1945 r.* Warsaw: Żydowski Instytut Historyczny, 2000.
Cohen, Boaz. *Israeli Holocaust Research: Birth and Evolution*. Abingdon, UK: Routledge, 2013. Originally a dissertation in Hebrew: "Holocaust Research in Israel: Trends, Characteristics, Developments, 1945–1980," Bar Ilan Univ., 2004.
——. "Rachel Auerbach, Yad Vashem, and Israeli Holocaust Memory." *Polin: Studies in Polish Jewry* 20 (2008): 197–221.
——. "Representing Children's Holocaust: Children's Survivor Testimonies Published in Fun Lezten Hurban, Munich 1946–1949." In *"We Are Here": New Approaches to Jewish Displaced Persons in Postwar Germany*, edited by Avinoam J. Patt and Michael Berkowitz, 75–96. Detroit: Wayne State Univ. Press, 2010.
——. "Setting the Agenda of Holocaust Research: Discord at Yad Vashem in the 1950s." In *Holocaust Historiography in Context: Emergences, Challenges, Polemics, and Achievements*, edited by David Bankier and Dan Michman, 255–92. Jerusalem: Yad Yashem; New York: Berghahn Books, 2008.
Cohen, Boaz, and Rita Horváth. "Young Witnesses in the DP Camps: Children's Holocaust Testimony in Context." *Journal of Modern Jewish Studies* 11, no. 1 (Mar. 2012): 103–25.
Cohn, Robert L. "Early Postwar Travelers on the Future of Jewish Life in Poland." *Polish Review* 53, no. 3 (2008): 317–40.
Crane, Susan A. "Writing the Individual Back into Collective Memory." *American Historical Review* 102, no. 5 (Dec. 1997): 1372–85.
Czop, Edyta, and Elżbieta Rączy, eds. *Z dziejów stosunków polsko-żydowskich w XX wieku*. Rzeszów, Poland: IPN, 2009.
Dasberg, Haim. "Late-Onset of Post-traumatic Reactions in Holocaust Survivors at Advanced Age." In *Das Schweigen brechen: Berliner Lektionen zu Spätfolgen*

der Schoa, edited by Alexandra Rossberg and Johan Lansen, 311–48. Frankfurt am Main: Peter Lang, 2003.

Datner, Szymon. *Walka i zagłada białostockiego ghetta*. Łódź, Poland: Wydawnictwa Centralnej Żydowskiej Komisji Historycznej w Polsce, 1946.

Davidovitch, Nadav, and Rakefet Zalashik. "Recalling the Survivors: Between Memory and Forgetfulness of Hospitalized Holocaust Survivors in Israel." *Israel Studies* 12, no. 2 (Summer 2007): 145–63.

Dean, Carolyn J. *Aversion and Erasure: The Fate of the Victim after the Holocaust*. Ithaca, NY: Cornell Univ. Press, 2010.

Dobroszycki, Lucjan. "Restoring Jewish Life in Post-war Poland." *Soviet Jewish Affairs* 3, no. 2 (1973): 58–72.

Donat, Alexander. *The Holocaust Kingdom: A Memoir*. New York: Holt, Rinehart and Winston, 1965.

Don-Yehiya, Eliezer. "Memory and Political Culture: Israeli Society and the Holocaust." *Studies in Contemporary Jewry* 9 (1993): 139–62.

———."Political Religion in a New State: Ben-Gurion's Mamlachtiyut." In *Israel: The First Decade of Independence*, edited by S. Ilan Troen and Noah Lukas, 171–92. Albany: State Univ. of New York Press, 1995.

Dubnow, Simon. "Let Us Search and Research: A Call to the Wise of Our People Who Volunteer to Collect Material on the Jews in Poland and Russia" (in Hebrew). *Pardes* 1 (1891): 221–42.

Duraczyński, Eugeniusz. *Wojna i okupacja, wrzesień 1939–kwiecień 1943*. Warsaw: Wiedza Powszechna, 1974.

Dworzecki, Marc. "The Day-to-Day Stand of the Jews." In *Jewish Resistance during the Holocaust: Proceedings of the Conference on Manifestations of Jewish Resistance*, 152–81. Jerusalem: Yad Vashem, 1971. Reprinted in *The Catastrophe of European Jewry: Antecedents, History, Reflections: Selected Papers*, edited by Israel [Yisrael] Gutman and Livia Rotkirchen, 367–99. Jerusalem: Yad Vashem, 1976.

Eisenbach, Artur. "Jewish Historiography in Interwar Poland." In *The Jews of Poland between Two World Wars*, edited by Yisrael Gutman, Ezra Mendelsohn, Jehuda Reinharz, and Chone Shmeruk, 453–93. Hanover, NH: Univ. Press of New England, 1989.

Engel, David. "Early Account of Polish Jewry under Nazi and Soviet Occupation Presented to the Polish Government-in-Exile, February 1940." *Jewish Social Studies* 45, no. 1 (Winter 1983): 1–17.

———. "Historical Writing as a National Mission: The Jews of Poland and Their Historiographic Tradition." In *Emanuel Ringelblum: The Man and the Historian*, edited by Yisrael Gutman, 117–40. Jerusalem: Yad Vashem, 2010.

———. "Patterns of Anti-Jewish Violence in Poland 1944–1946." *Yad Vashem Studies* 26 (1998): 43–85.

———. "Poland since 1939." In *The YIVO Encyclopedia of Jews in Eastern Europe*. New York: YIVO Institute for Jewish Research, 2010. At http://www.yivo encyclopedia.org/article.aspx/Poland/Poland_since_1939.

Engelking, Barbara. *"Jest taki piękny słoneczny dzień": Losy Żydów szukających ratunku na wsi polskiej 1942–1945*. Warsaw: Stowarzyszenie Centrum Badań Nad Zagładą Żydów and Wydawnictwo Instytut Filozofii i Socjologii PAN, 2011. Translated as *Such a Beautiful Sunny Day . . . : Jews Seeking Refuge in the Polish Countryside, 1942–1945*. Jerusalem: Yad Vashem, 2016.

Engelking, Barbara, Jacek Leociak, and Dariusz Libionka, eds. *Prowincja noc: Życie i zagłada Żydów w dystrykcie warszawskim*. Warsaw: Wydawnictwo Instytut Filozofii i Socjologii PAN, 2007.

Engelking, Barbara, Jacek Leociak, Dariusz Libionka, and Anna Ziębińska-Witek, eds. *Zagłada Żydów: Pamięć narodowa a pisanie historii w Polsce i we Francji*. Lublin, Poland: Wydawnictwo Uniwersytetu Marii Curie-Skłodowskiej, 2006.

Ezrahi, Sidra DeKoven. *By Words Alone: The Holocaust in Literature*. Chicago: Univ. of Chicago Press, 1980.

Felman, Shoshana, and Dori Laub. *Testimony: Crises of Witnessing in Literature, Psychoanalysis, and History*. New York: Routledge, 1992.

Field, Trevor. *Form and Function in the Diary Novel*. London: MacMillan Press, 1989.

Fink, Ida. *A Scrap of Time and Other Stories*. 1st American edition. New York: Pantheon Books, 1987.

Forecki, Piotr. *Od "Shoah" do "Strachu": Spory o polsko-żydowską przeszłość i pamięć w debatach publicznych*. Poznań, Poland: Wydawnictwo Poznańskie, 2010.

Frankel, Jonathan, ed. *The Fate of the European Jews, 1939–1945: Continuity or Contingency?* Studies in Contemporary Jewry no. 13. Oxford: Oxford Univ. Press, 1997.

Friedländer, Saul. *Nazi Germany and the Jews: The Years of Persecution, 1933–1939*. Vol. 1. New York: Harper Collins, 1997.

———, ed. *Probing the Limits of Representation: Nazism and the "Final Solution."* Cambridge, MA: Harvard Univ. Press, 1992.

———. "Trauma, Memory, and Transference." In *Holocaust Remembrance: The Shapes of Memory*, edited by Geoffrey H. Hartman, 252–63. Oxford: Blackwell, 1994.

———. *The Years of Extermination: Nazi Germany and the Jews, 1939–1945*. Vol. 2. New York: Harper Collins, 2007.

Friedman, Philip. *Roads to Extinction: Essays on the Holocaust*. New York: Jewish Publication Society of America; Philadelphia: Conference on Jewish Social Studies, 1980.

———. *To jest Oświęcim!* Warsaw: Państwowe Wydawnictwo Literatury Politycznej, 1945.

———. *Zagłada Żydów lwowskich*. Vol. 4. Łódź, Poland: Wydawnictwa Centralnej Żydowskiej Komisji Historycznej w Polsce, 1945.

Fuks, Marian. "20 lat *Biuletynu Żydowskiego Instytutu Historycznego*." *Biuletyn ŻIH*, no. 77 (1971): 3–16.

———. "The Institute for Jewish Studies in Warsaw (1928–1939)." In *Jewish Historical Institute: The First Fifty Years 1947–1997. Conference Papers*, edited by Eleonora Bergman, 29–35. Warsaw: Żydowski Instytut Historyczny Instytut Naukowo-Badawczy, 1996.

———. "Z działalności Żydowskiego Instytutu Historycznego w Polsce." *Kwartalnik Historyczny* 88, no. 3 (1981): 904–7.

Funkenstein, Amos. "Collective Memory and Historical Consciousness." *History and Memory* 1, no. 1 (Spring–Summer 1989): 5–26.

Gertsman, Ida. "Zajścia w Kielcach." *Biuletyn ŻIH*, no. 4 (1996): 23–24.

Gil, Idit. "The Shoah in Israeli Collective Memory: Changes in Meanings and Protagonists." *Modern Judaism* 32, no. 1 (Feb. 2012): 76–101.

Glaser, Barney, and Anselm Strauss. *The Discovery of Grounded Theory: Strategies for Qualitative Research*. Chicago: Aldine, 1967.

Główny Urząd Statystyczny Rzeczypospolitej Polskiej. *Drugi powszechny spis ludności z dn. 9. XII 1931 R*. Warsaw: Nakładem Głównego Urzędu Statystycznego, 1938.

Goldberg, Amos. "Jews' Diaries and Chronicles." In *The Oxford Handbook of Holocaust Studies*, edited by Peter Hayes and John K. Roth, 397–413. New York: Oxford Univ. Press, 2010.

Goldenberg, Myrna. "Memoirs of Auschwitz Survivors: The Burden of Gender." In *Women in the Holocaust*, edited by Dalia Ofer and Lenore J. Weitzman, 327–39. New Haven, CT: Yale Univ. Press, 1998.

Goodenough, Ward. *Description and Comparison in Cultural Anthropology*. Cambridge: Cambridge Univ. Press, 1970.
Gouri, Haim. "Facing the Glass Booth." In *Holocaust Remembrance: The Shapes of Memory*, edited by Geoffrey H. Hartman, 153–60. Oxford: Blackwell, 1994.
Grabowski, Jan. *Ja tego Żyda znam! Szantażowanie Żydów w Warszawie, 1939–1943*. Warsaw: Wydawnictwo Instytut Filozofii i Socjologii PAN, 2004.
Grabski, August. *Działalność komunistów wśród Żydów w Polsce (1944–1949)*. Warsaw: Trio, 2004.
———. *Żydowski ruch kombatancki w Polsce 1944–1949*. Warsaw: Trio, 2002.
———. "Żydzi a polskie życie polityczne (1944–1949)." In *Następstwa zagłady Żydów: Polska 1944–2010*, edited by Feliks Tych and Monika Adamczyk-Garbowska, 157–88. Lublin, Poland: Wydawnictwo Uniwersytetu Marii Curie-Skłodowskiej and Żydowski Instytut Historyczny im. Emanuela Ringelbluma, 2011.
Green, Anna. "Individual Remembering and 'Collective Memory': Theoretical Presuppositions and Contemporary Debates." *Oral History* 32, no. 2 (Autumn 2004): 35–44.
Greenspan, Henry. *On Listening to Holocaust Survivors: Recounting and Life History*. Westport, CT: Praeger, 1998.
———. "Survivors' Accounts." In *The Oxford Handbook of Holocaust Studies*, edited by Peter Hayes and John K. Roth, 414–27. New York: Oxford Univ. Press, 2010.
Gross, Jan Tomasz. *Fear: Anti-Semitism in Poland after Auschwitz. An Essay in Historical Interpretation*. New York: Random House, 2006.
———. *Neighbors: The Destruction of the Jewish Community in Jedwabne, Poland*. Princeton, NJ: Princeton Univ. Press, 2001.
———. *Sąsiedzi: Historia zagłady żydowskiego miasteczka*. Sejny, Poland: Fundacja Pogranicze, 2000.
———. *Strach: Antysemityzm w Polsce tuż po wojnie: Historia moralnej zapaści*. Kraków: Znak, 2008.
———. *Wokół Sąsiadów: Polemiki i wyjaśnienia*. Sejny, Poland: Pogranicze, 2003.
Gross, Jan Tomasz, and Irena Grudzińska-Gross. *Golden Harvest: Events at the Periphery of the Holocaust*. New York: Oxford Univ. Press, 2012.
———. *Złote żniwa*. Kraków: Znak, 2011.
Gutman, Israel [Yisrael], ed. *Major Changes within the Jewish People in the Wake of the Holocaust: Proceedings of the Ninth Yad Vashem International Historical Conference, Jerusalem, 1993*. Jerusalem: Yad Vashem, 1996.

Gutman, Israel [Yisrael], and Livia Rotkirchen, eds. *The Catastrophe of European Jewry: Antecedents, History, Reflections. Selected Papers.* Jerusalem: Yad Vashem, 1976.

Gutman, Yisrael. "Emanuel Ringelblum: A Historian and His Time." In *Emanuel Ringelblum: The Man and the Historian*, edited by Yisrael Gutman, 79–116. Jerusalem: Yad Vashem, 2010.

———, ed. *Emanuel Ringelblum: The Man and the Historian.* Jerusalem: Yad Vashem, 2010.

———. *Hajehudim be-Polin acharei Milchemet Ha'olam Hashniya.* Jerusalem: Merkaz Zalman Shazar, 1985.

———. *The Jews of Warsaw, 1939–1943: Ghetto, Underground, Revolt.* Bloomington: Indiana Univ. Press, 1982.

Gutman, Yisrael, and Shmuel Krakowski. *Unequal Victims: Poles and Jews during World War Two.* New York: Holocaust Library, 1986.

Gutman, Yisrael, Ezra Mendelsohn, Jehuda Reinharz, and Chone Shmeruk, eds. *The Jews of Poland between Two World Wars.* Hanover, NH: Univ. Press of New England, 1989.

Gutman, Yisrael, and Avital Saf, eds. *She'erit Hapletah, 1944–1948: Rehabilitation and Political Struggle.* Proceedings of the Sixth Yad Vashem International Historical Conference, Jerusalem, Oct. 1985. Jerusalem: Yad Vashem, 1990.

Gutwein, Daniel. "The Privatization of the Holocaust: Memory, Historiography, and Politics." *Israel Studies* 14, no. 1 (Spring 2009): 36–64.

Halbwachs, Maurice. *On Collective Memory.* Chicago: Univ. of Chicago Press, 1992.

Hallie, Philip Paul. *Lest Innocent Blood Be Shed: The Story of the Village of Le Chambon, and How Goodness Happened There.* New York: Harper and Row, 1979.

Hartman, Geoffrey H., ed. *Holocaust Remembrance: The Shapes of Memory.* Oxford: Blackwell, 1994.

Hayes, Peter, and John K. Roth, eds. *The Oxford Handbook of Holocaust Studies.* New York: Oxford Univ. Press, 2010.

Herzig, Jakub. *The Wrecked Life: The War Story of a Physician.* Translated by Adam Gillon. New York: Vantage Press, 1963.

Hilberg, Raul. *The Destruction of the European Jews.* New Haven, CT: Yale Univ. Press, 1961.

Hochberg-Mariańska, Maria, and Noe Grüss, eds. *The Children Accuse.* Translated by Bill Johnston. Library of Holocaust Testimonies. Portland, OR: Vallentine Mitchell, 1996.

———, eds. *Dzieci oskarżają: Materiały i dokumenty*. Kraków: Wydawnictwa Centralnej Żydowskiej Komisji Historycznej w Polsce, 1947.

Holocaust Survivors Testimonies. Catalog, vols. 1–5. Warsaw: Jewish Historical Institute, 1998–2007.

Horn, Maurycy. "Czterdzieści lat działalności w Warszawie Żydowskiego Instytutu Historycznego w Polsce." *Kalendarz żydowski*, 1987–88, 135–41.

———. "Działalność naukowa i wydawnicza Centralnej Żydowskiej Komisji Historycznej przy CKŻwP i Żydowskiego Instytutu Historycznego w Polsce w latach 1945–1950." *Biuletyn ŻIH*, nos. 133–34 (1985): 123–32.

———. "Scholarly Activity of the Jewish Historical Institute in Poland, 1947–1996." In *Jewish Historical Institute: The First Fifty Years 1947–1997. Conference Papers*, edited by Eleonora Bergman, 42–49. Warsaw: Żydowski Instytut Historyczny Instytut Naukowo-Badawczy, 1996.

———. "Szkic z przeszłości Żydowskiego Instytutu Historycznego w Polsce (1949–1966)." *Biuletyn ŻIH*, no. 110 (1979): 3–19.

———. "Żydowski Instytut Historyczny w Polsce w latach 1944–1949." *Biuletyn ŻIH*, no. 109 (1979): 3–16.

Hurwic-Nowakowska, Irena. *A Social Analysis of Postwar Polish Jewry*. Jerusalem: Zalman Shazar Center for Jewish History, 1986.

Jedlicki, Jerzy. "Dzieje doświadczone i dzieje zaświadczone." In *Dzieło literackie jako źródło historyczne*, edited by Zofia Stefanowska and Janusz Sławiński, 344–71. Warsaw: Czytelnik, 1978.

Jockusch, Laura. "Chroniclers of Catastrophe: History Writing as a Jewish Response to Persecution before and after the Holocaust." In *Holocaust Historiography in Context: Emergence, Challenges, Polemics, and Achievements*, edited by David Bankier and Dan Michman, 135–66. Jerusalem: Yad Vashem; New York: Berghahn Books, 2008.

———. *Collect and Record! Jewish Holocaust Documentation in Early Postwar Europe*. Oxford: Oxford Univ. Press, 2012.

———, ed. *Early Jewish Texts on the Holocaust: The Collections of the Central Jewish Historical Commission in Poland*. Göttingen, Germany: Vandenhoeck & Ruprecht, forthcoming.

———. "A Folk Monument to Our Destruction and Heroism: Jewish Historical Commissions in the Displaced Persons Camps of Germany, Austria, and Italy." In *"We Are Here": New Approaches to Jewish Displaced Persons in Postwar Germany*, edited by Avinoam J. Patt and Michael Berkowitz, 31–73. Detroit: Wayne State Univ. Press, 2010.

Kaczmarski, Krzysztof. *Pogrom, którego nie było: Rzeszów, 11–12 czerwca 1945 r.: Fakty, hipotezy, dokumenty.* Rzeszów: IPN, 2008.

Kahana, Boaz, Zev Harel, and Eva Kahana. *Holocaust Survivors and Immigrants: Late Life Adaptations.* New York: Springer, 2005.

Kamiński, Łukasz, and Jan Żaryn. *Wokół pogromu kieleckiego.* Vol. 1. Warsaw: IPN, 2006.

Kassow, Samuel D. *Who Will Write Our History? Emanuel Ringelblum, the Warsaw Ghetto, and the Oyneg Shabes Archive.* Bloomington: Indiana Univ. Press, 2007.

Katznelson, Yitzhak. *Vittel Diary, 22.5.43–12.9.43.* Western Galilee: Hakibbutz Hameuchaud, 1972.

Kenan, Orna. *Between Memory and History: The Evolution of Israeli Historiography of the Holocaust, 1945–1961.* New York: Peter Lang, 2003.

Kermisz, Josef, ed. *Dokumenty i materiały do dziejów okupacji niemieckiej w Polsce.* Vols. 1–3. Warsaw: Wydawnictwa Centralnej Żydowskiej Komisji Historycznej w Polsce, 1946.

———. *Instructions to Interview Jewish Survivors in Poland.* Translated by Anna Purisch and Daniel Purisch. In *Early Jewish Texts on the Holocaust: The Collections of the Central Jewish Historical Commission in Poland*, edited by Laura Jockusch. Göttingen, Germany: Vandenhoeck & Rupprecht, forthcoming.

———. *Instrukcje dla zbierania materiałów historycznych z okresu okupacji niemieckiej.* Łódź, Poland: Wydawnictwa Centralnej Żydowskiej Komisji Historycznej w Polsce, 1945.

Kersten, Krystyna. *Polacy, Żydzi, komunizm: Anatomia półprawd, 1939–68.* Warsaw: Niezależna Oficyna Wydawnicza, 1992.

———. *Repatriacja ludności polskiej po II wojnie światowej: Studium historyczne.* Wrocław, Poland: Zakład Narodowy im. Ossolińskich PAN, 1974.

Klibanski, Bronia. "The Underground Archives of the Bialystok Ghetto Founded by Mersik and Tennenbaum." *Yad Vashem Studies* 2 (1958): 295–329.

Klier, John Doyle, and Shlomo Lambroza, eds. *Pogroms: Anti-Jewish Violence in Modern Russian History.* Cambridge: Cambridge Univ. Press, 2004.

Kołodyńska, Agnieszka. "Interview with Bożena Szaynok: Jak to widzi Gross." *Gazeta Wyborcza*, July 8, 2006.

Kopciowski, Adam. "Zajścia antyżydowskie na Lubelszczyźnie w pierwszych latach po drugiej wojnie światowej." *Zagłada Żydów: Studia i Materiały*, no. 3 (2007): 178–207.

Kosinski, Jerzy. *The Painted Bird.* Boston: Houghton Mifflin, 1965.

Kowalski, Robert, ed. *Wokół legendy "Ognia": Opór przeciwko zniewoleniu. Polska–Małopolska–Podhale 1945–1956. Materiały z ogólnopolskiej konferencji naukowej zorganizowanej w Nowym Targu w dniach 9–11 III 2007*. Nowy Targ, Poland: Polskie Towarzystwo Historyczne i IPN, 2008.

Koźmińska-Frejlak, Ewa. "Asymilacja do polskości jako strategia adaptacyjna ocalałych z Zagłady polskich Żydów." *Kwartalnik Historii Żydów*, no. 2 (2013): 236–47.

———. "Kondycja ocalałych: Adaptacja do rzeczywistości powojennej (1944–1949)." In *Następstwa zagłady Żydów: Polska 1944–2010*, edited by Feliks Tych and Monika Adamczyk-Garbowska, 123–55. Lublin, Poland: Wydawnictwo Uniwersytetu Marii Curie-Skłodowskiej and Żydowski Instytut Historyczny im. Emanuela Ringelbluma, 2011.

Krall, Hanna, and Marek Edelman. *Shielding the Flame: An Intimate Conversation with Dr. Marek Edelman, the Last Surviving Leader of the Warsaw Ghetto Uprising*. New York: Holt, 1986.

Krystal, Henry, ed. *Massive Psychic Trauma*. New York: International Universities Press, 1968.

Kugelmass, Jack, and Jonathan Boyarin, eds. *From a Ruined Garden: The Memorial Books of Polish Jewry*. Bloomington: Indiana Univ. Press, 1998.

———. Introduction to *From a Ruined Garden: The Memorial Books of Polish Jewry*, edited by Jack Kugelmass and Jonathan Boyarin, 1–48. Bloomington: Indiana Univ. Press, 1998.

Kwiek, Julian. "Dzieje ludności żydowskiej w Tarnowie po II wojnie światowej." *Studia Judaica* 8, nos. 1–2 (2005): 187–211.

———. "'Ogień' wobec mniejszości narodowych." In *Wokół legendy "Ognia": Opór przeciwko zniewoleniu. Polska–Małopolska–Podhale 1945–1956. Materiały z ogólnopolskiej konferencji naukowej zorganizowanej w Nowym Targu w dniach 9–11 III 2007*, edited by Robert Kowalski, 243–58. Nowy Targ, Poland: Polskie Towarzystwo Historyczne i IPN, 2008.

———. "Zabójstwa ludności żydowskiej w Krakowskiem w latach 1945–1947: Fakty i mity." *Kwartalnik Historii Żydów*, no. 4 (2013): 679–95.

Lambroza, Shlomo. "The Pogroms of 1903–1906." In *Pogroms: Anti-Jewish Violence in Modern Russian History*, edited by John Doyle Klier and Shlomo Lambroza, 195–247. Cambridge: Cambridge Univ. Press, 2004.

Lang, Berel. "The Representation of Limits." In *Probing the Limits of Representation: Nazism and the "Final Solution,"* edited by Saul Friedländer, 300–317. Cambridge, MA: Harvard Univ. Press, 1992.

Langer, Lawrence L. *Holocaust Testimonies: The Ruins of Memory.* New Haven, CT: Yale Univ. Press, 1991.

———. "Remembering Survival." In *Holocaust Remembrance: The Shapes of Memory*, edited by Geoffrey H. Hartman, 70–80. Oxford: Blackwell, 1994.

Lejeune, Philippe, and Paul John Eakin. *On Autobiography.* Minneapolis: Univ. of Minnesota Press, 1989.

Levin, Abraham. *A Cup of Tears: A Diary of the Warsaw Ghetto.* Oxford: Blackwell, 1988.

Libionka, Dariusz. "Polska konspiracja wobec eksterminacji Żydow w dystrykcie warszawskim." In *Prowincja noc: Życie i zagłada Żydów w dystrykcie warszawskim*, edited by Barbara Engelking, Jacek Leociak, and Dariusz Libionka, 443–504. Warsaw: Wydawnictwo Instytut Filozofii i Socjologii PAN, 2007.

Libionka, Dariusz, and Paweł Reszka. "Święto zmarłych w Rechcie." *Karta*, no. 46 (2005): 122–35.

Liebman, Charles S., and Eliezer Don-Yehiya. *Civil Religion in Israel: Traditional Judaism and Political Culture in the Jewish State.* Berkeley: Univ. of California Press, 1983.

Łuczak, Czesław. "Szanse i trudności bilansu demograficznego Polski w latach 1939–1945." *Dzieje Najnowsze* 26, no. 2 (1994): 9–14.

Machcewicz, Paweł. "Wokół Jedwabnego." In *Wokół Jedwabnego*, vol. 1, edited by Paweł Machcewicz and Krzysztof Persak, 9–62. Warsaw: IPN, 2002.

Machcewicz, Paweł, and Krzysztof Persak, eds. *Wokół Jedwabnego.* Vol. 1. Warsaw: IPN, 2002.

Madajczyk, Czesław. *Polityka III Rzeszy w okupowanej Polsce.* Warsaw: Państwowe Wydawnictwo Naukowe, 1970.

Maltz, Moshe. "Pages about Pain and Death of the Jewish Settlement in Sokal." Translated from Yiddish to Hebrew by Tzvi Schussman; translated from Hebrew to English by Vered Dayan. In *Memorial Book of Sokal, Tartakow, and Surroundings (Ukraine)*, edited by Abraham Chomet, 277–317. Tel Aviv: n.p., 1968. At http://www.jewishgen.org/yizkor/sokal/sokal.html.

Mankowitz, Zeev W. *Life between Memory and Hope: The Survivors of the Holocaust in Occupied Germany.* New York: Cambridge Univ. Press, 2002.

Martens, Lorna. *The Diary Novel.* Cambridge: Cambridge Univ. Press, 1985.

Meducki, Stanisław, and Zenon Wrona. *Antyżydowskie wydarzenia kieleckie 4 lipca 1946 roku.* Kielce, Poland: Urząd Miasta Kielce, 1992.

Meerloo, Joost Abraham Maurits. "Delayed Mourning in Victims of Extermination Camps." In *Massive Psychic Trauma*, edited by Henry Krystal, 72–75. New York: International Universities Press, 1968.

Melchior, Małgorzata. "Jewish Identity: Between Ascription and Choice." *Polish Sociological Review* 109, no. 1 (1995): 49–60.

———. *Zagłada a tożsamość: Polscy Żydzi ocaleni "na aryjskich papierach." Analiza doświadczenia biograficznego*. Warsaw: Wydawnictwo Instytut Filozofii i Socjologii PAN, 2004.

Michlic, Joanna B. "Who Am I? Jewish Children's Search for Identity in Postwar Poland, 1945–1949." *Polin: Studies in Polish Jewry* 20 (2008): 122–48.

Michman, Dan. *Holocaust Historiography, a Jewish Perspective: Conceptualizations, Terminology, Approaches, and Fundamental Issues*. London: Vallentine Mitchell, 2003.

Moyn, Samuel. "Bearing Witness: Theological Roots of a New Secular Morality." In *The Holocaust and Historical Methodology*, edited by Dan Stone, 127–42. New York: Berghahn Books, 2012.

Murphy, H. B. M. "The Resettlement of Jewish Refugees in Israel, with Special Reference to Those Known as Displaced Persons." *Population Studies* 5, no. 2 (Nov. 1951): 153–74.

Müller, Beate. "Trauma, Historiography, and Polyphony: Adult Voices in the CJHC's Early Postwar Child Holocaust Testimonies." *History and Memory* 24, no. 2 (Fall–Winter 2012): 157–95.

Myers, D. G. "A Life beyond Repair: Review of James Park Sloan, *Jerzy Kosinski: A Biography*." *First Things* 66 (Oct. 1996): 58–64. At https://www.firstthings.com/article/1996/10/003-a-life-beyond-repair.

Nachmany-Gafny, Emunah. *Dividing Hearts: The Removal of Jewish Children from Gentile Families in Poland in the Immediate Post-Holocaust Years*. Jerusalem: Yad Vashem, 2009.

Nalewajko-Kulikov, Joanna. "Pierwsze wrażenia: Żydowski intelektualista w rzeczywistości odradzającej się Polski (na przykładzie Dawida Sfarda)." In *Zagłada Żydów: Pamięć narodowa a pisanie historii w Polsce i we Francji*, edited by Barbara Engelking, Jacek Leociak, Dariusz Libionka, and Anna Ziębińska-Witek, 229–33. Lublin, Poland: Wydawnictwo Uniwersytetu Marii Curie-Skłodowskiej, 2006.

Neale, Timothy D. "'... The Credentials That Would Rescue Me': Trauma and the Fraudulent Survivor." *Holocaust and Genocide Studies* 24, no. 3 (Winter 2010): 431–48.

Niederland, William G. "An Interpretation of the Psychological Stress and Defenses in Concentration-Camp Life and the Late Aftereffects." In *Massive Psychic Trauma*, edited by Henry Krystal, 60–86. New York: International Universities Press, 1968.

Niewyk, Donald L., ed. *Fresh Wounds: Early Narratives of Holocaust Survival.* Chapel Hill: Univ. of North Carolina Press, 1998.
Nora, Pierre. "Between Memory and History: *Les lieux de mémoire.*" *Representations* 26 (Spring 1989): 7–24.
Ofer, Dalia. "The Community and the Individual: The Different Narratives of Early and Late Testimonies and Their Significance for Historians." In *Holocaust Historiography in Context: Emergences, Challenges, Polemics, and Achievements,* edited by David Bankier and Dan Michman, 519–35. Jerusalem: Yad Yashem; New York: Berghahn Books, 2008.
———. *Escaping from the Holocaust: Illegal Immigration to the Land of Israel, 1939–1944.* New York: Oxford Univ. Press, 1990.
———. "Fifty Years After: The Yishuv, Zionism, and the Holocaust, 1933–1948." In *Major Changes within the Jewish People in the Wake of the Holocaust: Proceedings of the Ninth Yad Vashem International Historical Conference, Jerusalem, 1993,* edited by Israel Gutman, 463–95. Jerusalem: Yad Vashem, 1996.
———. "Gender Issues in Ghetto Diaries and Interviews: The Case of Warsaw." In *Women in the Holocaust,* edited by Dalia Ofer and Lenore J. Weitzman, 143–67. New Haven, CT: Yale Univ. Press, 1998.
———. "The Past That Does Not Pass: Israelis and Holocaust Memory." *Israel Studies* 14, no. 1 (Spring 2009): 1–35.
———. "The Strength of Remembrance: Commemorating the Holocaust during the First Decade of Israel." *Jewish Social Studies* 6, no. 2 (Winter 2000): 24–55.
———. "We Israelis Remember, but How? The Memory of the Holocaust and the Israeli Experience." *Israel Studies* 18, no. 2 (Summer 2013): 70–85.
Ofer, Dalia, and Lenore J. Weitzman, eds. *Women in the Holocaust.* New Haven, CT: Yale Univ. Press, 1998.
Patt, Avinoam J., and Michael Berkowitz, eds. *"We Are Here": New Approaches to Jewish Displaced Persons in Postwar Germany.* Detroit: Wayne State Univ. Press, 2010.
Penkalla, Adam. "Stosunki polsko-żydowskie w Radomiu (kwiecień 1945–luty 1946)." *Biuletyn Żydowskiego Instytutu Historycznego* 7, no. 3 (1995): 175–78; 6, no. 2 (1996): 57–66.
———. "Władze o obecności Żydów na terenie Kielecczyzny w okresie od wkroczenia Armii Czerwonej do pogromu kieleckiego." *Kwartalnik Historii Żydów* 208, no. 4 (2003): 557–77.
Penslar, Derek J. "Narratives in Nation Building: Major Themes in Zionist Historiography." In *The Jewish Past Revisited: Reflections on Modern Jewish*

Historians, edited by David N. Myers and David B. Ruderman, 104–27. New Haven, CT: Yale Univ. Press, 1998.

Pike, Kenneth L. *Language in Relation to a Unified Theory of the Structure of Human Behavior*. 2nd ed. The Hague: Mouton, 1967.

Polonsky, Antony. "Beyond Condemnation, Apologetics, and Apologies: On the Complexity of Polish Behavior." In *The Fate of the European Jews, 1939–1945: Continuity or Contingency?* edited by Jonathan Frankel, 190–224. Studies in Contemporary Jewry no. 13. Oxford: Oxford Univ. Press, 1997.

———. *The Jews in Poland and Russia*. Vol. 3: *1914–2008*. Oxford: Littman Library of Jewish Civilization, 2012.

———, ed. *"My Brother's Keeper?" Recent Polish Debates on the Holocaust*. London: Routledge, 1989.

Polonsky, Antony, and Bolesław Drukier. *The Beginnings of Communist Rule in Poland, December 1943–June 1945*. London: Routledge and Kegan Paul, 1980.

Polonsky, Antony, and Joanna B. Michlic. *The Neighbors Respond: The Controversy over the Jedwabne Massacre in Poland*. Princeton, NJ: Princeton Univ. Press, 2004.

Porat, Dan A. "From the Scandal to the Holocaust in Israeli Education." *Journal of Contemporary History* 39, no. 4 (Oct. 2004): 619–36.

Porat, Dina. *The Blue and Yellow Stars of David: The Zionist Leadership and the Holocaust 1939–1945*. Cambridge, MA: Harvard Univ. Press, 1990.

———. *Israeli Society, the Holocaust, and Its Survivors*. London: Vallentine Mitchell, 2008.

———. "The Role of European Jewry in the Plans of the Zionist Movement during World War II and Its Aftermath." In *She'erit Hapletah, 1944–1948: Rehabilitation and Political Struggle*, proceedings of the Sixth Yad Vashem International Historical Conference, Jerusalem, Oct. 1985, edited by Yisrael Gutman and Avital Saf, 292–93. Jerusalem: Yad Vashem, 1990.

———. "With Forgiveness and Grace: The Encounter between Ruzka Korczak, the Yishuv, and Its Leaders, 1944–1946." *Journal of Israeli History* 16, no. 2 (1995): 101–32.

Poświatowska, Halina. "Letter from Northampton, November 7, 1961." At http://www.koniczynka.art.pl/index.php?option=com_content&task=view&id=281&Itemid=108.

Prekerowa, Teresa. "Wojna i okupacja." In *Najnowsze dzieje Żydów w Polsce: w zarysie (do 1950 roku)*, edited by Jerzy Tomaszewski, 273–384. Warsaw: Wydawnictwo Naukowe PWN, 1993.

Quercioli-Mincer, Laura. "'Nie będziemy się więcej bać ludzi?' Powrót po Zagładzie w literaturze polsko-żydowskiej." *Kwartalnik Historii Żydów* 222, no. 2 (2007): 199–225.

Rączy, Elżbieta. "Zabójstwa dokonane na Żydach w województwie rzeszowskim w latach 1944–1947 w świetle akt organów bezpieczeństwa." In *Z dziejów stosunków polsko-żydowskich w XX wieku*, edited by Edyta Czop and Elżbieta Rączy, 128–44. Rzeszów, Poland: IPN, 2009.

Ram, Uri. "Zionist Historiography and the Invention of Modern Jewish Nationhood: The Case of Ben Zion Dinur." *History and Memory* 7, no. 1 (Spring–Summer 1995): 91–124.

Redlich, Shimon. *Life in Transit: Jews in Postwar Lodz, 1945–1950*. Boston: Academic Studies Press, 2010.

Rice, Monika. "The 'Gross' Effect: Polish–Jewish Historiography in Poland after 'Neighbors.'" N.d. At http://www.aapjstudies.org/manager/external/ckfinder/userfiles/files/Monika%20Rice%20PIASA%20.pdf.

Ringelblum, Emanuel. *Notitsn fun varsher geto*. Warsaw: Farlag "Yidish Bukh," 1952.

———. *Polish–Jewish Relations during the Second World War*. Edited by Joseph Kermish and Shmuel Krakowski. Evanston, IL: Northwestern Univ. Press, 1992.

Rosen, Alan. *The Wonder of Their Voices: The 1946 Holocaust Interviews of David Boder*. New York: Oxford Univ. Press, 2010.

Roskies, David G. *Against the Apocalypse: Responses to Catastrophe in Modern Jewish Culture*. Cambridge, MA: Harvard Univ. Press, 1984.

———. Introduction to *The Literature of Destruction: Jewish Responses to Catastrophe*, edited by David G. Roskies, 3–12. Philadelphia: Jewish Publication Society, 1989.

———, ed. *The Literature of Destruction: Jewish Responses to Catastrophe*. Philadelphia: Jewish Publication Society, 1989.

Rusiniak, Martyna. "Treblinka-Eldorado Podlasia?" *Kwartalnik Historii Żydów*, no. 2 (2006): 200–211.

Rzepliński, Andrzej. "Ten jest z ojczyzny mojej? Sprawy karne oskarżonych o wymordowanie Żydów w Jedwabnem w świetle zasady rzetelnego procesu." In *Wokół Jedwabnego*, vol. 1, edited by Paweł Machcewicz and Krzysztof Persak, 353–460. Warsaw: IPN, 2002.

Santner, Eric L. "History beyond the Pleasure Principle: Some Thoughts on the Representation of Trauma." In *Probing the Limits of Representation: Nazism* and the "Final Solution," edited by Saul Friedländer, 143–54. Cambridge, MA: Harvard Univ. Press, 1992.

Schatz, Jaff. *The Generation: The Rise and Fall of the Jewish Communists of Poland.* Berkeley: Univ. of California Press, 1991.

Schweid, Eliezer. "The Rejection of the Diaspora in Zionist Thoughts: Two Approaches." *Studies in Zionism* 5, no. 1 (1984): 43–70.

Segev, Tom. *The Seventh Million: The Israelis and the Holocaust.* New York: Hill and Wang, 1993.

Sfard, David. *Mit zich und mit andere.* Jerusalem: Farlag "Jeruszalaimer Almanach," 1984.

Shabtai, Kesev. *As Sheep to the Slaughter?* Bet Dagan, Israel: Keshev Press, 1962.

Shapira, Anita. "The Holocaust: Private Memories, Public Memory." *Jewish Social Studies* 4, no. 2 (Winter 1998): 40–58.

———. *Land and Power: The Zionist Resort to Force, 1881–1948.* New York: Oxford Univ. Press, 1992.

Shapira, Anita, and Ora Wiskind-Elper. "Politics and Collective Memory: The Debate over the 'New Historians' in Israel." *History and Memory* 7, no. 1 (Spring–Summer 1995): 9–40.

Shapira, Avraham, ed. *The Seventh Day: Soldiers' Talk about the Six-Day War.* Recorded and edited by a group of young kibbutz members. Translated and edited by Henry Near. New York: Scribner's, 1971.

Shoshkes, Henryk. *Poyln—1946.* Buenos Aires: Zentral-Farband fun Poylishe Yiden in Argentina, 1946.

Siek, Magdalena, Aleksandra Bańkowska, and Agnieszka Jarzębowska. "Morderstwa Żydów w latach 1944–1946 na terenie Polski na podstawie kwerendy w zbiorze 301 (Relacje z Zagłady) w Archiwum ŻIH." *Kwartalnik Historii Żydów* 231, no. 3 (2009): 356–67.

Siekierski, Maciej, and Feliks Tych, eds. *Widziałem anioła śmierci: Losy deportowanych Żydów polskich w ZSRR w latach II wojny światowej. Świadectwa zebrane przez Ministerstwo informacji i Dokumentacji Rządu Polskiego na Uchodźstwie w latach 1942–1943.* Warsaw: Rosner i Wspólnicy and Żydowski Instytut Historyczny w Warszawie; Stanford, CA: Hoover Institution on War, Revolution, and Peace, Stanford Univ., 2006.

Skibińska, Alina. "Powroty ocalałych." In *Prowincja noc: Życie i zagłada Żydów w dystrykcie warszawskim,* edited by Barbara Engelking, Jacek Leociak, and Dariusz Libionka, 505–99. Warsaw: Wydawnictwo Instytut Filozofii i Socjologii PAN, 2007.

———. "Powroty ocalałych i stosunek do nich społeczeństwa polskiego." In *Następstwa zagłady Żydów: Polska 1944–2010*, edited by Feliks Tych and Monika Adamczyk-Garbowska, 39–70. Lublin, Poland: Wydawnictwo Uniwersytetu Marii Curie-Skłodowskiej and Żydowski Instytut Historyczny im. Emanuela Ringelbluma, 2011.

Skibińska, Alina, and Dariusz Libionka. "'Przysięgam walczyć o wolną i potężną Polskę, wykonywać rozkazy przełożonych, tak mi dopomóż Bóg': Żydzi w AK. Epizod z Ostrowca Świętokrzyskiego." *Zagłada Żydów: Studia i Materiały*, no. 4 (2008): 287–323.

Skibińska, Alina, and Jakub Petelewicz. "Udział Polaków w zbrodniach na Żydach: Casus region świetokrzyski." *Zagłada Żydów: Studia i Materiały* 1 (2005): 114–47.

Śmietanka-Kruszelnicki, Ryszard. "Podziemie antykomunistyczne wobec Żydów po 1945 roku—wstęp do problematyki (na przykładzie województwa kieleckiego)." In *Z przeszłości Żydów polskich: Polityka, gospodarka, kultura, społeczeństwo*, edited by Jacek Wijaczka and Grzegorz Miernik, 249–77. Kraków: IPN, 2005.

Stankowski, Albert, and Piotr Weiser. "Demograficzne skutki Holokaustu." In *Następstwa zagłady Żydów: Polska 1944–2010*, edited by Feliks Tych and Monika Adamczyk-Garbowska, 15–38. Lublin, Poland: Wydawnictwo Uniwersytetu Marii Curie-Skłodowskiej and Żydowski Instytut Historyczny im. Emanuela Ringelbluma, 2011.

Stauber, Roni. "Confronting the Jewish Response during the Holocaust: Yad Vashem, a Commemorative and a Research Institute in the 1950s." *Modern Judaism* 20, no. 3 (Oct. 2000): 277–98.

———. *The Holocaust in Israeli Public Debate in the 1950's: Ideology and Memory*. London: Vallentine Mitchell, 2007.

———. *Laying the Foundations for Holocaust Research: The Impact of the Historian Philip Friedman*. Search and Research no. 15. Jerusalem: Yad Vashem, 2009.

Steinlauf, Michael C. *Bondage to the Dead: Poland and the Memory of the Holocaust*. Modern Jewish History. Syracuse, NY: Syracuse Univ. Press, 1997.

Stola, Dariusz. *Kampania antysyjonistyczna w Polsce, 1967–1968*. Warsaw: Instytut Studiów Politycznych Polskiej Akademii Nauk, 2000.

Strauss, Anselm, and Juliet Corbin. *Basics of Qualitative Research: Grounded Theory Procedures and Techniques*. Newbury Park, CA: Sage, 1990.

Szapiro, Paweł. *Wojna żydowsko-niemiecka: Polska prasa konspiracyjna 1943–1944 o powstaniu w getcie Warszawy*. London: Aneks, 1992.

Szarota, Tomasz. "Upowszechnienie kultury." In *Polska Ludowa 1944–1950: Przemiany społeczne*, edited by Hanna Jędruszczak, Krystyna Kersten, and Franciszek Ryszka, 408–70. Wrocław, Poland: Zakład Narodowy im. Ossolińskich, 1974.

Szaynok, Bożena. "The Jewish Pogrom in Kielce, July 1946: New Evidence." *Intermarium* 1, no. 3 (1997). At http://ece.columbia.edu/files/ece/images/kielce.html.

———. *Ludność żydowska na Dolnym Śląsku, 1945–1950*. Wrocław, Poland: Bellona, 2000.

———. *Pogrom Żydów w Kielcach 4 lipca 1946 roku*. Warsaw: Bellona, 1992.

———. "Polacy i Żydzi lipiec 1944–lipiec 1946." In *Wokół pogromu kieleckiego*, vol. 1, edited by Łukasz Kamiński and Jan Żaryn, 9–24. Warsaw: IPN, 2006.

———. "Problem antysemityzmu w relacjach polsko-żydowskich w latach 1945–1954." In *Zagłada Żydów: Pamięć narodowa a pisanie historii w Polsce i we Francji*, edited by Barbara Engelking, Jacek Leociak, Dariusz Libionka, and Anna Ziębińska-Witek, 235–46. Lublin, Poland: Wydawnictwo Uniwersytetu Marii Curie-Skłodowskiej, 2006.

Szlengel, Władysław. *Co czytałem umarłym: Wiersze getta warszawskiego*. Edited by and Irena Maciejewska. Warsaw: Państwowy Instytut Wydawniczy, 1977.

Tafet, Gersz, ed. *Zagłada Żydostwa Polskiego: Album zdjęć fotograficznych*. Łódź, Poland: Centralna Żydowska Komisja Historyczna w Polsce, 1945.

Taffet, Gershon. *Zagłada Żydów Żółkiewskich*. Łódź, Poland: Wydawnictwa Centralnej Żydowskiej Komisji Historycznej w Polsce, 1946.

Tłomacki, Andrzej. "Życie społeczno-religijne ludności żydowskiej powiatu bialskiego w latach 1944–1947." *Kwartalnik Historii Żydów* 214, no. 2 (2005): 209–26.

Tokarska-Bakir, Joanna. "Cries of the Mob in the Pogroms in Rzeszów (June 1945), Cracow (August 1945), and Kielce (July 1946) as a Source for the State of Mind of the Participants." *East European Politics and Societies* 25, no. 3 (Aug. 2011): 553–74.

———. *Legendy o krwi: Antropologia przesądu*. Warsaw: Wydawnictwo W.A.B., 2008.

———. "Następstwa Holokaustu w relacjach żydowskich i w pamięci polskiej prowincji." In *Następstwa zagłady Żydów: Polska 1944–2010*, edited by Feliks Tych and Monika Adamczyk-Garbowska, 775–811. Lublin, Poland: Wydawnictwo Uniwersytetu Marii Curie-Skłodowskiej and Żydowski Instytut Historyczny im. Emanuela Ringelbluma, 2011.

———. *Okrzyki pogromowe: Szkice z antropologii historycznej Polski lat 1939–1946.* Wołowiec, Poland: Wydawnictwo Czarne, 2012.

Tomaszewski, Jerzy, ed. *Najnowsze dzieje Żydów w Polsce: W zarysie (do 1950 roku).* Warsaw: Wydawnictwo Naukowe PWN, 1993.

———. "Niektóre problemy historiografii dziejów Żydów w Polsce XX wieku." *Biuletyn Żydowskiego Instytutu Historycznego*, no. 158 (1991): 65–71.

Troen, S. Ilan, and Noah Lukas, eds. *Israel: The First Decade of Independence.* Albany: State Univ. of New York Press, 1995.

Trunk, Isaiah. *Jewish Responses to Nazi Persecution.* New York: Stein and Day, 1979.

Tych, Feliks. *Długi cień Zagłady: Szkice historyczne.* Warsaw: Żydowski Instytut Historyczny, 1999.

Tych, Feliks, and Monika Adamczyk-Garbowska, eds. *Następstwa zagłady Żydów: Polska 1944–2010.* Lublin, Poland: Wydawnictwo Uniwersytetu Marii Curie-Skłodowskiej and Żydowski Instytut Historyczny im. Emanuela Ringelbluma, 2011.

Weitz, Yechiam. "The Holocaust on Trial: The Impact of the Kasztner and Eichmann Trials on Israeli Society." *Israel Studies* 1, no. 2 (Fall 1996): 1–26.

———. "Mapai and the 'Kastner Trial.'" In *Israel: The First Decade of Independence*, edited by S. Ilan Troen and Noah Lukas, 195–210. Albany: State Univ. of New York Press, 1995.

Wieviorka, Annette. *The Era of the Witness.* Ithaca, NY: Cornell Univ. Press, 2006.

Wijaczka, Jacek, and Grzegorz Miernik, eds. *Z przeszłości Żydów polskich: Polityka, gospodarka, kultura, społeczeństwo.* Kraków: IPN, 2005.

Wilkomirski, Binjamin. *Fragments: Memories of a Childhood, 1939–1948.* Translated by Carol Brown Janeway. New York: Schocken, 1996.

Winter, Jay, and Emmanuel Sivan. "Setting the Framework." In *War and Remembrance in the Twentieth Century*, ed. Jay Winter and Emmanuel Sivan, 6–39. Cambridge: Cambridge Univ. Press, 1999.

———, eds. *War and Remembrance in the Twentieth Century.* Cambridge: Cambridge Univ. Press, 1999.

Wistrich, Robert S. *Antisemitism: The Longest Hatred.* New York: Schocken Books, 1994.

Yablonka, Hanna. *The State of Israel vs. Adolf Eichmann.* New York: Schocken Books, 2004.

———. *Survivors of the Holocaust: Israel after the War.* New York: New York Univ. Press, 1999.

Yablonka, Hanna, and Moshe Tlamim. "The Development of Holocaust Consciousness in Israel: The Nuremberg, Kapos, Kastner, and Eichmann Trials." *Israel Studies* 8, no. 3 (Fall 2003): 1–24.

Yerushalmi, Yosef Hayim. *Zakhor: Jewish History and Jewish Memory*. Seattle: Univ. of Washington Press, 1982.

Young, James E. "When a Day Remembers: A Performative History of 'Yom ha-Shoah.'" *History and Memory* 2, no. 2 (Winter 1990): 54–75.

Zagłada Żydów: Studia i Materiały. Vols. 1–8 (2005–12).

Zaremba, Marcin. *Wielka Trwoga: Polska 1944–1947*. Kraków: Znak, 2012.

Żaryn, Jan, Leszek Bukowski, and Andrzej Jankowski, eds. *Wokół pogromu kieleckiego*. Vol. 2. Warsaw: IPN, 2008.

Żbikowski, Andrzej. "Morderstwa popełniane na Żydach w pierwszych latach po wojnie." In *Następstwa zagłady Żydów: Polska 1944–2010*, edited by Feliks Tych and Monika Adamczyk-Garbowska, 71–93. Lublin, Poland: Wydawnictwo Uniwersytetu Marii Curie-Skłodowskiej and Żydowski Instytut Historyczny im. Emanuela Ringelbluma, 2011.

Żebrowski, Rafał. "The Scholarly Tradition in Warsaw's Jewish Community in the Nineteenth Century." In *Jewish Historical Institute: The First Fifty Years 1947–1997. Conference Papers*, edited by Eleonora Bergman, 22–28. Warsaw: Żydowski Instytut Historyczny Instytut Naukowo-Badawczy, 1996.

Zerubavel, Yael. *Recovered Roots: Collective Memory and the Making of Israeli National Tradition*. Chicago: Univ. of Chicago Press, 1995.

Zimmerman, Joshua D., ed. *Contested Memories: Poles and Jews during the Holocaust and Its Aftermath*. New Brunswick, NJ: Rutgers Univ. Press, 2003.

Żyndul, Jolanta. *Zajścia antyżydowskie w Polsce w latach 1935–1937*. Warsaw: Fundacja im. K. Kelles-Krauza, 1994.

Index

Abramowicz, Yaakov, 188–89
Adamski, Józef/the Adamskis, 167, 170, 171, 177
Aleksandrowicz, Julian, 146, 166–77
Aleksiun, Natalia, viii, 39, 55
American Jewish Distribution Committee (JOINT), 21, 26, 35, 48–49, 103
Association for the Promotion of Skilled Trade (ORT), 26
Auerbach, Rachel, 51, 53–54, 55, 62, 96–97, 99–102, 107, 112
Aurbach, Berush (rabbi), 29
Auschwitz concentration and death camps, 61, 63, 133, 149, 150

Bałaban, Majer, 44
Baron, Salo, 51, 98
Bauer, Yehuda, 14, 21, 217n20
Baum, Zelman, 143–44
Begin, Menachem, 104
Belzec death camp, 55, 149
Ben-Gurion, David, 88, 89, 104
Berger, Mordko, 76
Berman, Jakub, 32
Berman, Kopel, 181–82
Biała Podlaska, 29, 69
Bialik, Hayim Nachman, 46
Białystok, 36, 73, 75, 80
Bierut, Bolesław, 32

Blatt Tojwie, 83
Blumental, Nachman, 51, 54, 55, 62, 96, 99, 100
Błoński, Jan, 11
Boder, David, 14
Browning, Christopher, 14
Brudner, Mania, 122

Camus, Albert, 145, 177, 224n31, 224n38
Caruth, Cathy, 225n45
Central Committee of Polish Jews (CKŻP), 21, 23, 26, 28, 32, 37, 40, 51, 61–62, 134
Central Jewish Historical Commission (CŻKH), 39, 41–43, 50–64, 67, 97, 98, 130–31, 184
Chełmno death camp, 80
children's testimonies, 8–9, 67–68
collective memory, 10–13, 195–99
communism: Jewish participation in, 31–32, 211n52; persecutions of Jews, 28–29, 221n6; support of Jewish institutions 67; terror and persecutions of Poles, 18–19
Częstochowa, 118, 141, 191–92

De-Nur, Yehiel, 107
Dinur, Ben-Zion, 92, 95, 99–100, 102

Dössekker, Bruno (Binjamin Wilkomirski), 162
Dubnow, Simon, 45–48
Dworzecki, Mark, 90
Dzierżoniów, 25

Eck, Nathan, 90, 96, 99, 100
Edelman, Marek, 172
Eisenbach, Artur, 45, 51, 61, 62
Engel, David, 35, 46, 212n67
Engelking, Barbara, 13
Epstein, Leon, 79

Field, Trevor, 164
Fink, Chawa, 123
Fink, Ida, 162
Friedländer, Saul, 14, 109, 197, 220n79
Friedman, Philip, 42, 45, 50–53, 54, 55, 56, 61, 63, 94, 97–99
Fuks, Cwija, 185–88

Garber, Szmul, 75
Gerber, Rafał, 45, 62
Gerstman, Ida, 134–36
Ghetto Fighters' House, 89, 95–96, 98
Gliksztajn, Ida, 181
Goldberg, Lejbko, 69
Goldblatt, Mojżesz, 69
Goldfein, Michał: comparison with Dr. Aleksandrowicz, 176–77; diary, 145–61; in fiction, 161–66
Grajewo, 69
Gross, Jan T., 9, 11, 29–30
Grubner, Jakub, 127
Gruenbaum, Dawid, 76
Gruenwald, Malkiel, 105

Gruszniewski, Pinches, 74
Gutman, Yisrael, 217n20

Halbwachs, Maurice, 10
Halpern, Israel, 99
Hampel, Symcha, 127–29
Herzig, Adam, 161, 163
Herzig, Jakub, 146, 150, 153, 157, 161, 163–66
Hilberg, Raul, 14, 52, 108
Hitler, Adolf, 1, 110–11, 136, 148, 155, 169, 189
Hofman, Lejb, 76
Hurwic-Nowakowska, Irena, 39, 127, 210n21

Israel, 8–9, 12; Eichmann trial, 8, 97, 106–9; Kasztner trial, 8, 105–6; reparations from Germany, 8, 104; Six-Day War, 8, 109–11
Israelis' attitudes toward survivors, 87–91

Jarkoni, Ida, 183–85
Jewish Historical Institute (ŻIH), 7, 41, 54, 61–64, 96, 112, 195, 197
Jewish Self-Help (Alleynhilf), 49, 53
Jockusch, Laura, 42, 45, 50, 60, 64
Judenrat, 59, 89, 105, 108–9
"Judeo-communism" (żydokomuna), 31–33

Kaminska, Ester, 119–20
Katowice, 61, 152–54, 160
Katznelson, Yitzhak, 49, 130

Ken, Hela, 81
Kenan, Orna, 91, 94, 108, 191
Kermisz, Josef, 45, 51, 54, 56–57, 62, 96, 99, 100
khurbn forshung, 43, 45–48, 94
Kielce, 29, 33, 35–36, 141; Pogrom, 20, 21, 34, 37–38, 40, 65, 120–21, 123, 125, 129, 134
Kindler, Dovid, 125
Kishinev Pogrom, 45–46
Klementów, 133, 143
Knoll, Roman, 30
Koplowicz, Ita, 3–5, 207n3
Korczak, Ruzka, 88
Koryska, Miriam, 137
Kosinski, Jerzy, 162, 166
Kosower, Rachel, 71–73, 75, 78, 138
Kostman, Samuel, 193–94
Kotarbiński, Tadeusz, 169, 224n32
Kovner, Abba, 51, 88, 90
Kraków, 1, 61, 120, 125, 127, 145, 166–67, 174–175, 192; Pogrom, 34, 134
Kuraś, Józef ("Ogień"), 33

Landsmanschaftn, 11, 105
Langer, Lawrence, 159, 176, 185, 195, 223n22
Laufer, Adela, 2
Lejeune, Philippe, 163
Lerer, Szmul, 68
Lerner, Icek, 77
Lipcer, Abram, 75
Lisikiewiczowa, Irena, 121, 179
Łódź, 51–55, 60–61, 63, 97, 141, 181–82, 187
Lubetkin, Zivia, 88
Lublin, 2, 29, 33, 35–36, 40–41, 51, 97, 121, 126, 128, 184
Lviv, 1, 51–53, 61, 125, 141, 189

Mackiewicz-Rotberg, Diana, 136–37
Magid, Elias, 70
Mahler, Raphael, 45
Mahler, Sara, 76
Majdanek concentration camp, 41, 55, 61
Mandelbaum, Avigdor, 121
Mark, Bernard, 62, 218n37
Markiewicz, Felicja, 138–39
Masłowska, Janina, 66
Melkman, Yosef, 100, 102
Międzyrzecz, 69, 70
Münz, Benedykt, 141

Nassan, Dawid, 78
Nasser, Gamal Abdul, 110–11
Nusenblatt, Chana, 120

Ordower, Eugenia, 142–43
Ofer, Dalia, viii, 93, 96, 110, 114
Oneg Shabbat, 43, 48–50, 96, 112
Organizational Committee of Polish Jews (KOŻP), 26
Ozer, Fayge, 117–19

Palestine, 2–3, 38, 81, 87, 120, 124–25, 155, 193
Pantofel, Moszek, 84–85, 139–40
Paporisz, Romuald, 122
Parczew, 115–16, 180
Paris, 95, 122, 154, 156
Pechter, Ida, 122
Pencyna, Pesla, 132–33
Perelman, Jakob, 115–17, 126–27, 179–81
Perelman, Nuchim, 78

Pistrąg, Feiwel, 141
Polish behavior toward non-Jewish Poles, 3, 18–19, 34
Polish behavior toward Jews, 3, 4; negative attitudes, 73–78, 120–22; positive, 79–82, 123–24; violence, 29–38, 68–73, 119–20
Polish Center for Holocaust Research in Warsaw, 13
Polish Committee of National Liberation (PKWN), 26, 32, 39
Polish Security Office (UB), 19
Poświatowska, Halina, 167, 224n32
Pregerowa, Gizela, 144–45

Radom, 121
Radomsko, 128–29
Rajzman, Samuel, 77
Rakocz, Henryka, 121–22
Ramat Gan, 3
Red Army, 2, 31, 71, 75–76, 80, 137, 141, 184
Reiner, Róża, 77
Reis, Salomon, 173
Ringelblum, Emanuel, 43, 45, 48–50, 53–54, 64
Roskies, David, 222n8
Rzeszów, 36; Pogrom, 34, 134, 144

Sawicz, Anna, 183
Schiper, Icchak, 44–45, 51, 55
Schorr, Mojżesz (rabbi), 44
Seibald, Ester, 123
Sfard, David, 28
Shabtai, Keshev, 108–9
Shenhabi, Mordechai, 94
Shneurson, Yitzhak, 95

Siekierka, Władysław, 74, 78
Sobibor death camp, 55, 69, 84
Sommerstein, Emil, 125
Sosnowiec, 1–5
Soviet People's Commissariat for Internal Affairs (NKVD), 19
Soviet Union, 5, 19, 21–22, 26, 27
Stalin, Joseph, 1, 17, 65
Starachowice, 14
Stecki, Henryk, 71
Steinlauf, Michael, 12
Szeptycki, Andrzej (archbishop), 123
Szlengel, Władysław, 172
Sznajd, Anna, 189–90
Szpannberg, Rywa, 84
Szpannberg, Cypa, 84

Tarnów, 76, 127, 133, 145, 150–53
Tel Aviv, 3, 96, 100, 182, 192
Tiefenbrun, Lieba, 133–34
Tokarska-Bakir, Joanna, viii, 221n3
Treblinka Death Camp, 25, 53
Trunk, Isaiah, 14, 45, 51, 62

Ukrainian Insurgent Army (UPA), 19
Ulicki Eli, 76, 80
Underground (Polish), 18, 24, 32–33, 35, 75, 96, 114–15, 133, 160, 171, 173–75; AK, 4, 24, 33, 69, 72, 75, 114, 116–19, 120, 167, 180–82, 185, 187, 189; NSZ, 24, 32–33, 36, 75, 114, 116, 117, 120, 180
Urman, Rywka, 173

Vilna, 43, 47, 51, 88, 137; Ghetto, 88, 137

Warhaftig, Zerah, 90
Warsaw, 4, 35, 49, 53, 61, 125–26, 137, 141; Ghetto Uprising, 63, 88, 172; Great Deportation, 50, 53; Uprising (1944), 3, 170, 172, 174
Weber, Alta, 126
Weksztajn, Anatol, 82
Wissenschaft des Judentums, 43, 45–46
Wittelsohn, Chaim, 1–3, 81, 207n1
Wrocław, 117, 187

Yablonka, Hanna, 106, 108
Yad Vashem (YV), 7, 54, 90, 92–102, 112, 167, 168, 196–98, 218n29; Department for the Collection of Testimonies, 3, 54, 96–97, 100, 101, 112, 178, 181, 184
Yiddish Scholarly Institute (YIVO), 43, 47–48, 51

Zbąszyń, 49
Zionism, 86–87, 91, 93, 131, 179, 181, 191, 193–94, 196, 198
Złoczów, 1
Zomper, Adam, 124, 191–94
Zuckerman, Yitzhak ("Antek"), 88
Żbikowski, Andrzej, 35–37
Żurawski, Mieczysław, 80

Monika Rice teaches courses on the Holocaust, Jewish–Christian relations, and women's spirituality at Seton Hall University and Gratz College. She has received a number of prestigious fellowships and grants and has published articles, essays, and reviews in edited volumes and academic journals. Her research focuses on the inner lives of Polish Jews.